Italian and Irish Filmmakers in America

FORD, CAPRA, COPPOLA, and SCORSESE

Lee Lourdeaux **Italian and Irish**

FORD, CAPRA,

Temple University Press
Philadelphia

Filmmakers in America

COPPOLA, and SCORSESE

Temple University Press, Philadelphia 19122
Copyright © 1990 by Temple University.
All rights reserved
Published 1990
Printed in the United States of America

The paper used in this publication meets the minimum
requirements of American National Standard for
Information Sciences—Permanence of Paper for Printed
Library Materials, ANSI Z39.48-1984

Library of Congress Cataloging-in-Publication Data
Lourdeaux, Lee.
    Italian and Irish filmmakers in America : Ford,
Capra, Coppola, and Scorsese / Lee Lourdeaux.
        p.   cm.
    Includes bibliographical references.
    ISBN 0-87722-697-0 (alk. paper)
    1. Catholics in motion pictures.   2. Italian
Americans in motion pictures.   3. Irish Americans
in motion pictures.   4. Ethnicity—United States.
5. Ford, John, 1894–1973.   6. Capra, Frank,
1897–   .   7. Coppola, Francis Ford, 1939–
8. Scorsese, Martin.   9. Motion pictures producers
and directors—United States—Biography.   I. Title.
PN1995.9.C35L68   1990
791.43'65222—dc20   89-20396
                                               CIP

To Kay and Elaine, and Mary and Vito.

I wanted to be a painter, but I wasn't doing that. I began to see that the priests and the nuns were talking about God, and heaven, and hell, and religious vocations. And I started to say, Well, at least with a religious vocation a priest or a nun might have more of an inside line to heaven—into salvation, if you want to use that word. They might be a little closer to it than the guy on the street because, after all, how can you practice the Christian beliefs and attitudes that you are learning in the classroom in your house or in the street? . . . Later on, obviously, it didn't work out, and I wound up finding a vocation in making movies with the same kind of passion.

—Martin Scorsese

Nobody leaves the Catholic Church.

—Jimmy Breslin

Contents

Acknowledgments

To embark on a cultural history of several hundred films requires encouragement and frequent assistance. In the early stages of my research, the late Gerald Mast generously gave me access to the superb film collection at the University of Chicago. Later on, Charles Silver of the Museum of Modern Art and Emily Sieger of the Library of Congress arranged for numerous screenings with efficiency and great courtesy. For help with the picayune details that pester every historian, I am indebted to librarians Ken Berger, Johannah Sherrer, and Jane Vogel at Duke University.

Outside the usual institutional resources, William K. Everson was a paragon of generosity, taking time away from his duties at New York University to screen rare prints from his private collection. After I set hand to keyboard, Terry and Maureen Tilley commented with acute insight on an early draft of my introduction.

Every writer also needs skilled editors to follow a manuscript through production, and I am fortunate to have had two good ones: Janet Francendese and Richard Gilbertie. To them and all the staff at Temple University Press, I am sincerely grateful. In that same spirit, I add a personal note of thanks to my parents and Valeria.

Italian and Irish Filmmakers in America

FORD, CAPRA, COPPOLA, and SCORSESE

Introduction: The Design of the Book

This book groups one Irish- and three Italian-American filmmakers together with D. W. Griffith in order to trace the gradual uphill path of two ethnic cultures in American film. The path was built in three stages.

In the 1910s, D. W. Griffith used Irish and Italian characters to touch the fears and address the needs of Anglo-American moviegoers: He probed nativist fears in scenes of ethnic violence, and he responded to Anglo needs with subtly distinctive Irish and Italian values. In the 1920s, a second stage commenced with the release of several hundred mainstream films featuring stereotypical ethnics and supposedly set in urban ghettos, in Ireland and Italy, and in exotic locales. Throughout this stage, social reality conformed to Anglos' romantic fantasies; attractive Irish and Italian women had to be separated from their unsavory brothers and fathers. By 1930, this ethnic picture had degenerated into sensational street portraits of ruthless gangsters.

The third stage of Catholic ethnicity was the ascendancy of filmmakers actually raised in Irish and Italian families, starting with John Ford. Over a fecund fifty-year career, he used the major landscapes of 1920s ethnic films (America, Ireland, and foreign lands) to explore and better understand the tensions in his hyphenated Irish-American identity. He confronted crude Irish-American stereotypes, faced political hatreds back in the old country, and experimented in faraway places with social religious values.

Unlike the American-born Ford, Frank Capra was a first-generation immigrant who wanted to leave the Sicily of his childhood behind him. So, he threw his considerable talents into picturing Italian family values in family-like institutions across America. Moreover, by matching Catholic social ethics with American populism, Capra

3

gradually figured out how to satirize the worst aspects of the WASP success ethic and still marry off an all-American (ethnic) guy to a savvy Anglo gal.

Two generations later, Francis Coppola and Martin Scorsese emerged on the national film scene. If the older filmmakers had been consistently upbeat about their church and its social relevance, the young Italian turks were highly critical of religion and society. Coppola has spent most of his career critiquing the American success ethic, especially its father figures, while relying on basic Italian family values to make his case. An effusive, out-going man, he makes films that are profoundly concerned with private identity issues and yet mirror postwar American society. Scorsese, on the other hand, has a passionately visible concern for religion lived in the streets. Educated by Irish nuns and priests, he pits both Irish- and Italian-American culture against a WASP success ethic.

All four directors have only occasionally pictured the Irish or Italian community on screen. This seeming Anglo conformity, in four outstandingly popular oeuvres, proved to be a Trojan horse that permanently changed Anglo-American film and society; America turned partly ethnic by following the directors' essentially Irish and Italian visions.

The precise function of Irish and Italian ethnicity in film is a complicated matter. Ethnic characters, always a strong sell at the box office, create a sense of the Other who can be ridiculed and admired at the same time; the quiet ridicule maintains sufficient distance for viewers to feel comfortably different, while admiration means to be attracted to positive social values proven by experience. These film ethnics have remained surprisingly resilient in American cinema, perhaps because they afford much more than a simple list of virtues. Their socioreligious values form a tight web of interrelated life strategies that help individuals, families, and communities on screen to survive and grow.

Any reading of ethnic identity in film must take into account tensions both within the ethnic community and between the ethnics and mainstream society. Consider, for example, the conflict of Roman institutionalism within modern American Catholicism. Although rarely pictured on screen (as in *Going My Way*), this crucial historical tension may lead either to revitalized civil institutions, as it does in Capra's films, or to harsh satire of insensitive organized religion, as it does in Scorsese's work.

Each of my chapters on a particular director begins with his earliest exposure to ethnicity and religion, followed by his later, day-to-day interactions with writers, actors, and editors. The remainder of the chapter is devoted to the canonical and social importance of a director's Irish or Italian family values. Because my ethnic arguments for each director and for 1920s film depend on a precisely chronological reading, I have provided at the end of the book a list of all film titles, organized chronologically by chapter.

A major challenge of writing ethnic film history is to sketch clearly the strong undercurrent of positive ethnic values beneath surface assimilation. To this end, Chapter 1 lays out a model for both the Catholic and ethnic sides of cultural identity. Catholic life in America becomes readily visible to outsiders when viewed through the lens of theological insight; basic theological principles bespeak everyday religious life. Specifically, the ideas of the First Vatican Council (1869–70) afford a rich source of definitions for Irish and Italian filmic identity. The writings of Richard McBrien, a Catholic theologian sensitive to the American scene, and David Tracy, a philosophical theologian interested in art and religious culture, have not only helped me establish an ontological footing for Catholic filmic language and audience reception, but helped me define the core religious visions of my ethnic subjects. Without McBrien's and Tracy's critical insights, this cultural study would be smaller in every way.

Let me also stress the historical import of the Irish and Italians arriving as a cultural force in an historically Protestant country. Long ago, Protestant and Catholic cultures in the West established an ontological and aesthetic balance that has provided Western civilization with two fundamentally different yet complementary world views. As for Judaism, which is essentially different and which I discuss briefly in my first chapter, it has surface similarities with both Catholicism and Protestantism.

Ethnicity, the second side of Irish and Italian identity, is seemingly more manageable, though ethnic history and sociology speak only for carefully circumscribed, lived experience, not the dream land of movie screens. Still, the many books available on Irish America and the few on the Italian-American experience helped me distinguish between the two cultures and connect major historical tensions of family and community to the screen world. Much the same was true for books on American cultural history: They showed me the conflicts of ethnics trying to assimilate into WASP America. What is more, a director's hyphenated vision, part ethnic and part mainstream, can magnify cracks in the national character and vice versa.

This turn-about convinced me that, at least for Anglo, Irish, and Italian audiences, assimilation is reciprocal.

Scholarship in religion and ethnicity is not enough, however. The familial stories on screen require a close understanding of a director's own family background; the filmic locus of ethnic history and theological insight is family relationships. So, I turned to family psychology, especially parent-child and sibling relationships as developed over an entire canon; early identity issues colored each director's ethnic values and inevitably influenced his creative career as a whole.

My readers may well wonder at this point if this is a book of auteur criticism. Do I attempt to rediscover the director's personality by gathering together recurrent motifs and personal filmic devices? My treatment of directors is akin to that of Gerald Mast's, who defends his study of Howard Hawks by carefully distinguishing between the initial auteurist approach of François Truffaut and his own idea of the filmmaker as a traditional storyteller and implied author.

Mast believed that Hawks' work could not be fully appreciated within the confines of auteur theory.

> The contribution of Howard Hawks to a film cannot be illuminated (as can [Douglas] Sirk's) by his separation from or antagonism to his content or script or performers. His contribution *is* the whole film: "his acting style, his script, and his visual style are all one." (1982, 29)

Mast goes on to point out that auteurist critics typically catch only the "bits of themes and business that link the films. . . . Picking through the Hawks films to reveal these consistent bits both fails to demonstrate the value of individual films and tends to collapse Hawks's career into one giant work, making little distinction between the concerns and quality of any one of them" (1982, 29).

Mast then shifts from the heavily freighted term "auteur" to the traditional idea of a storyteller.* Later, in a footnote, he confides that his term is

> synonymous with the term "implied author," coined by Wayne Booth in *The Rhetoric of Fiction*. It describes the narrative condition that someone telling the story—not precisely the author but not precisely the narrator of the story either—takes a *moral*

---

*See also Andrew Sarris's "Notes on the Auteur Theory" and Pauline Kael's "Circle and Squares," in Mast and Cohen (1985), including Mast's remarks on the debate and another version of his Hawks essay, pp. 521–71.

attitude toward the events and characters of the story (such and such a person or deed is in error, such and such a person or deed is honorable, etc.) without which there can be no story. (1982, 39)

It is Booth's idea of "moral attitude," in the fullest cultural and sociological senses, that is my goal when I discuss directors' films.

Mast closes by placing Booth's idea of the "implied author" within contemporary film studies. "Cinema semioticians make a similar point in very different language, distinguishing between the living human being and the creative persona who can be identified by a series of consistent stylistic codes and thematic motifs" (1982, 39). My book likewise focuses on the creative persona that grows over time in a director's canon.

To appreciate the advantage of my interdisciplinary approach to film history, consider Peter Wollen's comments on three Ford films in his seminal revision of auteur theory (1972). Today Wollen sounds astonishingly naive, given Ford's strong ethnic background and lengthy canon. He strangely begins at the end of Ford's canon for his overview and employs only vague cultural antinomies to summarize Ford's achievement.

My chapters on the four filmmakers start at the beginning of each director's canon, relying on a precise nexus of ethnic childhood values to trace each creative persona. This nexus of values, moreover, provides a cultural and aesthetic schema for each director's narrative experiments; moral attitudes acquired in childhood help account for a film's style, themes, and box-office success. Thus, this book uses a director's identity themes to elucidate a complex array of cross-cultural tensions—ethnic versus WASP, Catholic versus Protestant, and sometimes even Irish versus Italian.

On the broad canvas of American history, my book is about four ethnic filmmakers who have enjoyed fabulously successful careers in a national cinema with historic roots in Anglo-Protestant culture. Imagine a mighty river called Protestant-American life that must suddenly contend with another cultural force, which history and philosophy tell us possesses equal strength and which typically moves toward a reciprocal balance of cultural power. Irish and Italian popular culture in America, following heavy immigration in the 1890s, gradually increased from a trickle to a wide river. The emergence of these ethnic forces was greatly accelerated by the movies, which permanently altered the nation's cultural landscape.

One conundrum of generalizing about religious-ethnic signs in

American film is how to distinguish between ethnic Catholic and general Christian values. Because this potential confusion is intrinsic to cultural history in general, let us turn to the example of two national cultures. Consider the following travel fantasy. At the start of a vacation to Thailand with a friend, I order a beef dish prepared in the traditional Thai manner. My friend asks me to explain what is distinctly Thai about my meal. To reply, I first need to describe not only the dish's ingredients but also their special combination. I might mention cultural attitudes toward beef to get a full sense of Thai culture.

The Thai recipe is similar to the configuration of core socioreligious values in an Irish- or Italian-American film. Just as the recipe comprises ingredients like saffron, so an Italian film comprises essential ethnic principles of social and religious communion, principles that cannot be distinguished from Christian communion unless we closely examine the cultural context, unless we explain both where an ingredient came from and how it interacts with other basic elements; it is the ingredient *as part of* the recipe that made my meal distinctively Thai. Thus, only by recognizing the distinctive interrelation of basic values at the outset can we hope to observe cultural identity.

My focus on core values is nothing like the "images of" approach adopted by Les and Barbara Keyser in *Hollywood and the Catholic Church: The Image of Roman Catholicism in American Movies*, the only film history of American Catholics. The Keysers chronicle Hollywood's many images of Irish and Italians, priests and nuns. But they introduce ethnic identity and religious culture in only a piecemeal fashion. Because the most visible signs of Catholic life—the sacraments, church liturgies, and buildings—seldom appear in films by Catholic-born directors, we should be skeptical of any history based on lists of explicitly ethnic signs like names, clothing, and colloquial verbal expressions. After all, ethnic Catholics, like American Jews, disguised their visible differences from mainstream society in order to take part in the Anglo-American dream. The Keysers's "images of" approach gleans a film's surface, passing over the background yet essential issue of the narrative schemata that organize cultural values.

To undertake an interdisciplinary history of four ethnic, Catholic-born filmmakers is especially difficult today, given the state of affairs in both film studes and religious studies. One of the earliest statements of the common ground between the two fields is a long-neglected French essay about religion in film. In 1954, Amédée Ayfre discussed signs of divine presence and absence in *Conversions aux Images*, arguing that Europe's best filmmakers had four basic responses to God. To take only the first case, Ayfre said a director implies divine presence by using filmic absence. He asserted that the faithful if agonized Robert Bresson employed absence to mask divine presence, while the anticlerical Luis Bunuel used it to refuse that presence (1954, 39, 45). However elusive Ayfre's conceptual framework, the point remains that a director's fundamental beliefs (both antireligious and religious) are essential for understanding cultural identity in his work. Ayfre, with no American bias for materialist readings of culture, realized that the first link between religion and film is a fundamental sense of presence and absence, which I discuss in terms of similarity and difference.

Ayfre's overarching statements undoubtedly strike American scholars of religion as overly subjective. John May fears indeed the "ever-present subjectivist tendency in criticism. . . . A discussion of the religious or sectarian dimensions of cinema ought to be confined, as far as possible, to the language of film itself" (1982, 26). May's severe answer is to limit the historical study of religion in film to the "autonomy of cinema as an artistic form."

More recently, film historian Leo Braudy has adopted a more balanced view of filmic identity. It is Francis Coppola's and Martin Scorsese's ethnic background, he says, that accounts for their impact on American cinema. "Unlike the Protestant (and often Jewish) denigration of visual materiality in favor of verbal mystery," Braudy writes, "such directors mine the transcendental potential within the visual world" (1986, 19).

Religious studies should be of some help, given its lively interest in culture and theology. But scholars in the field, says Giles Gunn, have restricted themselves to "cognitive, psychological, and political approaches [to religion]," rarely treating "particular religious formations *as* a culture, that is, as a more or less systematically organized and experienceable way of life" (1985, 619). Part of the problem is that many basic attitudes of Irish- and Italian-American life do not show up on screen in obvious ways; Italian anti-clericalism and a superstitious Irish attitude towards the Eucharist are essential aspects of ethnic identity but hard to pinpoint in film. Moreover, Irish- and Italian-American directors filtered out the facts of social history and well-known church symbols in order to look all-American, and of course to sell more tickets. Because this filtering process limits the relevance of social history, Jay Dolan's first-rate study *The American Catholic Experience* (1981) sheds little light on the melodramas, musicals, and murder mysteries of ethnic Catholic filmmakers.

My book does not attempt to survey Hollywood's endless fascination with Italian and Irish images. In any case, the Mafia gangsters and Irish whiskey drinkers who have strode across American screens for decades mostly reflect the desires of WASP movie audiences. This is a project for another book. Also not included are several well-known directors with Irish or Italian names, since for a variety of reasons their canons do not develop religio-ethnic values. Although Leo McCarey should be mentioned in any survey of Irish-American films, the shape of his canon and the sparse information available on his childhood discouraged his inclusion here. The same is true of directors like Robert Altman and Brian De Palma. As for Alfred Hitchcock, his roots are not in immigrant America but in Anglo Catholicism, an entirely separate topic.

My book brings together four Catholic-born ethnic directors and D. W. Griffith in order to trace the impact of two ethnic cultures on American film. Those cultures emerged in the 1910s, endured stereotypes through the 1920s, and then found shrewd spokesmen who understood the business of pleasing Anglo-American audiences, while still expressing a uniquely ethnic vision.

Standing a few feet from her crucifix, the young (Catholic) woman in Pippa Passes *(1909) is one with Nature. (Museum of Modern Art/Film Stills Archive)*

CHAPTER 1

Irish and Italian

In the early 1900s when the American film industry was just getting on its feet, several million Irish and Italians immigrated to America looking for prosperity. They had fled the grinding poverty of Kilkenny and Catania, endured terrible hardships at sea, and then signed up for twelve-hour shifts in American factories. But at least they could feed a large family and gradually build up some savings. Nothing in their ethnic values or their religion prevented them from subscribing to the country's Anglo-Protestant ethic of hard work, private ownership, and success.

Of course, the Irish and Italians also brought with them cherished memories of the old country and religious principles that set them apart. This chapter defines and groups together three core principles as one powerful force, as a cultural imagination that eventually shaped the course of American cinema.

America's reaction to the flood of Irish and Italian newcomers was extremely mixed. Liberal Protestants, whose pragmatic faith had been badly shaken by World War I, envied Catholic immigrants for their confidence and ruddy innocence (May 1959). But immigration also led to crowded tenements and streets packed with shouting street vendors. At times, Irish and Italian neighborhoods suggested nothing so much as social anarchy.* The immigrants poured into New York, Chicago, and San Francisco until 1924, when the tide was sharply curtailed by legislation.

Angry nativists fearful of immigrant unrest were comforted by the fact that the Catholic Church in America appeared to be a rule-bound institution. Irish and Italian immigrants attended mass weekly

---

*Strong anti-Catholic feelings contributed to the rise of the Ku Klux Klan after World War I. See Curry (1972), p. 7.

Immigrants and the Movies

and went to confession almost as often. Infant baptisms and first communions created a rhythm for ethnic Catholic life, even for anti-clerical Italian fathers (Cordasco and Bucchioni 1974, 10). Above all, the Catholic Church conveyed an impression of institutional unity because of its doctrinal laws and ecclesiastical hierarchy. At a more basic level, the Church in America was a cohesive social structure from top to bottom; unlike their Protestant peers, most Catholic bishops had grown up in poor neighborhoods.

Did such a hierarchical institution belong in a democracy? So asked both virulent nativists in America and ecclesiastical bureaucrats in Rome. The question was academic. The Irish and Italian newcomers secured their position in America by their determined industry and fervid patriotism. Equally important, Anglo America needed these confident ethnics and their culture to shore up their own Anglo-Protestant heritage.

As Catholic immigrants strove to get ahead in America's big cities, they held onto their religious practices. They might avoid their mother tongue, neglect customs practiced for centuries, and forget the regional identity of their childhood. But they still practiced their religion. When everything from the old country seemed either no longer necessary or an embarrassment, the Irish and Italians looked to their local parish for cultural stability and continuity.

Throughout this period of immigration and limited assimilation, the Jewish and Catholic communities maintained cultural identities separate from the Protestant mainstream. In time, Protestants, Catholics, and Jews did relax distinctions of class and ethnicity, but they kept their differences of faith. This separateness was the chief structural pluralism in a social process distinctive for its acculturation towards Anglo conformity (Herberg 1955, 33; Gordon 1964, 235).

Among the various ethnic Catholics working in Hollywood, it was the Irish and the Italians who had the most lasting impact. Irish and Italian filmmakers would change the values, if not the surface signs, of Hollywood's products. In movie theaters nation-wide, this surface acculturation was actually a reciprocal assimilation that allowed Anglo-American moviegoers to take what they wanted from ethnic cultures.

Framing Ethnic Culture

Before we turn to the three principles of ethnic Catholic culture and their relation to American cinema, let us consider first the writings of two scholars who have grappled with the issue of filmic cultural vision.

In *Transcendental Style in Film*, Calvinist-raised Paul Schrader proposes and praises a filmic style that transcends materiality. Unfortunately, Schrader's idea of divine presence denies the ethnic Catholic concept of it as everywhere immanent; unwittingly, he repeats the ancient argument for gnosticism, in which a privileged disciple reveals the secret of a universal spirit trapped in the material world. Because he believes that "the enemy of transcendence is immanence," he places French Catholic filmmaker Robert Bresson among three great artists who try to "extract the universal from the particular" (1972, 8, 3).

Leo Braudy, on the other hand, has noticed the transcendental potential of the visual world, citing the films of Francis Coppola and Martin Scorsese as specifically Catholic examples. Both directors, he says, have a "Catholic way of regarding the visible world. . . . Unlike the Protestant (and often Jewish) denigration of visual materiality in favor of verbal mystery, such directors mine the transcendental potential within the visual world. Objects, people, places, and stories are irradiated by the meaning from within . . ." (1986, 19). Following Braudy's lead, what cultural terms may we use to pin down a sense of ethnic culture?

The central cultural beliefs in a film are an experiential nexus that permeates its narrative codes of ethnicity, social class, and family dynamics. Given this nexus, non-ethnic moviegoers should ask not so much what it is they *understand* of Irish or Italian film culture, but rather what it is they *experience*. If ethnic filmic presence depended on an audience's conscious recognition of values, then only explicit surface labels (name, country, religious symbols) would pass muster.

But Irish- and Italian-American culture runs much deeper than filmic images of priests, nuns, and churches; it is severely limiting, for both an ethnic group's identity and an audience's experience of it, to assume that ethnic identity stems from a one-to-one correspondence between filmic sign (visual, verbal, aural) and the particular culture. Far better to begin with the integrated perspective of someone from that culture, such as a director who has adapted culturally determined schemata.

The art historian E. H. Gombrich describes the importance of an artist's schemata for the history of painterly representation. There "is no neutral naturalism. The artist, no less than the writer, needs a vocabulary before he can embark on a 'copy' of reality" (1969, 87). Gombrich next argues that his concept of a schema is preferable to separate material signs such as the words in a sentence.

> Everything points to the conclusion that the phrase the "language of art" is more than a loose metaphor, that even to describe the visible world in images we need a developed system of schemata. This conclusion rather clashes with the traditional distinction, often discussed in the eighteenth century, between spoken words which are conventional signs and painting which uses "natural" signs to "imitate" reality. It is a plausible distinction, but it has led to certain difficulties. (1969, 87)

By the time Gombrich has finished explaining "certain difficulties," it is clear that artists, whether visual or verbal, employ cultural schemata that they change in the creative act of making, though they may seem at first glance only to copy nature. Gombrich's idea of schemata is the basis for my own argument that a film's implied author can be discovered in the carefully configured values that a filmmaker uses to make something new. Gombrich's idea that schemata are easily overlooked also helps account for the subtlety with which a nexus of ethnic values is seemingly swallowed whole into WASP narratives.* Working with the schemata of two ethnicities, I have noted the changing balance, over seventy years of filmmaking, of reciprocal assimilation between Irish or Italian and WASP cultures.

For centuries, communion, mediation, and sacramentality have been the basic principles of Catholic identity. None of these terms is

---

*See also Gombrich's "principle of the adapted stereotype" for the artist's or filmmaker's usually unconscious practice of adapting a given stereotype to his or her own sense of reality (p. 71).

unique to Roman Catholicism; they could hardly be expected to individually represent one cultural vision, given a Catholic ontology that stresses similarity before difference. They nonetheless enable us to chronicle ethnic identity in American film when viewed as configured elements of a cultural vision.*

The most readily apparent of Catholicism's three principles is communion. WASP Americans have long envied the way Irish and Italian immigrants enjoy community life in their parishes and neighborhoods. Essential to this sense of community, says theologian Richard McBrien, is the Catholic belief that "no relationship with God, however intense, profound, and unique . . . dispenses entirely with the communal context of *every* human relationship with God" (1981, 1181). Irish and Italian cultural vision differs from that of Protestants, McBrien continues, insofar as there is "*not* simply an individual personal relationship with God or Jesus Christ that is established and sustained by mediative reflection on Sacred Scripture, for the Bible itself is the Church's book. . . . [Catholics] are radically social beings."

While the idea of communion is present in some form in all faiths, the Irish's and Italians' extraordinary sense of church community in America has been evident to non-Catholics. "Especially to a Protestant," writes Baptist theologian Langdon Gilkey, there is "a remarkable sense of humanity and grace in the communal life of Catholics. . . . Consequently the love of life, the appreciation of the body and the senses, of joy and celebration, the tolerance of the sinner, these natural, worldly and 'human' virtues are far more clearly and universally embodied in Catholics and in Catholic life than in Protestants and in Protestantism" (1975, 17–18). Gilkey wrote in the 1970s, following the surge of interest in ethnicity and the release of *The Godfather*. The Church's ideal was to strive for a *societas perfecta* or perfect

---

*In *The Jew in American Cinema* (1984), Patricia Erens limits the scope of her commentary to types identified as Jewish by name, by associates, or by references to Jewish holidays. Otherwise, as Erens quotes one authority, "Jew is a three-letter word and beyond this there is no common agreement on any definition of precisely who or what is Jewish" (xii). Although Erens refuses to define the symbolic content of Jewish culture, she ably fills in the details of Jewish life in discussions of several dozen films.

See also Thomas Cripps' *Black Film as Genre* (1978), in which he leaves his key term, blackness, vague by attaching it quickly and briefly to the general complexity of "twoness," as when African Americans work in a white-owned and operated industry. Otherwise, Cripps relies on negative contrasts for a sense of cultural identity: Black genre films, he says, are not preachy films and not blaxploitation.

society (Dulles 1974, 27). In everyday life and family activities, communion especially meant the parish. Until the late 1940s, Irish and Italian religious communion was most visible in institutional forms like the sacrament of Holy Communion, which joined the worshipper with God and, by analogy, the temporal church on earth with the Communion of Saints.

Early American filmmakers had their own use for Irish and Italian community in family melodrama, the genre that had dominated nineteenth-century theater and then early cinema. Ethnic films of the 1920s pictured not a husband rescuing his wife and child but large families and congested neighborhoods. These films reflected the Irish-American part of town, where community meant saloons, police stations, and city politics, and the Italian-American section, where community meant large families and usually at least one vengeful relative. In both cases, the ethnic plot promised assimilation into Anglo America through marriage: The Irishman, for example, weds a rich Anglo American with a social pedigree. A firm ethnic sense of communal identity was of course not unique to either Irish or Italian culture. But in films like *Pippa Passes* (1909), the sense of community with others was carefully qualified by and linked to two other ethnic Catholic principles.

The concept of mediation is closely related to community, in the sense that individuals in a group need a mediator to resolve conflicts. In theology, God's presence in the world is mediated by nature, by human action, and by symbols—including filmic ones. Catholic theologian Richard McBrien writes that the "created realities not only contain, reflect, or embody the presence of God. They make that presence effective for those who avail themselves of these realities. . . . [For the Catholic] the universe of grace is a mediated reality: mediated principally by Christ, and secondarily by the Church and by other signs and instruments of salvation outside and beyond the Church" (1981, 1180).

In 1920s film, Irish cops seemed necessary to control the mob instinct of immigrants. While these Irishmen promised social order, the Italian gangster on screen was hardly so virtuous, with his fierce drive for power, money, and sex. Only after the 1960s, when a fuller sense of the Italian family was finally accepted in American culture, did an Italian man on screen mediate in family disputes between brothers, or two male cousins, or the heads of warring families.

Mediation is also evident in filmic scenes of Catholic confession, a sacrament that by tradition reconciles individuals to God and society.

In Catholic popular culture, confession usually but not necessarily requires a priest as the mediator or representative of Christ. The penitent assumes the roles of the accuser and the accused, regretting sin not just from fear of punishment, but because it separates him or her from divine love. For this reason, Catholics have traditionally believed that frequent confession sharpens the individual conscience, focusing it on opportunities for God's love. In actual practice, the focus was also on guilt. On screen, the biblical idea of confession as a return to the beloved appears regularly in 1920s Irish and Italian romantic comedies. All these forms of confession on screen helped draw WASP moviegoers closer to Irish and Italian community life.

Of the three principles, none "is more characteristic of Catholicism or more central to its identity than the principle of *sacramentality*," writes McBrien. Yet sacramentality is the most elusive to define, especially in popular culture. According to McBrien's theological definition of the concept, "the Catholic vision sees God in and through all things: other people, communities, movements, events, places, objects, the world at large, the whole cosmos. The visible, the tangible, the finite, the historical—all these are actual or potential carriers of the divine presence" (1981, 1180). Thus, Catholic sacramentality includes not only the Church's official sacraments and liturgical symbols—candles, bells, and crucifix—but also a remarkably broad sense of divine, incarnate representation. Because of this, Catholics, unlike Protestants, do not feel compelled to choose between the world and God; rather, God's revelation is mediated through the world. As a result, Anglo Americans have been deeply suspicious of the Irish and Italians for celebrating the material world and communal life; consequently, so-called Italian-American films like *Prizzi's Honor* chiefly confirm Anglo social prejudices by depicting an ethnic group of gangsters.

Historically, Italians have always celebrated the sacramental nature of dance, song, and the visual arts, while the Irish have restricted their religious sensibility to saints' statues and rosaries. In Ireland, the combination of French Jansenism and political oppression (Chapter 2) prevented the people from exploring the rich, often sensual sacramental aesthetic readily found in other Catholic societies. In Hollywood, a strong Irish-American presence initially limited the sacramental in film. Both Irish and Italian filmmakers discovered that official signs of sacramentality, like a baptism or a crucifix, were clumsy ways to introduce their cultural background to Anglo-

American audiences. Not until the 1970s did the joyful, festive spirit of Italian America flourish in the works of Coppola and Scorsese.

Filmic forms of sacramentality are often less explicitly ethnic than either mediation (Irish cops or Italian crooks) or communion (Irish and Italian families in a Lower East Side neighborhood). But sacramental presence can be seen in its acculturated form in films with an underlying ethnic narrative. When John Ford directs a confessional narrative and lingers on Western landscapes in long, worshipful shots, he adds his Irish-American vision to America's cult of the West.

By comparison, the Protestant and Jewish faiths have essentially different world visions. According to its historical roots, each religion depicts the believer's relationship to God, church, and community. Protestantism, which loosely encompasses many Christian denominations, is based on Martin Luther's concept of justification by faith alone: We cannot be redeemed by works and merits since only the grace of God, given through Jesus Christ, saves us. From this perspective, a Catholic devotionalism of rosaries and penances suggests that churchgoers are trying to work their way to heaven. But from the Catholics' sacramental viewpoint, objects, places, and people are all paths of grace to God.

Protestantism also stands on the principle of Scripture alone, which means that the Bible by itself is normative for Christian faith and doctrine. Here again, to many Protestants the Catholics' sacramental emphasis on symbol and mystery seems misplaced, even superstitious. The greatest source of disagreement between the two faiths has been their differing views on the priesthood. Protestants assert that a minister is a layman to whom a special function has been assigned, while Catholics support a hierarchical priesthood in which the priest is elevated to the role of a Christ-like mediator.

Judaism's distinctive history helps distinguish it from Christian faiths. Jews bear witness to a Lord of history who intervenes in Israel's life. Inseparable from this historical fabric is the language of Hebrew in which Jews stress a covenant with God: The actualization of past blessings and future hopes depends on righteous action in the present. In this light, the idea of mediation through a saviour would seem to encourage delay and uncertainty. Moreover, Jews are wary of any religion that relies on signs and symbols, lest they detract from worship of the one true God. Yet, in the 1910s, both American Jews and Catholics had, especially in the eyes of Protestants, an admirable self-confidence. Jews felt secure because of their belief that God has created harmony and order throughout nature, while ethnic Catholics were confident because they felt part of an enduring institutional church.

Jewish writers and producers in Hollywood repeatedly shied away from the historical facts of their faith (the people, the land, the language), preferring instead all-American types who embody traditional active Jewish virtues, such as righteousness in deed, piety of heart, and education of the mind. Italian and Irish film writers and directors, on the other hand, were accustomed to a life of accepted suffering; their characters face life's trials by offering up their troubles to God, while keeping in mind Christ's own pain on the cross.

When any of the three major faiths is pictured in American film, it must pass through the filter of civil religion. Such is the case in the 1949 educational movie *One God—The Ways We Worship*. Produced with the advice of a Catholic priest, a Jewish rabbi, and several Protestant ministers, the film advances a postwar, assimilationist perspective in which Judaism and Catholicism are implicitly inferior to Protestantism. The film's narrator favors a watered down religion of the Word and, in the end, characterizes the three faiths nearly as one, since all share a belief in one God. In short, the film champions the bland camaraderie of American civil religion.

The Catholic section opens with a tracking shot down the center aisle of an immense stone church, where the narrative voice-over intones the prescription, "straight and narrow as the path of life that leads to God is the way that leads to the high altar." This restrictive, Irish based morality would make sense to Protestant moviegoers raised on puritanical mores. But they might be put off by the visible separation of the individual worshiper from God: The communion railing bars entry to the altar area, and the prison-like tabernacle keeps Christ under lock and key. (For Catholics in 1949, the railing would have symbolically marked priests as a separate class, while the tabernacle was a sacred sanctuary.) The life-size crucifix and holy statues, moreover, would appear to overemphasize self-sacrifice and suggest peasant superstition. Finally, the narrator interrupts to explain that Catholic (sacramental) life is "enriched by the beauty of many symbols." Catholic culture, it seems, affords much beauty, however oddly expressed.

The importance of religious ritual to Catholics also stands out here. They prize genuflection, Eucharistic consecration, and the sign of the cross. And they "study a year to know the sacraments." For Baptism, they believe not so much in a soul saved for Jesus as in an institutional event: The sacrament means "the Catholic Church has a new member." Unlike Protestants, who for centuries have argued fiercely over theology and divided into sects, American Catholics in the late 1940s saw themselves as part of a worldwide institution based on legalistic sacraments and age-old rituals.

The film's exposition of Judaism in America is briefer. The narrator first distinguishes between orthodox and reformed Jews, and then describes in a few words the major holy days and sacred objects like the menorah. He draws as well implicit ties to civil religion: Passover celebrates freedom, and the pledge to the Torah leads to America's own Pledge of Allegiance.

The film's crowning section is Protestantism. Watching this segment, Protestant filmgoers would feel progressive as they viewed the third and thus most enlightened of the faiths. The narrator begins by mentioning that not "all Protestants observe the same form of worship," a sense of division that promotes a loosely knit pluralism in which "every member is free to interpret [the Bible] as he believes"; consequently, "the Bible takes the place of the Church as the final authority." The key Protestant sacrament is baptism with its definitive rebirth: "The old sinful self is buried in the water and the new person is raised up." Equally important, Protestant preachers stress the practical application of Scripture to everyday life, not the Catholics' invisible communion or sense of centuries' old restrictions. Tying together all these Protestant beliefs is a buoyant optimism in a male-oriented religious culture: As the film closes, two Protestant men, ready for the world, shake hands outside a church door.

This film's overly general portrait of Protestantism highlights unity, while ignoring its rich "principle of prophetic protest" (Marty 1972, 294). Uppermost is a fundamentally vague civil religion—with its practicality, friendly optimism, and above all freedom of interpretation for every citizen. The film's ending seems so innocuous because its makers had no clear idea of the cultural and theological boundaries of religious identity.

American Catholics watching *One God—The Ways We Worship* would have noticed Catholic values overlooked by general audiences. In the 1940s, they would have seen a cathedral as the industry of the same brick-and-mortar bishops who had built thousands of churches in America, not to mention seminaries, hospitals, colleges and more than ten thousand grammar schools and high schools (Cogley 1973,

269). The Irish-dominated hierarchy had pushed for continual expansion in order to accommodate millions of new Catholic immigrants. With their fervent institutionalism, the bishops fostered a new American clericalism, reinforcing Catholics' sense of their Church as a confident authority that brings order to the turmoil of a new life in a new country.

The cathedral's interior would also have had particular meaning. The communion rail is both a holy place, where priests distribute sacred hosts, and a symbolic border separating clergy from laity. Behind the altar hangs a huge crucifix, a visible sign of the suffering Christ who consoles immigrants wearied by the struggle to survive and assimilate. And comforting, too, were the sounds of Latin, since it suggested an international Church. If few immigrants actually understood the ancient language, they had plenty of statues, side altars, and rosaries. Altogether, the mediational clergy, symbols, and sacraments contrasted sharply with Protestants' reliance on grace directly from God. "If Protestants would deny the incarnational mediations of Christian faith by an emphasis upon the overpowering graciousness of God, then Catholics would stress the sacramental, ecclesiastical, juridical, hierarchical, and cultural instruments of Divine Presence" (Happel and Tracy 1984, 89).

Catholic identity in *One God—The Ways We Worship* is so acculturated that all distinctions among the Irish and the Italians and other ethnic Catholic groups are lost. This is the melting pot of both American education and film culture, a pot that permits a sense of (Catholic) institutionalism because, by the 1940s, Americans viewed it in private industry and public works as regrettably necessary. They would likewise accept worshippers of different faiths as workers striving for the same prosperity and career success.

Although both Irish and Italian filmmakers have achieved impressive successes at the box-office, it is an entirely different matter for their ethnicity to count in a country dominated by the Protestant idea of success. Umberto Eco, speaking as an Italian novelist who wants to "be taken seriously" by the Anglo-American literary establishment, sums up the fundamentally different idea of success in Catholic and Protestant cultures. "We are a Catholic civilization, which is exactly the opposite of what Max Weber told of the Protestant civilization," Eco says. "For the Protestant civilization, economic success is a sign of the benevolence of God, while for our civilization, poverty and suffering are proofs of his benevolence. Success, on the contrary, is the proof that God is ready to send you to hell" (1989, 79). While neither Italian immigrants to America nor their descendents would agree with Eco's extreme and overly general view of success as a sign of hell, his point remains that Catholics have a very different view of success, a view that not only complicates their immigrant identity but also stymies their acceptance in the Anglo mainstream.

To understand the Catholic cultural slant on issues such as economic success, let us consider the spirit behind both Irish and Italian Catholic cultures—the analogical imagination (Tracy 1981, 405–56). While Protestants stress the interpretation of the biblical Word and the consequent gap between God's text and humanity, Catholics emphasize the image as an analogue of sacramental reality. The concept of the analogical was first introduced by Aristotle, then revised by Thomas Aquinas, and later resurrected by the Council of Vatican I (1869–70). According to this tradition, analogous relationships among various realities (self, others, world) clarify the relation of each to a prime analogue—the event of Jesus Christ as mediated by tradition. The prime analogue ultimately sets the order of the relationships among the analogies (Tracy 1981, 408). An analogical vision of ordered similarities is at the root of communion (you are finally more like me than you are unlike me), mediation (because we are all essentially alike, humans resolve their differences through some form of mediation), and sacramentality (humans are finally drawn in similarity to the divine presence everywhere immanent, including in one another). The similarity in difference of analogical language reflects God's sacramental relation to the world and all its signs.

Protestant culture, on the other hand, traditionally derives its strength from difference in similarity. According to theologians David Tracy and John Cobb, the theology of Jürgen Moltmann was always "faithful to the Reformation heritage." In his work one "sees the dialectical logic of contradiction disclosed in the central symbol of the crucified one challenging, at its roots, all claims to the possibilities of an analogical vision informed by the logic of ordered relationships" (1983, 20).

Tracy and Cobb also provide the clearest and most recent description of analogical language.

[It is] the predominant language employed by Catholic theologians from Thomas Aquinas to Karl Rahner and Bernard Lonergan. . . . [In] the model for theology articulated in the first Vatican Council (1869–70) . . . theology is the partial, incomplete, analogous but real *understanding* of the mysteries [that which cannot be fully explained] of the Catholic faith. It achieves this understanding in three steps: First, by developing analogies from nature to understand that mystery. Second, by developing —by means of the analogy—interconnections among the principal mysteries of the faith (Christ, Trinity, Grace). And third, by relating this understanding to the final end of humanity. (1983, 18)

Thus, in three steps, analogical language comprises the central mysteries of the Catholic faith.

To extrapolate Tracy and Cobb's description to film language and culture, let us turn to one of D. W. Griffith's most well-known Biograph shorts, *Pippa Passes*, which relocates Robert Browning's long poem about Italy to America. A Catholic reading does not, however, deny alternate readings, such as Pippa as a feminine figure of the filmmaker as artist and pacifist. This 1909 one-reeler is the story of three men who reform their lives after hearing Pippa's sweetly innocent voice and guitar. The sinful trio comprises an alcoholic father who abuses his wife, a poet-figure who expects his girlfriend to be a virgin, and a young soldier who is tempted to murder his superior in order to take the man's wife.

Just as the first step for analogical language is to note an analogy with Nature, we observe that Griffith begins by linking Pippa closely with her nearby garden. Especially for Catholic audiences, this compassionate young spirit is part of an accepting, sensuous Nature. Her vibrant voice creates, moreover, the divine in music, just as the film's innovative and strikingly back-lit images suggest a holy presence. Unlike the brutal men found outdoors in *Fools of Fate*, both Pippa and Nature are incarnations of God's forgiving grace.

Like the second analogical step, the film uncannily interconnects the principal mysteries of the Catholic faith: grace, as just explained; Christ, as identified with Pippa in the opening and closing shots of a crucifix nearby her; and the Trinity, as established by inverted portraits of the three repentant men. The implicit image of Trinity arises from a father who gives up alcohol, a young officer or son figure who stands in a filial relation to his superior officer, and a poet-figure who writes by inspiration (as close as American secular imagery comes to the Holy Spirit).

The third step of analogical language—to relate the understanding of Catholic mysteries to humanity's final end—occurs in the film's closing eschatological vision of divine good will: The fate of humankind need be no more troubled than Pippa's trustful sleep. Thus,

Griffith, working intuitively with religion, used various analogical steps to approach ethnic Catholic culture.

Later Irish- and Italian-American filmmakers eschewed Griffith's heavy directorial hand, especially the forced similarity between Pippa and the sinners who hear her sacramental song. Still, the insightful Protestant Griffith introduced a remarkably confident young woman to an uncertain post-Victorian world of authoritarian men and subservient women. With her crucifix, Griffith's Pippa herself is a Christ-figure and prime analogue: For each male sinner, she is analogous to the better self within. Although the difference or lack of analogy between Pippa and each character is at first most striking, it is the overpowering spiritual similarity between her and the men that finally accounts for their conversions.

Griffith had hit upon the Marian tradition of the mediational virginal woman. According to tradition, Pippa is not just an idealized figure but an active sign of divine presence. Among Protestant Americans, it was not just Griffith who was fascinated with the Catholic tradition of the Virgin Mary. In *Mont-Saint-Michel and Chartres* (1904), Henry Adams complained vehemently about the absence of Marian values in industrial Anglo America (1933).

Within Irish and Italian cultures, the Virgin Mary has been a pervasive and potent force, especially during tough times for immigrant families in America.

> The nineteenth century witnessed a popular and official resurgency in the veneration of Mary throughout the Catholic world. Indeed so great was this revival that leaders of the church call the years between 1850 and 1950 the Marian Age. The papacy demarcated this era by defining two controversial dogmas about the Mother of Christ: the Immaculate Conception, in 1854, and the Assumption of the Virgin, in 1950. The many reported apparitions of the Virgin throughout southern and western Europe, some of which gained widespread fame and church approval, were another sign of the rise in Marian fervor. (Atkinson, Buchanan, and Miles 1985, 173)

Symbolically, the Virgin Mary is a key figure for the analogical imagination, as she consoles anxious sinners with a compassion like God's own love. The sociologist and religious historian Andrew Greeley has summed up the rich tradition of Marian symbolism. As a Madonna holding an infant Jesus, Mary epitomizes maternity; as the Virgin full of grace, she renews inspiration; as the desired one of Yahweh, she represents the highest spiritual ecstasy; and in the traditional pieta, she understands the death of all living creatures (1977, 127, 151, 179, 205).

For the Irish and the Italians, the figure of the Virgin Mary has taken on diverse meanings. To the former, she can be used to justify the manipulative control of a long-suffering mother—in a twisted version of the Mater Dolorosa. To the latter, she can be a naive symbol of uncritical maternal love. Filmmakers like John Ford and Francis Coppola had to work against the grain of these cultural contexts to recover potential positive values of Marian tradition.

The assimilation of ethnic Catholic and especially Marian values into American film is a complex story with two sides. American filmmakers like Griffith envied the young Irish woman's vital spirit and the Italian man's warmly compassionate nature. But they also insisted on the proviso that neither figure be associated with unruly immigrant mobs; social anarchy was the dark side of immigration. When later WASP filmmakers pictured an Irishman or an Italian, the figures often revealed little more than clichés about ethnicity: An Irishman's confession is superficial without a strong sense of community and mediation. By comparison, Irish- and Italian-American filmmakers, writers, and actors expressed their ethnic roots with an analogical imagination. For them, the filmic sign was a way of creating sacramental places and actions and people.

The story of Irish and Italian culture in American film is finally one of reciprocal assimilation. At first, filmmakers like John Ford and Frank Capra adjusted their ethnic backgrounds to accommodate Hollywood stereotypes. But once they discovered that the success ethic was a strong common bond between Anglo-America and their immigrant cultures, they began to configure new socio-religious values lacking in mainstream society.

Filming Ethnicity Piecemeal: D. W. Griffith's Women and Other Precedents

D. W. Griffith created a virtual encyclopedia of American popular culture in a canon of several hundred films, including family melodramas, historical epics, literary adaptations, and pastoral tableaux. By birth a Methodist and by nature a Victorian moralist, Griffith thus had plenty of leeway to explore Irish and Italian cultures for new ways of challenging mainstream Protestant audiences. Though at first he fed nativist fears of ethnic anarchy, he soon turned to positive ethnic figures, especially celibate Catholic priests and vivacious Catholic young women. When he later took up socially sensitive issues, such as the social implications of rigid Catholic institutional-ism, he stuck to foreign lands of long ago. Eventually, he tried his hand at an epic-size analogical narrative about contemporary oppression of the working-class Catholic ethnic.

The first two American films with Catholic figures took a decidedly downbeat Anglo-Protestant view. *The Execution of Mary Queen of Scots* (1895) is a thirty-second reenactment of a famous Catholic beheading. *The Land Beyond the Sunset* (1904) more subtly expresses cultural anger against the ethnic minority: A Catholic boy meets with an accidental death. The film also strongly suggests WASP envy of Catholic innocence, as discussed earlier. The film's Anglo-Protestant ambivalence towards ethnicity would later serve as a starting point for D. W. Griffith's own experiments with ethnic life.

The Land Beyond the Sunset was produced by the Edison Company in conjunction with the Fresh Air Fund, a Protestant charity that carried out the social gospel by taking slum youngsters into the countryside. As the film opens, a Catholic boy works hard selling newspapers but still is beaten by his drunken mother. One day, he slips out of the house to join local boys, led by a Catholic priest, on a trip to the country.

In the film's most remarkable scene, the visuals shift from the gritty detail of city slums to the radiant beauty of an untrodden land-scape. According to William Everson, an historian of early cinema, the film is

> the screen's first genuinely lyrical film. . . . For once, the prosaic Edison script wound up in the hands of a director—or, more likely, cameraman/director—who had an eye for pictorial com-position and who seized the opportunity of an outdoor location to frame his shots with symmetry and beauty. . . . The first shot [in the country] is of an empty field, picturesque with flowers and trees; from behind the camera, the children suddenly rush into the frame, communicating a feeling of joy and wonderment. (1978, 34–35)

Thus, one of the first American films to touch on Catholic life was also the first to celebrate a basic sensual pleasure in Nature.

The film's sense of sacramental Nature began with a communal perspective, even as filmmakers in general continued to think of the Irish and the Italians simply as part of the new masses. Here, the boys eventually settle down to listen to the priest's story of a child who, like many of them, has been mistreated. The unhappy boy in the story is rescued by fairies who place him in a small boat, taking him to "the land beyond the sunset." After the story has ended, the group returns to the city, though the boy from the broken home stays behind. Evidently not missed, he imitates the story's character: He finds a small boat and sets out to sea for "the land beyond the sunset." Although he dies, he seems at least to have escaped his terrible slum life. The film's ending includes a final, implicitly Irish link between mother and son: the equally fatal traits of her drunkenness and his escapist imagination.*

This bleak vision of ethnic life in effect suggests a harsh Protestant condemnation of basic Catholic ethnic identity: The communal spirit of immigrants is compromised by deleterious poverty and alcohol; the boy's vision of a spiritual and sacramental world, here palpably present in Nature, becomes the superstitious, largely Irish idea of fairies; and the mediational figure between city and countryside, the well-meaning priest, overlooks one boy because individuals do not count amid the Romish masses. Just as bad is the young boy's death, the result of his naively imitating a fantastical ethnic story. His death undercuts the earlier communal pleasure of the boys at play; in fact, the desire for unspoiled play (as opposed to industrious work) leads to the story's fatally make-believe world. For contemporary Anglo moviegoers, the underlying moral would have been clear: The sensuous pleasures of Catholic ethnics and their priests lead them to confuse everyday reality and quasi-religious fantasy, with disastrous results.

To rise above religious prejudice and conventional ethnic stereotypes, American film had first to examine its own Protestant identity. D. W. Griffith used Irish-American culture to challenge Protestant audiences, assimilating mostly Irish ideas piecemeal into Anglo Protestant culture. It would take more than ten years for an integrated sense of either Irish or Italian identity to appear on screen. Still, at least Griffith's early ethnic images and characters provided sharp points of contrast to the Anglo norm.

In American cinema Griffith is justly famous for innovations in narrative structure, camera work, and mise-en-scène. His experiments with Irish and Italian figures are much less well known, despite

---

*It will be necessary throughout this chapter and the next to include detailed plot summaries, since few if any of my readers will have seen these films.

the strong religious streak in his work. This Methodist Kentuckian had many reasons to feel an affinity for both cultures. He too was an outsider in New York City; he too was steeped in a visual aesthetic; and he too had a strong social conscience. Relying heavily on metaphor, he critiqued social institutions, championed women's virtues in men, and pictured ethnic environs in realistic detail. All these interests would later appear in the canons of America's Irish- and Italian-American filmmakers: John Ford would work hard to achieve a sacramental sense of environment; Frank Capra would praise traditionally feminine virtues in Marian men; and Francis Coppola would stress metaphor and the analogical imagination. But it was Griffith who first explored these topics.

Griffith's ready interest in ethnic material should not, however, be mistaken for a full understanding of either Irish or Italian culture. Always the Victorian moralist, he sought to preserve the status quo. He may occasionally have lauded so-called feminine traits like gentleness in men, but he found them chiefly in women. And he tried to restore women to a Victorian social norm, not rework its WASP assumptions.

As a social moralist, Griffith was highly critical of his second home in the North, especially the poverty, crime, and moral degradation everywhere visible in New York's less affluent neighborhoods. Given his Victorian sense of the vulnerable family and of overwhelming social evils, he believed that men and women will easily fall to greed, lust, and jealousy, unless they inculcate firm moral standards. In Griffith's films, the husband often saves his terrified family, thus defining himself as an heroic, all-powerful father.

Initially, Griffith's socioreligious view was that of a dark Protestantism. *The Devil* (1908) portrays evil as a pop-up Satan who entices a husband into adultery. In the closing scene, the devil tricks the husband into both murdering his wife and taking his own life. In films like *For Love of Gold* (July 1908) and *Money Mad* (November 1908), Griffith returned to a similarly righteous bleak vision of human nature.

As a Protestant director, Griffith idealized women in stories of sin and salvation. In *The Resurrection* (March 1908) the heroine may fall to sin, but she discovers salvation, both for herself and her former lover, by privately reading the Bible. Adapted from a story by Tolstoy, *The Resurrection* is about an officer of the czar's army who debauches an innocent country maid, though he later repents and brings her a Bible in prison. At first, she angrily flings the good book at him as he leaves, but then later retrieves it. When he again returns with a reprieve, she chooses to remain in prison as a missionary for those in need of similar consolation. In the closing shot, maid and officer kneel on a wintry tundra beside a huge, plain cross.

The film's ending, a reflection of the social gospel in contemporary Protestantism, is bleak in more ways than the frozen landscape. The couple may finally be reunited, but has little hope of a permanent happiness; even as Griffith champions a social gospel, he essentially pictures Protestant Scripture as isolating the soul (Handy 1971, 156–70). This woman's isolation helps account, in films like *Pippa Passes* and *Intolerance*, for the solitude of Griffith's later Catholic women.

Griffith also created a Protestant niche for the minister who saves a young woman from the world's temptations. In his view, the cleric is as likely to be tempted as the woman he saves. In 1909, for example, he directed two films about Protestant ministers who rescue fallen women out of sexual attraction as much as for salvation. *A Strange Meeting* (June 1909) clearly exemplifies the social gospel: A Protestant minister saves a sinful woman, a drunkard and a thief, by first knocking down a belligerent fellow and then dragging the woman from a raucous party. This righteous reformer has clearly overcommitted himself. In the film's closing shot, he touches only the young woman's hand—a discrete but still overtly sexual gesture. Even the final image of the couple beside a large, plain cross cannot compensate for the odd determination of this dedicated clergyman.

By late 1909, Griffith was suspicious of young, marriageable ministers who preach social reform. And ministers in church pulpits were likewise demanding that movies be sanitized. If some ministers held up Biograph films as exemplary models, Griffith was tough on his admirers (May 1980, 66). In his second film about a romantic reformer, *To Save Her Soul* (November 1909), he acidly satirized the reformist spirit. A minister "crazed with jealous love" pursues a young choir member who has decided to become a professional singer, an assuredly evil profession. Because male lust is reason enough for murder and despair, Griffith shows sexual attraction blinding the Protestant reformer. In the film's last scene, the holy fanatic pulls the singer away from a banquet in her honor and then forces her to stand beside a large, plain cross. Thus, the film stresses not the virtue of social reform, as in *A Strange Meeting*, but the reformer's rationalized sexual desire. Griffith's Protestant culture here viewed secular arts, like singing, as pathways to sin, just as it had painting in *The Devil* and music in *A Strange Meeting*. Add to this a Protestant sense of divine justice, as in *Money Mad*, and Griffith was clearly ready for an alternative religious culture.

The weakening of Protestant cultural identity on screen proved to be the perfect entrance chord for Catholic ethnics. It was at this time, too, that Griffith felt at liberty to experiment with Irish and Italian figures, since his titles already numbered in the hundreds. He knew that these figures had strong box-office appeal for immigrants living just a few blocks from his studio. These filmgoers delighted at the familiar sight of Irish cops, priests in Roman collars, and big Italian families. WASP audiences, for their part, were ready for filmic ethnics like the Catholic priest, as long as he substituted for the conventional husband in Victorian family plots.

Because Griffith was raised by Methodists in Louisville, Kentucky, he seems at first glance to have little in common with Irish and Italian immigrants (May 1980, 68). Yet, like them, he was an outsider living in the North and had a strong moral conscience. Equally important, he was a brilliant reader of the American scene, one who knew intuitively which Irish or Italian values might fill gaps in Anglo-Protestant culture on screen. Towards this end he adopted a two-pronged approach: celibate Catholic priests and vivacious Irish-American women.

At first, Griffith had to assuage WASP fears that immigration only breeds social anarchy. This widespread fear was partly a response to the rugged appearances of the impoverished newcomers, and partly the anxiety of an identity crisis within American Protestantism itself. To counter the supposed threat of new Irish and Italians, Griffith portrayed their priest as someone capable of controlling large groups: The hierarchic Catholic clergy ruled immigrant masses who might otherwise commit every conceivable social evil. In this view, the priest functions much as a neighborhood cop—to keep the peace. Serving as a social guardian and in later decades as a social worker, the priest mediated in effect between the Protestant mainstream and Irish and Italian cultures.

Griffith further soothed nativist fears by suggesting that celibate priests and virginal women possess sufficient sexual self-control to help keep other immigrants in line. So that celibacy might buttress the nineteenth-century image of the Victorian woman, Griffith showed the Catholic priest saving this standard-bearer of morality from temptation, while never falling for her himself. Similarly, Griffith required the high-spirited Irish woman on screen to resemble both the traditional Irish widow and the Virgin Mary. Thus, she would rescue

WASP American culture, which sorely needed a stronger sense of female presence.

Griffith's films about immigrants, virginal women, and Catholic priests gradually explored the distinctive cultural identity of Catholic ethnics. Over the years, Griffith attempted many sociological overviews of contemporary problems, ending in 1931 with a heavy-handed depiction of alcoholism. So, Griffith, like later filmmakers, first approached ethnicity by filming a quasi-documentary. In 1909, *At the Altar* played to contemporary Anglo fears of ethnic anarchy with careful social detail. The film was a clichéd tableau of an Italian family at supper, complete with violin and checkered tablecloth and clearly reflecting Protestant ambivalence towards immigrants. On the one hand, the Irish's and Italians' confident sense of religion and community was to be envied, especially by Protestants raised on a dour individualism. But the Italians also posed the threat of social anarchy. (In real life, Italians were mostly conservative, especially about private property, says historian James Hennesey [1981, 215]). So, Griffith exploited the stereotype of the jealous and vengeful Italian: A rejected suitor plants a booby-trap, a loaded gun, behind the couple's wedding kneeler. Then an alert cop uncovers the gun, although most of the narrative is devoted to the cop's long race to the church.

Griffith's story is a shrewd blend of WASP and ethnic desire. The long suspenseful rescue rests on a cruel, nativist irony: What if one of the Italians, a group rumored to hide firearms in their church, should be shot by a concealed gun? This Anglo fantasy of ethnic self-destruction focuses especially on the wedding couple as a threatening symbol of immigrant fertility, already suggested by the large Italian family. Yet, the policeman's last-minute rescue shows that neither Griffith nor his Protestant audience wanted tragedy finally to strike such an enviably close family.

After Griffith had portrayed immigrants in a quasi-documentary, he turned to the leading figure in any Irish or Italian community—the parish priest. Like many Protestants, he was alternately fascinated and repelled by this celibate figure. If the priest were to be assimilated into family melodrama, the most popular filmic genre of the period, then he had to seem not foreign and peculiar but rather like other American men. Griffith believed he had to spell out a priest's attraction to women, especially his desire to marry. So, he pictured the Catholic cleric as implicitly part of a romantic couple. Griffith's *A Baby's Shoe* (April 1909) shows the Catholic priest as fully capable of sexual, romantic attraction. Like many of Griffith's Biographs, the film opens with a social problem. A destitute mother with two children leaves her baby girl on the doorstep of a well-to-do Protestant home. Years later the daughter unwittingly falls in love with her brother. When the secret of their past is uncovered, the brother, a Catholic, is so profoundly shocked that he joins the priesthood. As he swears an oath to join the clergy, a nun stands nearby holding his clerical clothing. The image of the nun and the young man side by side, with another nun watching (or chaperoning) in the background, suggests the image of a couple; this is no less than Griffith's clever substitution for the conventional couple of Victorian melodrama.

Griffith further developed a sense of family in the film's Catholic statues. In the church sacristy, a room where vestments and altar cloths are stored, a large white statue of the Virgin Mary stands on the right, a large white crucifix on the left, and a grey statue of Saint Joseph at the center in back. Together, these statues suggest a Holy Family. Lest we overlook the familial ties, Griffith's priest stands close to Mary's statue, while an orphan boy reaches out his arms towards the maternal figure; the kindly priest and the statue of Mary serve throughout childhood as the boy's substitute parents. Years later, a young woman seems to displace the Holy Mother in the young man's life: He meets an attractive woman and returns to the sacristy where the Virgin Mary's statue has been moved to center rear, a weaker position in the family triangulation. But in the final three-shot, after the discovery of the siblings' true identities, we once again see a young man, a priest, and a background statue of Mary; Griffith returned to his original and basically Anglo-American idea of Catholic celibacy: *A Baby's Shoe* rationalizes why a red-blooded fellow would dedicate himself to clerical celibacy. The Catholic priesthood, in this Protestant view, compensates for personal circumstances that have prevented the full expression of sexual desire in marriage.

In Irish and Italian cultures, on the other hand, religious celibacy meant for women a marriage to Christ and for men an almost brotherly relationship. Teresa of Avila, a Renaissance religious writer often praised by the American Catholic clergy, told her Carmelite nuns that Christ is the spouse of every religious sister (1961, 50). In this light, Irish and Italian audiences watching *A Baby's Shoe* would believe that the Virgin Mary mediates between the young man and the family-like communion of the Church: Her symbolic presence in the nuns, as well as in the statue, saves the young man from the pessimism and isolation of thwarted love.

Griffith soon learned to rely less on clumsy icons for assimilating ethnics into family melodrama. Sacramentality in Nature, he discovered, was less overt and more appealing. *Pippa Passes*, for instance, opens with a darkened screen that slowly fills with sunlight, revealing a young woman asleep in bed. (As her name suggests, she was Italian in Griffith's source, a long poem by Robert Browning.) The innovative opening with sensuous sudden lighting highlights several key objects that establish Pippa's ambiguous religious identity: a (Catholic) crucifix over her bed, a guitar, a large (Protestant) Bible, and a simple Renaissance dress. Responding to this scene, Irish and Italian audiences would likely have noticed the crucifix, while Protestants would have recognized the weighty Bible. Both audiences were expected to identify with the young woman who picks up her guitar and sings, "God's in his heaven. All's right with the world!" Pippa represents not only God's ubiquitous, sacramental presence in Nature and society but also a faint-hearted civil religion.

Although in the last scene Pippa's sign of the cross before prayers suggests a distinctly Catholic identity, not all her traits resonate with Catholic culture. True, she has an astonishing, feminine understanding of sinners as in Marian tradition. But her repentance seems outside all sense of community. Specifically, she does not take on others' suffering, as would a truly Italian Marian figure. More than this young woman would be necessary to get WASP moviegoers to seriously entertain the ethnic idea of suffering as a form of social communion with others.

After Pippa's (Italian) appearance in Griffith's Anglo canon, his Catholic priests no longer need a childhood reason to chose celibacy. In *The Way of the World* (March 1910) a young priest puts on working clothes and preaches Christian virtues. When he fails to change the world, except for one woman convert, his failure helps create a sense of Catholic separateness typical of the immigrant Church in America. This separateness appears as a church high on a hill, where celibate Catholic priests do not evangelize, as do their Protestant brethren. This portrait of separateness raises a question that troubled many Protestants. How can an institution that seems so cut off from mainstream America be part of a democracy?

Griffith approaches the topic of church-state relations in his opening shot of church bells ringing out over the countryside, where "the multitude heeds them not." (Years later in Hollywood, the image of church bells would be a sure sign of a Catholic Church, from *The Bells of St. Mary's* to *Vertigo*.) Two priests, one young and one much older, survey their empty church. Then the younger cleric decides to follow "the master's footsteps" and go "into the world." After eagerly changing into workman's clothes, he in effect lives the Protestant social gospel: He brings gifts to the poor, he turns the other cheek when struck, and he rescues a modern-day Magdalene. In short, he epitomizes the Protestant belief that the gospel should embody an "enthusiasm for humanity" and cure social evils (Handy 1971, 160). But slowly the gospel fails: A matron refuses to take in the Magdalene character, leaving the disguised priest with his arms open in the image of a cross.

Griffith, who said he was a hard-working American with "little time for sex," thoroughly approved of celibate priests and an age-old institution that kept them separate yet available to a sinful, secular society (May 1980, 71). He avoids any overtone of romance for the celibate priest: Only after the penitent woman has approached the older cleric for forgiveness does the young cleric appear briefly to give her a cross to wear. More important, he only discovers his true clerical identity once he has failed in the world and returned alone to his church. Then, wearing his Roman collar, he hears the woman repent. The moral ("Not in vain if one is saved") is clear: The better path is to remain separate from a fallen society, or so at least seemed the Catholic Church to Griffith. As in *Pippa Passes*, he initiated conversion not through the Protestant Word and reason but through the sensuous sound of music, specifically the last shot of tolling Catholic bells.* (In America's big cities, Catholic church bells were rung several times each day, either to mark the Angelus, a prayer to Mary, or to call worshipers to daily mass.)

In other ways, however, Griffith's two Catholic priests resemble Protestant clergy, especially as a critique of contemporary Protestant culture. The young priest's dramatic shift from the naive optimism of the social gospel to a more hard-headed realism foreshadowed the change in the 1920s among neo-orthodox theologians like Reinhold Niebuhr, who would struggle to adapt liberal Protestantism to the times (Hutchison 1976, 290). Griffith foresaw the theologians' future task in popular film culture.

As for the issue of Catholic separateness in democracy, Griffith evidently believed that the church should acknowledge the secular world but stay out of it, as most forcefully symbolized by clerical

---

*Another example of the well-known sound of Catholic bells across the country is William Carlos Williams' poem "The Catholic Bells," in his collection *An Early Martyr*.

celibacy. High on a hill of eternal values, his priest remains available as the church bells summon the sinful masses. Besides serving his Victorian pessimism about human nature, Griffith's passive image of church helped to counter the nativist fear that Catholic immigrants were not only separate but wanted to overthrow the government and establish an American theocracy controlled by Rome. In real life, both young and old Catholic priests had their hands full building an institution big enough to cope with the religious, educational, and social needs of millions of immigrants.

This separation between church and people further suggests that the Protestant individualist Griffith had not yet learned how to picture the strong sense of community within the Catholic Church. His priests address a secular society entirely preoccupied with farm work and frenetic parties. Like the nearly invisible Pippa, Griffith's young cleric must don a disguise before crossing the great gulf between sinner and church. Of course, if the cleric had offered more than an isolated sanctuary, he would be asserting an openly Catholic presence in everyday American life. Griffith had not yet found a way to portray a Catholic sense of community without setting off a nativist alarm.

By 1910, Griffith could claim family melodrama as his metier. It was to be expected, then, that he would first introduce a mainstream story of Catholics in a family narrative. *In Life's Cycle* (1910) is about an average American boy who becomes a Catholic priest and reunites his family. Here Griffith tried not only to present Catholics as part of everyday America but to show implicitly what they could contribute. Veering away from his earlier Victorian films, Griffith defined the family in terms of a man with conventionally feminine as well as masculine virtues: A young Catholic priest openly shows his emotions and has a finely tuned intuition.

In Life's Cycle is the story of Vincent and Clara, first seen as children placing flowers on their mother's grave. Like the future cleric in *A Baby's Shoe*, Vincent seems to compensate for an absent mother figure by adopting the virtues of Marian tradition; Griffith used the young man to explore traits commonly associated with women. After Vincent eventually leaves home for a Catholic seminary, he reveals an unusually strong sense of empathy and intuition. A novice in the seminary, he looks deeply troubled at the very moment Clara, many miles away, falls for a low-life charmer. And when he later visits his mother's grave for the first time without his fallen sister, he openly weeps for his sibling.

Vincent is also a forgiving Marian mediator. Years pass and a destitute Clara returns with her baby to her mother's grave, where Vincent finds her, rejoices at her return, and reunites her with their aged father. In effect he reestablishes her familial identity. The reunion, as already implied in the opening scene from childhood, implies another one of Griffith's substitutions for a married couple, comparable to the nun and the pledged young man in *A Baby's Shoe*. Lit by cameraman Billy Bitzer, the reunion is a tight close-up with vertical placement that defines relationships: Vincent in his Roman collar stands above the others, followed by the elderly father, the baby, and finally Clara. Thus, once again, Griffith uses a family model to justify the elevated role of the celibate Catholic priest. Moreover, Griffith subtly introduces the idea of mediation through Catholic institutionalism (Vincent in his Roman collar), a view that the young seminarian himself reinforces: "I am happy in the call of the Church," he says. In real life, such personalized institutionalism was typical of celibate priests who dedicated themselves to urban, family-like parishes. But given Griffith's non-ethnic cast and rural setting, he seems to speak mostly to WASP moviegoers. He was in fact acculturating urban ethnicity as a goodly priest who restores the chief myth of national identity in the early 1900s, namely, an all-American country family.

Vincent's role as family mediator is only possible because of his almost clairvoyant (Catholic) compassion. Like the young man in *A Baby's Shoe*, he may initially choose the priesthood to compensate for an absent mother, but he also adopts a positive role in the world as a mediator. Once the figure of the Catholic priest had an active role in the secular world, Griffith was ready to take up the volatile issue of Catholic institutional authority in a democracy. For this he turned to another country and another time.

The Oath and the Man (1910) is about a minor event in the French Revolution, itself a tale of social anarchy. War was of course one of Griffith's enduring interests, as seen later in *Judith of Bethulia*, *Intolerance*, and *Birth of a Nation*, where he often juxtaposed gentleness and violence, the noble family and the debauched individual. *The Oath and the Man* stresses French loyalty to the Church, especially to priests who mediate between angry mobs and fallen noblemen. Significantly, the priest acts not for the sake of the new republic but in accord with basic religious principles. So, his symbol is the flower, a sign of a peaceful nature that reconciles warring factions.

The film's initial protagonist, a perfumer, is quite the opposite.

Just as making perfume requires crushing flowers, so the perfumer believes that mob anarchy and consequent political violence is necessary for a better government. But he has a personal motive as well: He wants to kill the nobleman who has seduced his wife. But then the priest mediates for peace: He puts aside his flowers and holds up a crucifix, an apparently more powerful peace symbol that seals the perfumer's oath not to harm the fallen nobleman, whom he allows to leave with his unfaithful wife. (The presumably Catholic tolerance of immorality here would have struck Protestant filmgoers.) When French mobs later overrun the nobleman's estate and the perfumer has his adversary at sword's point, the priest again holds up his crucifix to remind the perfumer of his oath.

Griffith's priest is also an emblem of national patriotism, as he dons his tricorne hat of revolutionary colors. (According to French history, the Catholic lower clergy did contribute to the overthrow of the *ancien régime*.) His lay clothing adds an ambivalent touch to his mediation. Audiences not antagonistic to Catholicism would interpret the shift from clerical to secular clothing as a sign of the true patriot; and the French tricolors would immediately link the Revolution with its American precedent. Audiences with an anti-Catholic attitude, noting the interference of the priest in politics, would view the change as a further sign of deceit. For either audience, the priest would at least seem capable of controlling a mob.

The political acceptance of Catholics, as the title *The Oath and the Man* suggests, lies in the odd loyalty of the Irish and the Italians to a rule-bound Church and its priests. To worried Protestants, the idea that priests could serve as both religious and secular mediators might seem un-American. Griffith took this into account when in 1916 he filmed *Intolerance*, which included another story of Catholic anarchy in Renaissance France.

First, however, Griffith associated the popular negative image of the corrupt Italian with a keen critical conscience. *Pippa Passes* had suppressed its literary Italian subject, and *At the Altar* had depicted a vengeful Italian lover. The feature length *The Avenging Conscience* (1914) was only slightly more positive with its portrait of the Italian immigrant as a sneaky, lowlife blackmailer. Based on Edgar Allan Poe's poem "Annabel Lee" and his short story "The Tell-Tale Heart," the film is about a young man whose father does not approve of his girlfriend. The son appears to murder his father by immuring him in brick beside the family hearth. But an itinerant Italian accidentally witnesses the murder and proceeds to blackmail the son.

Suddenly, Jesus appears with the admonition, "Thou shalt not kill," followed by a vision of the crucifixion. When the murderer kneels to beg God's forgiveness, his confession seems inadequate, in Catholic terms, because he does not confess to another human being. Not surprisingly, then, the son still refuses to confess his crime when a detective knocks on his door.

Griffith focused here on the Catholic tradition of a critical conscience. In a religious twist on the "The Tell-Tale Heart," the murderer confuses the sound of tapping in his room with his victim's heart and then envisions devils beckoning him to hell. When he imagines himself roped to a chair with a skeleton, his guilty conscience has erupted. Finally, he breaks down and confesses, only to flee to a barn where he commits suicide, after which his girlfriend jumps from a cliff. Yet the story is not over. The so-called sinner discovers that he has only been dreaming, and that his father will accept his girlfriend after all.

Griffith's trick ending is a facile answer to a deeply disturbed dream of conscience. The Protestant idea of confession here is limited to a strictly private act between the sinner and God; the young man does not hesitate to confess in private to Jesus but fails in public. Similarly, he can neither express nor confess his anger towards his father. Without the social dimension of Catholic confession (telling one's sins to another), the young man feels tortured in his Protestant dream of guilt and retribution.

Not surprisingly, Griffith's idea of ethnicity here is piecemeal. The sneaky Italian blackmailer personifies a persistent conscience, and the medieval devils call the supposed murderer to hell. As narrative devices, these ethnic figures are as clumsy as the statues in *A Baby's Shoe*. What is worse, the son awakens without acknowledging his desire to kill, a repression similar to one suggested by the earlier Italian Pippa, a mediator who magically turns anger and guilt into repentance. Without a comparable feminine figure, the young man ignores his anger and displaces his guilt on the Italian, who ironically serves as a punishing conscience.

As Griffith further explored the idea of a critical conscience, he discovered that at best it depended not on a medieval hell but on Marian concern for the offended. *Intolerance*, along with its other ethnic aspects, has this Catholic sense of compassion. Released in 1916, Griffith's second epic was his longest feature film and also his most immigrant Catholic one. From the beginning of his career, he had exploited film narrative and extended the length of his films. But he had never attempted anything so monumental as the nearly four-hour *Intolerance*. Pauline Kael considers the film to be not just "the greatest film ever made in this country" but "the greatest film ever made" (Roud 1980, 452). Griffith's epic reveals cinematic traits developed in dozens of smaller projects, traits that explain his affinity to an Irish and Italian aesthetic and that are often found in later works by Irish- and Italian-American filmmakers. First, Griffith often turned to metaphors in *Intolerance*, like the two doves signifying gentleness and peace as they pull a small toy cart. Second, Griffith placed vibrant realistic detail at the center of public scenes. Third, he both criticized social institutions and showed his concern for little people like the laborer, the peasant, and the maid.

Griffith's complex narrative has four simultaneous, parallel plots to point up age-old intolerance: In Babylon, an evil high priest betrays the just king Belshazzar; in Judea, the Pharisees betray Christ; in Renaissance France, the Catholic king has his soldiers slay the Protestant Huguenots; and in modern America, the working-class (Catholic) Boy is convicted falsely of murder, while (Protestant) social reformers visit his wife to take away their baby. The overwhelming impression is that all organized religion and socioeconomic groups perpetrate evil in the name of their beliefs. Structurally, Griffith balances a modern scene of Anglo Protestants oppressing Catholic ethnics with a Renaissance picture of Royalist French Catholics slaughtering Huguenots. Perhaps because of Griffith's vague moralisms and vast historical concept, critics have found the film's structure and intellectual points confusing (Mast 1981, 69).

An ethnic reading of Griffith's epic, however, would be more in line with contemporary filmgoers. In the 1910s, audiences would have recognized the film's strongly ethnic character. The modern story is pivotal to the fundamental moral question posed by Griffith: Will intolerance occur in America as it has in past world history? Although the modern protagonist seems at first to be only a vaguely lower-class worker, contemporary audiences would have assumed that he was Catholic, probably Irish, after the modern story's conclusion: a Catholic priest hears the Boy's confession and accompanies him to the gallows. Contemporary filmgoers also often viewed the labor conflict between factory workers and industrialists as Irish organizers versus WASP owners. Modeled on a well-known labor struggle in Massachusetts, this social struggle leads to a series of ethnic stereotypes. The Boy flees to a large industrial city, where he finds work from a machine politician; like any unemployed Irish worker, the Boy first seeks help from his own kind. The big city pol epitomizes an evil vice lord: He has the Boy arrested on a false charge and then tries to seduce the wife, the Dear One. Griffith's acerbic portrait of the Irish political machine is balanced by his equally black portrayal of (Protestant) women reformers: As soon as the Boy is in jail, the goodly women take custody of the couple's baby. Thus, the combined injustice of Catholic and Protestant social institutions deprives a new ethnic family of basic freedoms.

In Renaissance France, Griffith neatly reversed the social power structure by pitting royalist Catholic troops against innocent Protestant Huguenots. Like *The Oath and the Man*, the Renaissance subplot turns to a time in France before the Enlightenment, when the Catholic crown and aristocracy oppressed Protestants. In 1572, the devious queen mother, Catherine de Médicis, persuades her son, Charles IX, to slaughter the Huguenots on Saint Bartholomew's Day. For American Protestant audiences, the queen's figure sums up several Italian clichés: vengeance, shady political intrigue, and a relentlessly self-critical conscience. First, the queen acts out of vengeance, as might be expected from her Italian name: A flashback shows her memory of Protestants killing Catholics. Like the guilt-ridden son in *The Avenging Conscience*, however, she is suddenly stricken with remorse on the morning of the massacre; though this repentance is too late, the (Catholic) conscience asserts itself in even the most wicked of historical characters.

Griffith also strongly believed that America's WASP ruling class, with its heartless female reformers and exploitive managers, badly needed the warm maternal love and confession associated with modern ethnic culture. Within the context of the film's other mothers and sons, the veneration of a Mary-like figure (the Dear One who "Endlessly Rocks the Cradle" and is "Uniter of Here and Hereafter") unifies the film's several narratives and focuses its moral themes. The Dear One seems indeed to emulate Mary's virtue and moral strength, when she begs the true murderer to confess out of pity. Irish and Italian audiences would probably even have seen her as a modern Mary figure, because of the dark shawl she wears over her head.

Griffith also used analogical thinking commonly associated with Irish and Italian cultures. His analogical-like imagination is most evident in the accelerando of jump cuts for a fast-paced, four-part climax. An earlier film like *Pippa Passes* prepared for these structural analogies by presenting three proportional scenes of salvation that demonstrate, to use a Catholic scholastic phrase, "analogy of proportionality" (Ricoeur 1977, 278). Despite the many contrasts in the four stories—monarchy versus democracy, pagans versus Christians, the twentieth century versus the Renaissance and Biblical times—the plots are finally more similar than different. For instance, the costumes (a major visual aspect of any film epic) may initially contrast the simple clothes of the working class with the finery of the rich. But in the end an underlying similarity surfaces: the sin of intolerance. In sum, Griffith amplified metaphor to an analogical structure and aesthetics that were typical of immigrant Catholic culture.

Still, the underlying use of religious culture in such a complex narrative would have been unclear to general audiences. Part of the problem is Griffith's didactic moralizing, especially in the figure of an archetypal mother. His critics have also complained that *Intolerance* barely relates this visionary material to the Dear One's rescue of her husband. Thus, the modern ending seems like a lucky coincidence that depends, if anything, on the wife's lone (Anglo) determination. It would take more than an analogical-like narrative and the piecemeal introduction of a Mary-like mediator to assimilate Irish and Italian identity into American film.

Despite Griffith's strongly intuitive approach to Irish and Italian values that appealed to WASP America, he created little more than fragmented pictures of ethnic identities. Although one could glimpse a few Irish and Italians among his characters, audiences had to wait until the end of the 1920s for full expressions of those immigrant cultures.

Condemned by a WASP judicial system, the ethnic Catholic laborer in Intolerance *(1916) seeks consolation from his priest. (Museum of Modern Art/Film Stills Archive)*

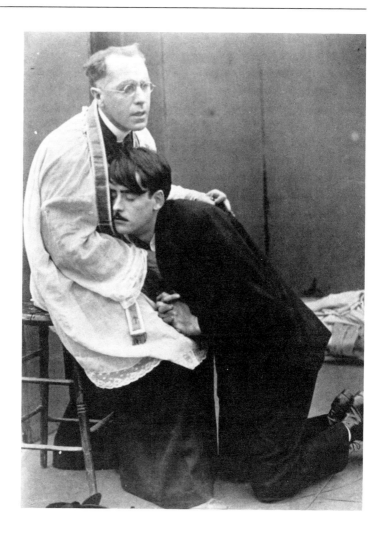

Mary Pickford, as the Little Evangelist in The Hoodlum *(1919), demonstrates that the ethnic ghetto can be a safe, even fun, place. (Museum of Modern Art/Film Stills Archive; courtesy of First National)*

CHAPTER 2

Irish and Italian Immigrant

In the 1920s, Griffith's experiments with Catholic priests and nuns were quickly forgotten. Filmmakers mostly believed that Irish and Italian ethnics on screen had to suit mainstream melodrama. From the kindly Irish cop to the scolding Irish widow, from the Italian criminal to the Neapolitan hurdy-gurdy man, ethnic filmic stereotypes reflected not so much immigrant neighborhoods as the fears and desires of WASP audiences.

Still, the closer movies got to Irish and Italian cultures, the more likely they were to capture brief moments of ethnic reality; the realistic tendency in American cinema was never entirely absent. The filmic Irish son, for example, was true to life when he both strove for success and struggled with a manipulative widowed mother. And filmic Italians naturally prized familial ties. Sometimes, Irish and Italian religious cultures appeared as well, if in subtle guises; religion and ethnicity turned out, after all, to be inseparable in popular culture. When a film was especially culturally accurate, such as *Peg O' My Heart*, it was typically set in the old country.

Still, ethnic life consistently turned into fantasy whenever a young woman was the filmic subject. A favorite screen figure in several dozen films, the Irish young woman was a non-threatening example of the success ethic, as she climbed from ethnic rags to WASP riches. She was usually aided by a wealthy Anglo Protestant who would marry her in order to revitalize his own sense of success, even if his girlfriend deftly criticized his Anglo attitude of superiority. At her most astute, this young woman pointed to a major cultural division: an Irish dialogical art of expressive analogues based on community versus an Anglo culture of surface signs rooted in individualism.

The history of Irish and Italian immigrants at the turn of the century began with a staggering number of newcomers. By 1920, the

Stereotypes in the 1920s

United States had absorbed eighteen million emigrés in less than fifty years, with four and a half million from Ireland and close to five million from Italy. In their native countries, these peoples had a strong sense of regional identity; they saw themselves first as Sicilians and Neapolitans, and only second as Italians (Herberg 1960, 12). But in America, families in multiethnic neighborhoods had only their religion, their native tongue, and a few folk customs to recall the past.

The ethnic waves of Irish and Italians were threatening to the Anglo majority, who noticed the seemingly undivided unity and discipline of the Roman Catholic Church. Although within the Church the Irish and Germans fought bitterly for control of the hierarchy, outside the " 'moderates throughout the country were no less disturbed than [Ku Klux] Klansmen about the threat that America would go Catholic by immigration' " (Hennesey 1981, 237).

By the mid 1920s, however, Anglo Americans had several reasons to feel less intimidated. The restrictive immigration laws of 1921–1924 relieved much anxiety. And the Reed-Johnson Act reduced immigration particularly from eastern and southern Europe. Also, the Catholic hierarchy had not proved to be much of a threat, because they had devoted their energy to meeting the needs of the many new arrivals; they spent their time constructing a large institution of churches, schools, and seminaries. (By 1921, there were 130 Catholic colleges and universities, and eight years later 163 [Hennesey 1981, 237].) Yet the furious expansion did not mean that the Catholic Church in America was buzzing with new theological studies that might change the larger culture. To the contrary, the Catholic Church was not an intellectual force but a pragmatic leviathan. In 1907, the Vatican had come down hard on theologians who favored ideas of modernism and Americanism; consequently, native American contributions to

Catholic theology all but ceased for fifty years (Hennesey 1981, 217). Meanwhile, Catholic ethnic culture was visible everywhere in the immigrant neighborhoods of America's big cities.

In the same period of the Church's institutional expansion, the film industry was also enjoying explosive growth: From 1910 to 1930, film production doubled three times. In the 1920s over 150 films with Irish and Italian characters were produced, though few prints are extant today. So, the film industry could easily afford to accommodate Irish and Italian stereotypes, as long as the stories appealed to the Anglo Protestant majority. Actors named O'Brien or Moore were hired to serve as stereotypical guides to ethnic neighborhoods built on studio lots. Thus continued the process of reciprocal assimilation between Anglo-American and Irish and Italian cultures on screen.

Irish America Pays a Price for Success

The Irish easily assimilated into America because they spoke English and lived according to puritanical sexual mores learned long ago from French Jansenists. The Irish, with their simple sensibility in the visual arts, had little in common with established German Catholics, who enjoyed the aesthetic excess of Baroque church architecture. And unlike many French and Italian Catholics, the Irish had little sense of aristocracy and were known for a feisty commitment to democratic politics. To WASP Americans, the Irish were famous both for their saloons and for the sobering figures of the parish priest, the street cop, and the strict straw boss. For all these reasons, Hollywood elected the Irish to serve as role models of assimilation for other immigrants.

The Irish have always been strongly devoted to the Virgin Mary. Watching her son die on Calvary, she seems to earn her later assumption into heaven. Irish priests linked this powerful maternal figure to confession: A sinner should resist temptation not only because of Christ's agony on the cross, but also because of Mary's sorrows by her son's side. And so, part of one's penance after confession was usually the recital of several prayers known as "Hail Marys."

One basis of Irish penitential guilt was the Irish mother: For a son to disobey Irish mores was to hurt a totally caring mother. Within the Irish family, the mother maintained both social and sexual prohibitions. Her firm moral authority partly compensated for her earlier subservience to a father and older brothers. Once her husband died, as so many did from manual labor, she had to manage the family's meager savings with great care. In Irish plays such as *Playboy of the Western World*, she appeared in the stereotype of the strong-willed, independent widow. On studio sets, she was the Irish-American mother who strictly chaperoned her daughter and shaped her career. In 1912, for example, Lillian Gish's Irish stage mother visited the Biograph studio, where she ran across an old Irish-American friend, Gladys Smith, soon to be renamed Mary Pickford. Mother Gish's judgmental Irish temperament was quickly evident. Gladys "has fallen from grace," she later said. "The poor girl must be very poor indeed to have so degraded herself [as to take a job in film]" (Pickford 1955, 148). Consequently, on screen, the Irish daughter's mixed image of Catholic innocence and Irish self-sufficiency gradually changed the filmic stereotype of the dependent Victorian woman.

Irish immigrants in general had few opportunities in the film industry, despite Ireland's long tradition in theater. These poor newcomers lacked the education to work as scriptwriters, producers, or directors. They were mostly country people with little background in entrepreneurship. As filmgoers, they did venture frequently outside their neighborhood to watch Irish types played by actors with Irish names. But who usually hired these actors and who wrote their lines?

Jewish movie producers and scriptwriters were highly sensitive to the Anglo-Protestant majority, especially to virulent nativists who condemned immigrants across the board. As Jews changed their names and downplayed their own religious heritage in the fishbowl of Hollywood life, they seemed to assimilate to the point of Anglo conformity. As sensible businessmen and shrewd readers of American audiences, Jewish producers soon realized that movies about ethnics need not necessarily provoke nativist anxiety; they could just as easily soothe it. If the ethnic influx was a smoldering issue across the country, then perhaps one exemplary group might allay reactionary fears by reaffirming the conventional image of the melting pot. Producers like Harry Cohn, William Fox, and Louis B. Mayer turned to Irish-American actors and stereotypes to escort Protestant audiences through a mixed ethnic neighborhood.

Irish-American actresses first appeared in D. W. Griffith's Victorian plots, where they bolstered religious themes. He assigned Lillian Gish quasi-religious roles in films with ethnic titles such as *The Madonna of the Storm* (1913). And he capitalized on the Irish innocence and confidence of Gish's screen persona, two traits that, as historian Henry May has noted, American Protestants were keenly aware they lacked (1959).

Mary Pickford's star persona likewise subtly reflected her ethnic background. Pickford was closely attached to her mother, an Irish Canadian.* Widowed in her mid-twenties with three very young children, Mrs. Smith was determined to keep her small family together, which meant excluding suitors interested in her daughters. As Pickford herself recalled, "No man would have seemed suitable in mother's eyes. Mother was not only mid-Victorian, she was antediluvian in this respect" (1955, 133). As for contracts and salaries, "to the very last day she lived [my mother's] word was law" (1955, 86). Pickford was the victim of this isolating, lifelong attachment. After her mother's death, she felt consoled by telling her mother in heaven, "I pray every night that I will go over to your side. . . . It gives me infinite peace to know that so long as I can dream I shall have my Mother with me" (1955, 304).

But constant maternal support also had its rewards. Pickford never lacked for gumption when it came to furthering her career. With her mother's full support, the thirteen-year-old Pickford boldly presented herself to impresario David Belasco. "I've got to make good between now and the time I'm twenty, and I have only seven years to do it in," she told the veteran Broadway producer. "Besides, I am the father of my family and I've got to earn all the money I can" (1955, 93). Pickford's unswerving attachment to her mother, typical of the Irish, helps account for her screen mixed-image of conviction and vitality and childish innocence.

Confidence was one of the chief traits of immigrant Irish culture. After all, the Irish belonged to a Church that had endured for centuries. Unlike liberal Protestants, the Irish had not watched their religious ideals defeated by World War I; in their separateness, ethnic Catholics maintained not just innocence but also a firm conviction envied by Protestants (Halsey 1980, 51). And Catholic immigrants' confidence in their own community was strengthened by their frequent use of the Church's sacraments.

Pickford, like Gish, started out at Biograph with Victorian types. In films such as *A Feud in the Kentucky Hills* (1909), she had to fit the mold of the helpless woman. But Griffith soon noticed that Pickford's palpable vitality could be used for roles other than an abstracted heroine, and he placed her in films such as *In Old Kentucky* (1909), where the Civil War plot has plenty of room for a vibrantly dynamic woman. Eventually, he asked her to star in *To Save Her Soul* (1909), the Bio-

*Pickford's father was a Methodist who died in an accident when she was five.

graph short, mentioned earlier, in which a young chorister leaves her Protestant church to begin a career as a professional singer; the accompanying dark portrait of a jealous minister was a daring satire of the Anglo Protestant attitudes that had long prevented strong images of women.

Pickford finally left the Biograph studio to create a real-life version of the Horatio Alger story. Between 1914 and 1918, she established the filmic persona of a resourceful heroine, while earning both a personal fortune and exuberant public acclaim. Her forceful image on screen and off demonstrated to immigrant men and women that if a movie actress could make a fortune, surely they could too.

Success was, however, only one part of Pickford's star appeal. She also let WASP filmgoers try out ethnic values absent in their own culture. *Tess of the Storm* (1914), a seminal film in Pickford's early career, shows a specifically Irish approach to politics through community. Pickford's Tess, a self-sufficient mountain girl, demands that unfair game laws be repealed so that she may live happily with her father, a hunter. But Mr. Graves, the local sheriff, forbids "poaching in the forest." After Graves's daughter has an illegitimate child, subsequently raised by Tess, the old man discovers the child's true identity and yields to Tess's request to change the game laws.* The entire story sums up an age-old Irish-British conflict with a typically Irish resolution: The intricate web of community allows Tess, here a surrogate mother, to resolve a legal issue that is a matter of basic (Irish) survival.

Tess's ethnic identity is first apparent in several allusions to Irish culture. Tess's name is Irish, and she initially appears on screen dancing an Irish jig. More importantly, Griffith's plot conflict was a thinly disguised version of Great Britain's hegemony over the Irish through repressive laws. And Tess herself reveals an Irish, legalistic knowledge of baptism when she christens the baby: As long as the proper ritual is followed, anyone may perform the sacrament. (In real life, knowledge of sacramental formulas was the rule, since all Catholic children had to learn the definitions and proper circumstances for the seven sacraments.) Despite Tess's ostensible affiliation with a Protestant church, she undoubtedly struck Irish-American audiences as one of their own. In her actions they might recognize a localist Irish

---

*Throughout this chapter I include many plot details because prints of the films are either rare or lost. The details not only convey a film's distinct flavor but also support my arguments about specific audiences' desires.

approach to politics based on maternal love, patience, and suffering. Two decades later, Frank Capra would restore this localist ethnic social vision in his all-American political comedies.

After Pickford succeeded in roles ranging from rags to riches, WASP audiences trusted her to guide them into immigrant neighborhoods. Because the allure was vaguely exotic, Pickford's first step towards the Lower East Side in film was a trip to a deserted tropical island. *Hearts Adrift* (1914) was a film fantasy about what it means for a young Victorian woman to become modern and independent. An American traveller (Pickford) takes an ocean cruise that ends with her stranded on a deserted island. After she teaches herself to build a hut, catch food, and make her own clothes, she is content to live on her own. But then a young man drifts ashore and the two strangers fall in love, improvise a marriage ceremony, and are blissfully happy together. But when the man's wife is suddenly washed ashore, the desperate first woman jumps into an active volcano with her child.

To Irish-American filmgoers, the island romance would likely have seemed doomed from the start since it lacked any sense of community. For the Irish, romance is always headed towards a marriage witnessed by others. By contrast, the isolating effect of this mainstream male fantasy (the discovery of a beautiful woman alone on a deserted island) is clear. The film, in a suicidal offer, proposes a simple existence, an independent life, and an understanding mate to contemporary women; this self-sufficient woman would never fit into conventional life on the mainland.

After Pickford played the independent woman in an exotic locale, she chose a variety of foreign roles that gradually transformed her Victorian persona, preparing her for an ethnic neighborhood. Her heroines were Italian, Japanese, Dutch, and of course the accepted Irish. This open model of analogous foreign identities for Pickford's star persona legitimated ethnicity in general and paved the way for Anglo-American audiences to enter an ethnic neighborhood.

Pickford's next ethnic-related character allowed audiences the condescension of social reformers. In *The Eternal Grind* (1916), Pickford played an impoverished young woman in a New York sweatshop. And in *Poor Little Peppina* (1916), she contributed to a multiethnic story based on a common Anglo fantasy: A baby is stolen by gypsies and later raised by Indians, Hindus, and Italians. The curiously exotic plot suggests that, on the one hand, filmgoers might think of themselves as somehow related to various ethnics. The ending, on the other hand, asserts that newly arrived Italians are no better than homeless gypsies and uncivilized Indians.

By 1919, *The Hoodlum* gave mainstream audiences a socially acceptable reason to enter an ethnic neighborhood: Their adored Pickford was the Little Evangelist, a social worker in the Irish part of town. To better serve her clients, she adopts local slang and even dances in the street. Her job, in effect, gives her permission to enjoy the full life of the Irish community. That festive atmosphere reinforced WASP impressions of Irish vitality and confidence, essential virtues as well of Pickford's screen persona. With her communal identity at the fore, her Little Evangelist ironically reforms not the Irish but her own capitalist father, who generously promises to become a social guardian.

In summary, ethnic assimilation shifted from Lillian Gish's innocence to Pickford's confident, multi-ethnic persona. Pickford was soon ready to take audiences into urban ethnic neighborhoods, where her glamorous face promised vitality and excitement, traits not nearly as evident in earlier Biograph heroines. Thus, Pickford capitalized on her theatric Irish expressiveness by showing spunk and independence, sharp humor and a special spontaneity.

Yet, Pickford's role as a social worker in *The Hoodlum* was also a guise for letting audiences indulge in the "cult of fun," as it was known in the 1920s. Her role mediated between threatened WASP audiences and the ethnic communities they wanted to visit. The festive atmosphere pictured there was a filmic approximation of ethnics' communal life, as vibrant in its way as the glow of Pickford's face on screen. But the visit was always temporary, and ethnic community life appeared mostly not in character development but in outdoor dance numbers. So, by the end of Pickford's career, her still youthful figure was hard to distinguish from the popular Gibson girl. The persona of "Little Mary" with girlish curls had prolonged the image of the Irish child-woman.

Pickford in the end enjoyed only limited success with ethnic identity. America badly needed a mischievous Irishman to help it laugh at Victorian social conventions. And Mack Sennett fit the bill. Born Mikall Sinnott to Irish, working-class immigrants in Quebec, Sennett toiled at the American Iron Works before becoming an actor at the Biograph with Mary Pickford. By late 1910, he was directing short films of his own. Like Griffith, he saw the inadequacy of Protestant reformers and wickedly satirized reformist beliefs in family and society. Nothing was sacred to him. Whereas Griffith had chipped away at Victorian clichés and middle-class assumptions, Sennett blasted Anglo-American conventions with comic violence and vulgarity. With quick, often low humor, he ridiculed restrictive mores, especially surface proprieties of dress, courtship, and social etiquette. In films like *Riley and Schultze* (1912), he also parodied ethnic subjects such as the Irish cop. From 1912 to 1915, his Keystone period, he was perhaps most effective because he had complete control over productions (Mast 1979, 44).

Sennett was safe from his critics as long as the Anglo-American establishment of journalists and cultural commentators did not feel threatened by his low comedy. He might be criticized for vulgarity but never for social criticism, even while lambasting sacred cows like social order and the police who protected it. Half joking, Sennett claimed that his films "reduced convention, dogma, stuffed shirts and Authority to nonsense, and then blossomed into pandemonium" (Mast 1979, 53). For this reason, some audiences, like later film historians, dismissed Sennett's antics as tasteless humor. Ironically, the Americans who most feared this anarchy also thoroughly enjoyed his social farces. To exaggerate social anxieties on screen was permissible, even funny.

The first appearance of Irish characters on an American screen is as far back as *Levy and Cohen—The Irish Comedians* (1903), which presented Irishmen as examples for all immigrants who learn baseball. Sennett's comedies of crude manners gave Anglo-American audiences a foretaste of 1920s ethnic comedies written and directed by Anglo Protestants. His so-called primitivism was typically a send-up of competitive individualism. His freewheeling farce was a first step towards the vital ethnic community that would later replace Victorian scenes of isolated vulnerable families. In particular, Sennett's uses of strong slapstick, accelerando editing, and topsy-turvy finales forced the issue of community. For example, by the end of *A Healthy Neighborhood* (1913) all the characters seem part of an unruly extended family of child-adults. (Although Sennett rarely treated explicitly Irish material, he eventually wrote and produced *Molly O'* [1921] and directed *Clancy at the Bat* [1929].)

After Sennett's immensely popular low comedies he featured Irish characters in the 1920s, starting with the nineteenth-century stereotype of a superstitious, lucky people. In *All Soul's Eve* (1921), a sorrowful sculptor discovers that his dear murdered wife has been reincarnated in his Irish servant girl, and so he decides to marry the poor immigrant. The Irish woman's assumedly superstitious character, in effect, let Anglo-American men indulge in some magical thinking of their own. *Hold Your Horses* (1921), on the other hand, was a laughably literal treatment of Irish magical ideas in which an Irish American receives anything his heart desires because of a horseshoe scar on his chest. He has only to wave a red flag and make his request. Released by Goldwyn Pictures, the film clearly uses both the Anglo-American woman and the Irish as the butt of filmic humor: In the end, the Irishman waves his flag in front of his nagging Anglo-American wife, a boorish upper-class woman, so that she will instantly enjoy his bad manners. But the Irish character needed even more luck than this to find his way into mainstream 1920s films.

Ambitious Irish young men were not at first welcome on screen in the social mainstream. Initially, the filmic Irishman grew out of Irish folklore as interpreted by Anglo-American culture. Nineteenth-century American newspapers had sketched him as part of an "indolent, feckless, good-humored, and irresponsible folk" (Shannon 1963, 132). He was, in short, a leprechaun. In real life, Irish-American men often worked as manual laborers and helped build the U.S. railroads. By the early 1900s, most big cities had policemen, firemen, and politicians of Irish descent. As the "lace-curtain" or middle-class Irish established themselves, the old stereotypes eventually began to change. All this was reflected in the filmic Irishman who chiefly acted as a mediator serving the cultural needs of WASP America.

Filmmakers gradually realized that the Irish immigrant struggle to succeed perfectly suited the Anglo success ethic. One version of the popular Horatio Alger story was *Fortune's Mask* (1922), in which an Irishman rises from the position of worker to that of a Central American ruler. In *The Scrapper* (1922), the cheerful Irishman proves himself a first-rate construction engineer, a promotion from nineteenth-century associations with manual labor and the railroad. And in *Conductor 1492* (1924), an Irish immigrant's bravery earns him the respect of his Protestant employer.

The success plot formula entertained Anglo-American and immigrant audiences alike with Irish strength, courage, and often bravery: the prizefighter in *Blarney* (1926), the builder in *Mountains of Manhattan* (1927), the fireman in *One of the Bravest* (1925), and of course the local policeman in *Riley the Cop* (1928). Although the stereotype of the drunken Irishman in *Sweet Daddies* (1926) was still strong, most 1920s films offered an upbeat Irish character with a cheerful disposition and lots of social charm. Added to this was the Irish cop's image of law and order. His communal attitude not only assured Protestant audiences that the new ethnic masses would be kept in line, but that the Irish would serve as a role model for other ethnic groups. Not until *Kathleen Mavoureen* in 1930 did an Irish gangster on screen seriously challenge the dominant association of the Irish with social order.

The Irish, unlike filmic Italians, were seldom seen back in the old country. (John Ford addressed this neglect in *The Shamrock Handicap* [1926] and *Hangman's House* [1928].) The majority of 1920s Irish films were about recently arrived immigrants in plots that appealed equally to ethnic and nonethnic audiences. These films idealized recollections of the old country. In one typical filmic fantasy, the Irishman dreamed that perhaps relatives back in Ireland had become wealthy and died, leaving their fortune to their American relative. *Little Miss Hawkshaw* (1921) was just such a story about a surprise inheritance left to one of New York's working class. But the fantasy of sudden wealth reinforced, in effect, the nineteenth-century stereotype of the Irish as always wanting something for nothing.

In a few Irish films, wealth corrupted the traditional Irish sense of community. *The Supreme Passion* (1921) pictured a crooked New York politician returning to Ireland to convince a young girl and her father to emigrate. Later the pol forces the innocent lass into a marriage contract, though she later escapes wedlock by burning her wedding veil and claiming she has been disfigured. Once back in Ireland, she quickly weds her true love. The film's true disfigurement is, however, not the lass's hoax but the older, successful immigrant's betrayal of Irish communal values. He even cheats his precinct voters.

Sometimes, the image of a corrupt success ethic took a much subtler form. *Come On Over* (1922) is about a young Irish girl who immigrates by herself to New York, after first waiting months for her Irish beau to send for her. When she gets to town, she overlooks rumors about her beau's attachment to his employer's daughter because a friend gives her a pretty dress to wear for her surprise reunion. The middle-class dress, in effect, assuages her suspicions and defines her assimilation into American culture.

A comparably materialistic accommodation was true for the Irish male immigrant. *Made in Heaven* (1921) is about an Irish husband who agrees to a marriage of convenience, in which he holds his Anglo-American wife to the letter of their arrangement. But after he gets a sudden windfall from a patent on firemen's poles, she falls in love with him. Although the Irishman's opening rescue of his future wife (he saves her from a burning building and from a demanding millionaire) mitigates the crassness of her final profession of love, money is still the basis of their marriage. Produced by Goldwyn Pictures, the film reflected not so much the dynamics of assimilation from an Irish perspective as its Anglo-Protestant scriptwriter, William Hurlbut.

Not surprisingly, few of the films about Irish immigrants criticize Protestant American culture. Given the Anglo-American perspective of these Irish success stories, they repeatedly cheer individualism, job competition, and financial rank. None of these films expresses the values of Irish Americans in an integrated way.

Still, films about strong spirited Irish characters, like an independent widow or a lively colleen, brought Anglo America a step closer to Irish culture. Typically, a widow leaves Ireland with her son to search out an American relative already well established. *The Man with Two Mothers* (1922), for example, is a success story that highlights the central importance of the mother-son relationship in Irish culture, even though the film's resolution asserted Anglo-American values. Ostensibly, it is the success story of young Dennis O'Neill, an immigrant to New York City who takes over his aunt's prosperous junk business. But that plot is also a frame for discussing the aunt's dislike of Dennis's poor widowed mother, who has accompanied him to America; it seems Widow O'Neill reminds the aunt of her own humble origins. Dennis indirectly resolves the conflict between his two mother figures by uncovering crooks in the family business: His (Irish) heroism makes his aunt so grateful that she is willing to tolerate his mother.

The central mother-son dynamics of the Irish family is evident here in various narrative cues. The supposedly helpless widow lives in an apartment so near her son that she can signal to him anytime she desires, in effect, manipulating his life. Likewise, the demanding aunt clearly values motherhood most of all: She gives Dennis the family business and is willing to tolerate her closest competitor—his mother. At the same time, he must prove that he will save the family business; the aunt is really a new American version of the controlling Irish mother. For both women, the son may be forgiven anything as long as he remains obedient.

Sociologist Andrew Greeley has aptly summed up the strategy of the Irish mother in real life: "There is not enough chicken soup to go around; and if you don't love Mother enough, you'll go to bed hungry" (1972b, 269). By threatening to withhold emotional support, the conventional Irish mother starves her son's emotions and makes him dependent. In *The Man with Two Mothers*, the son's success and emotional stability depend equally on the two mothers in his life. On the one hand, Dennis needs the worldly successful aunt while, at the same time, he must keep his penniless mother nearby if he is not to feel guilty in his new success. The widow's proximity is only a subtler version of Mrs. Bryan's demand for attention through her business.

In real life, the Irish son's dependency stemmed partly from Irish devotion to the Virgin Mary: In a twisted version of Marian devotion, the son feels responsible for his long-suffering mother. *The Man with Two Mothers* translates this oppressive dynamic into the specific terms of American success: The aunt's threat of financial starvation is as bad as the mother's implicit threat of emotional deprivation. It is hardly surprising that, given these two manipulative widows, Dennis has few emotions left over for his own wife, who is meagerly presented and accurately labelled as "Mrs. O'Neill's daughter." As for the Anglo-American side of the immigrant story, Dennis's success in business permits him to reconcile the differences between his two mother figures.

After the filmic types of the Irish widow and her son came the Irish colleen. Almost as independent as the widow, she had an ethnic vitality and Irish sense of community that heightened her image of self-confidence on screen. With her clever turns of phrase, she was irresistible to Anglo-American moviegoers. Her character offered not just Mary Pickford's spunky vitality to the bored, inevitably upper-class Anglo husband. Her own desire for success also rekindled his. Also, because she knew all about poverty firsthand, she was in effect an early Irish mediator between the haves and the have-nots.

Anglo-American moviegoers first met the Irish young woman through her social superior, a fellow always respected by Americans —the British gentleman. The two figures together suggest a double cultural vision that was fundamental to 1920s Irish-American films and their success. *Peg O' My Heart* (1922) features a British country gentleman who meets and eventually marries Peg, a poor peasant girl from Ireland. Her character neatly sums up Irish culture: Peg shows strong emotions bordering on sentimentality, a sensitivity to injustice bordering on rebellion, a wit close to impertinence, and a conservative attitude towards romantic courting that could seem prudish. Each ambiguous trait would appeal to WASP and ethnic audiences in quite different ways. Irish immigrant audiences would likely have identified with the socially acceptable version of each trait (sentimentality, wit, and conservative romance). Anglo nativist audiences, on the other hand, likely chose negative ethnic qualities (rebelliousness, impertinence, and sexual prudishness).

Adapted by Mary O'Hara from the successful stage play, *Peg O' My Heart* opens with Peg O'Connell celebrating Irish family life: She dances a jig to the tune of her father's fiddle. Peg's mother, originally from aristocratic British stock, lies in bed ill, a sure sign that a British woman cannot easily assimilate into Irish society; marriage to an Irishman means virtual expulsion from her own family. (Mother O'Connell has written to her English relatives, the Chichesters, for medical assistance but received only indifferent letters.) For solace, she has only her loving family and the Catholic crucifix on her bedroom wall. When she finally dies, her husband immediately associates her needless death with the frustrations that sparked the Irish Rebellion. Peg sums up this communal vision of Irish politics, when she says after an illegal meeting, "And pity them as would silence the voice of the people!"

Peg's journey to England was a model of reciprocal assimilation for American ethnic audiences. Her father learns that she will receive a large inheritance, provided she live with her Anglo relatives, the Chichesters. He sends her off, telling her nothing of her expected wealth. In England (as in later films set in America), it is not Irish Peg but the Anglo Chichesters who must change: She resents her relatives' expectation that she adopt their snobbish Anglo behavior, and she particularly ridicules English interior decoration and what is, in her eyes, her cousin's lack of manly behavior; she likes neither the Anglo aesthetic nor the effeminate manners it fosters in men.

Peg herself lives according to an Irish creed of determined self-sacrifice for a divinely chosen group. To rejuvenate the selfish Protestant Chichesters, Peg teaches them Irish virtues like familial mediation, and her first lesson is that of self-sacrifice. "I can sacrifice myself for those who would do the same for me," she says. So, she later puts aside her pride and warns her cousin Ethel that a favored admirer is actually a cad. Still later, Peg, knowing Ethel is guilty, even takes the blame for a jewelry theft.

Peg's communal vision is at first surprisingly effective. Deeply moved by Peg's repeated self-sacrifices, Ethel breaks down and confesses. Although the English Gerald also humbles himself by traveling to Peg's rural home and asking her forgiveness, the couple's subsequent return to the English upper class leaves unresolved a basic cultural conflict that is most visibly apparent in Peg's final nervousness. While Peg waits in line to meet British royalty, she fiddles with her hands, a certain sign of her inexperience; the Irish woman is unsure of herself when it comes to controlling the surface appearances of clothes, social manners, and polite conversation. Irish-American audiences, however, would have understood Peg's twisted handkerchief as a natural response to her swift rise in social standing. Later Irish-American heroines would translate this nervousness into unpredictable clumsiness.

Peg O' My Heart also captures a distinctly Irish sense of humor, mixing self-deprecation and criticism of others. For the Irish, one must be able to laugh at misfortune, whether it be an unexpected bump or the sudden appearance of British soldiers. When Peg accidentally hits her father on the head at the end of a political speech, and then laughs, the silly and the politically serious join in one comical moment. The Irish, moreover, are famous for a pessimistic cast of mind that often expects misfortune (Shannon 1963, 9). This attitude fosters a closed sense of community that, in turn, ridicules pompous pride; an Irish community sometimes values social humility to the point of repressing individual worth. For example, Peg teases anyone who considers himself above others. She announces one visitor to the Chichesters, "It's that little man who thinks himself so much." Likewise, she undercuts her new posh surroundings in simple actions, such as washing her dog in the Chichesters' formal fountain.

Peg alludes to the cultural gap between herself and her relatives when, soon after her arrival, she complains about the deceptive nature of English social life. She dislikes the deception of her relatives' feigned concern for her, the cad's supposed love for her cousin, and the mansion's seeming look of substantial wealth; as an Irish woman, she prefers to orient herself according to analogous relations and straightforward symbols of religion, class, and character. When her new British beau turns out to be not a farmer but a wealthy gentleman, she concludes in an exasperated voice, "Nobody tells the truth around here." Peg's humor has a culturally significant underside. Honesty to her means putting the similarities of identity before differences, which helps her establish her sense of community. The issue of Irish honesty reaches a climax when Peg playfully asks Jerry to admit his love for her: She asks him to "make a confession" of his love, when he has said only that he wants her to stay in England because he values her friendship.

Peg: Everybody tells lies here.

Jerry: Peg o' my heart.

Peg: Do you want to make a confession?

Jerry: Damn your rebellious Irish character!

Peg knows she will be able to trust her beau, when love is as honest as a statement in confession. (The narrative does not ask whether love ever could, or should, strive to attain such a mark.) In the end, Jerry must travel to Ireland to prove the sincerity of his love, which is his roundabout way of confession.

The cultural issue of an honest appearance is evident even in the simple expressiveness of Irish country arts, as opposed to the controlled surfaces of British high culture. One intertitle especially calls attention to this underlying cultural conflict: "Peg continued to display Irish rebelliousness in her battle against culture." Peg has grown up with simple entertainments that foster personal expression in community—like the jig, the fiddle, and the occasional song. WASP culture, by contrast, is the decorative arts in the Chichesters' home, where the desire to control surfaces is entirely foreign to Peg.*

The visual crux of the film's double cultural vision—the ethnic versus the Anglo mainstream—is the contrast between a dialogical art of expressive analogues and a decorative culture of surface signs. The film's ending in no way resolves this crux. It merely asserts an ideal reconciliation in which "love united England and Ireland." More accurately, the ending turns on the assimilation of British Sir Gerald into Irish culture through his heartfelt confession. On the other hand, the film also stresses Peg's limited assimilation into British society. Immigrant assimilation is framed finally by a socially powerful Anglo culture, epitomized here by a royal British reception.

The high point of the Irish young woman in 1920s cinema was the well-known stage and film role of Irene, played by Colleen Moore. *Irene* (1926) translated the assimilationist plot of *Peg O' My Heart* to the American scene, adding an Irish widow figure. In real life, Moore was a good example of an American actress who, with the help of her Irish background, created an image of independence for herself, both off screen and on. Born Kathleen Morrison to an Irish irrigation engineer in Michigan, she attended a convent school and at seventeen left for Hollywood, where she started her career with obscure roles in B pictures. She eventually became one of the top paid stars of the 1920s. (As shrewd a businesswoman as Mary Pickford, Moore published *How Women Can Make Money in the Stock Market.*) Moore initially appeared in films with all-American titles such as *A Hoosier*

---

*For one of the clearest articulations of this Catholic personalism, see "Totalitarianism and Personalism," pp. 96–102, in Jacques Maritain's ([1943] 1986) *The Rights of Man and Natural Law.*

Romance (1918) and *Little Orphan Annie* (1919). By 1924, she was known for her independent energetic spirit in films like *The Perfect Flapper, Painted People* and *Flirting with Love*. Her greatest success, however, was her Irish-American role in *Irene* (1926), which was followed by *Smiling Irish Eyes* (1929).* *Irene* had been a popular musical comedy when John McCormick, Moore's future husband, adapted it for the screen. The film version traced Irene O'Dare's assimilation into the upper crust of Anglo-American society. For a bored WASP young man and an immigrant young woman, the Irish neighborhood was an ideal meeting ground. We first get to know this part of town in a series of Irish clichés: An Irish policeman brings Irene's father home drunk, while her mother washes clothes to support the family. The mother is, in effect, a widow. This working-class woman is also "every ounce a lady," especially about sexual morality. (Irene herself later reflects Irish mores by deftly putting off an aggressive date named Flaming Bob.) Mrs. O'Dare also knows how to dish out Irish ridicule in salty put-downs. Complaining to her husband, she says, "You'll be smokin' in hell for all eternity. Can't you stop smokin' in Philadelphia?"

Irene shares this self-confident, ironic view of life when she spoofs the affectations and decorative arts in a palatial Anglo-American home. Like the Irish heroine in *Peg O' My Heart*, she immediately suspects pomposity and gorgeous surfaces. After entering the wealthy home of the Marshall family as a decorator's assistant, Irene uses a fancy lampshade as a hat to playact the manners of the idle rich. Later, she seems to excel as a model because she does not regard decorative expensive clothes seriously, but adopts instead a playful attitude. It is Irene's suspicion of conspicuous consumption and her secure sense of her own family-based identity that prove so attractive to young Donald Marshall. When he discovers her playacting with the lampshade, he is fascinated by her lively imagination and feels all the more dissatisfied with the ease of his own family's success. In short, he is looking for a vital life-style outside his own Anglo-Protestant heritage.

Irene's first link to Donald is on the common ground of success and the social gospel. Unwittingly, she woos him by telling him of her prayerful hopes: "I'm always praying for a chance to meet nice people—so I can be somebody—and take care of Ma and Pa and the

---

Irene was remade again in 1940 with Anna Neagle and Ray Milland.

kids." Donald recognizes here the traditional American dream of success, a vision for which he no longer can strive because his family
long ago attained it. Infatuated, he insists on helping Irene and offers
her a job modeling. Her prayers have been answered: She will finally
acquire wealth and be able to join WASP society, while maintaining
her Irish identity with her family. In the end, of course, she must
choose between the two.

Irene unintentionally sums up her cultural dilemma at a department store window. Hired to demonstrate a mattress in a large window display, she bounces on the mattress like an Irish pixie, trivial-
izing wealthy consumption for an amused crowd of onlookers. After
she takes an especially big bounce and disappears above the window's edge (an emphatic frame within the frame), she suddenly falls
safely back on the mattress. Her game is in effect a framing metaphor
for her later social mobility: Her romance will propel her into the
WASP upper class, but only for a short time. In the end, she will fall
back to her Irish neighborhood, the only place she could ever really
be sure of honest romance.

As the lampshade scene highlighted private consumption by the
wealthy, so the department store scene calls attention to public consumption and leads directly to the later fashion show. The show, a
secular ritual based on the theme of the four seasons, allows Irene's
imagination to triumph once and for all over earnest materialism.
At first, the show seems to be Donald's supreme attempt to cata-
pult his new girlfriend into his own social sphere. But cultural conflicts quickly arise. Irene almost loses the chance to model because
Madame Lucy, the effeminate male director of Marshall's salon, does
not find her sufficiently serious. Like the male cousin in *Peg O' My
Heart*, Madame Lucy seems, in this ethnic young woman's eyes, ineffectual and silly. By implication, Donald's own masculinity is at stake
if he succumbs to an inherited Anglo wealth of glamorous surfaces;
the character of Madame Lucy sheds new light on Donald, as he tries
to recover not only his family's sense of the success ethic, but also
his sexual identity as a man.

Has Irene, on the other hand, sold out her Irish background
for her new social position? She succeeds in passing as a well-bred
model in Donald's/Madame Lucy's fashion show. Even Mrs. Marshall, Donald's haughty mother, commends the young woman. But
at this crucial moment, Mrs. O'Dare arrives to save her daughter
from what she regards as scandal. Then Donald's mother, surmis-

ing Irene's background, accuses her of "angling" for her son. So, Irene adopts the traditional tack of the Irish when confronted by the oppressive British: She relies on semantics and the law to defend herself, her mother, and their background. "I don't want your son—and you can't insult my mother and me. We're not common—we're just poor—and that's no crime!" Having reaffirmed her ties with her Irish neighborhood, Irene returns home with her mother.

Like the safe fall back onto a mattress in the department store window, Irene's fantasy narrative ends happily with marriage and material success. Her Donald, like Sir Gerald in *Peg O' My Heart*, descends to the Irish ghetto to confess his mistake and propose marriage. Now, however, the WASP young man must be reconciled with the insulted angry "widow." Although in America the beau evidently does not need to make a confession on screen, we infer that he has done so from Mrs. O'Dare's response, "Go on with ye—with that gift of blarney, ye'd talk forgiveness out of anyone." Significantly, Mrs. O'Dare refers to Donald as if he had turned Irish; his confession has made him, at least in her eyes and those of Irish filmgoers, part of the immigrant community.

Donald's limited assimilation reverses the initial expectation that only Irene will change to improve her circumstances. Although she finally leaves her neighborhood, she does not cast off her cultural heritage. Her biggest achievement, her marriage to Donald, is the direct result of turning down fine clothes when forced to choose between her ethnic family and superficial WASP high fashion.

Yet, Irene is far from reconciled to Donald's Anglo-American background. Like the heroine in *Peg O' My Heart*, she has the equivalent of nervous hands. Though she imitates her social betters, she is at other times persistently awkward: She loses her mother's laundry and later accidentally rips a fashion dress. Her unarticulated worry seems fully justified. Even her marriage to Donald will not bring together the Irish O'Dares and the blue-blooded Marshalls. But at least the reciprocal assimilation between the two families introduced Anglo-American moviegoers to an ethnic neighborhood with real Irish traits and values.

In summary, 1920s ethnic films provided partly authentic roles for Irishmen and women. The filmic Irishman was often a model for the assimilated immigrant because he championed law, social order, and hard work. Otherwise, he might serve as a comic foil for the Anglo success ethic. The filmic Irish woman, for her part, served two purposes. She might ridicule WASP consumption, provided she also marry an Anglo hero. And she was the safest guide for WASP filmgoers curious about the urban ethnic ghetto.

Immigrant Italians for Anglo-American Audiences

Americans have long envied Italian immigrants for their unshakable belief in the family. But in the 1920s, other filmic desires were more pressing. Italian immigrants on screen seemed a backward, superstitious lot who threatened WASP social order. So, Italian young men had to be punished as lawbreakers, and their sisters hastily separated from gangster fathers. Both exclusions worked against any sense of the Italian family, and set up later fantasies: Only in film did an Italian young woman act independently of her family, marry an Irish young man, and, most incredible of all, fix a troubled Protestant marriage. At the same time, the hard-working Italian man degenerated into a despicable husband, paving the way for later half-mad gangsters like Scarface. In sum, the general public seemed most happy assimilating Italian young women and punishing their violent brothers.

The history of Italian immigration to America was but a brief sentence in 1860, when America had taken in only 10,000 Italians. Most were from northern Italy where they had worked as artists, artisans, and merchants—all highly skilled workers and solidly middle-class. But from 1880 to 1924, five million Italians sailed to America, the majority from southern Italy and Sicily where they had been common laborers and farmhands (Cogley 1973, 124). Their subsequent, well-documented success in this country is impressive. From 1905 to 1925, the number of Italian men who headed households and engaged in various skilled trades nearly doubled (from 15.7% to 30.6%), while the number of Italian men working as unskilled laborers dramatically decreased (from 55.5% to 28.1%) (Briggs 1978, 114). In the film industry, however, few Italians were actors or directors. If a producer needed someone to play an Italian street merchant, he usually hired an Irishman or some other ethnic for the part.

By the mid-1920s, the range of jobs held by Italians broadened slightly to include electricians and radio repair men. (The positions required technical training seldom learned by the Irish.) Filmic stereotypes of Italian immigrants, however, remained lower class: waiters and florists, icemen and grocers. One exception was the literary character of the Italian nobleman, which allowed directors to exploit Americans' mixed feelings about social titles. As for the dark-eyed and beautiful Italian women on screen, they acquired an independence not permitted them in real life. (In 1925, only 10% of Italian immigrant women worked outside the home as skilled craftswomen [Briggs 1978, 115]). Movie fantasies of Italian women said more about the male public's need for a vital, ethnic woman than they did about the patriarchal Italian family.

Italian men, unlike immigrant Irishmen, were not in general committed to the Roman Catholic Church in America. If Italian wives and children went to confession regularly, fathers and older sons mostly ignored church laws. Still, even Italian men who no longer went to mass kept a family tradition in which baptisms and First Communions and saints' feast days set the rhythm of each month.

Italians are admired generally for their "clear, logical, and skeptical thinking, a fine natural perception of beauty, and a gentleness of manner" (Briggs 1978, 121, 136). Movie audiences during the 1920s, however, perceived Italian culture largely in terms of passion. In its crudest form, passion meant strong feelings like lust, jealousy, and revenge. These were the traits of Italian characters in films that climaxed with a fire, a typhoon, or even a volcanic eruption. But along with the modern denotations of passion as a "sexual impulse" or an "outburst of anger," it also appeared in its original form: For centuries the word denoted *passio* or compassion, as exemplified by Christ's sufferings as a sacrificial mediator (*Oxford Dictionary of English Etymology* 1966). Italian filmic characters sometimes reflected this original meaning when they suffered for others. As a trait, Italian Catholic suffering mediated for others and fostered community.

Essential to the communal identity of Italian Americans is a sense of themselves *in famiglia*. Even an outburst of joy or bad temper on screen implied a trust in community, as if it were all one family. Add maternal Marian devotion and a rich aesthetic sensibility, and Italian immigrants have had much to offer Anglo Protestant America, with its isolating, often austere individualism.

One filmic metaphor for the complex, occasionally violent dynamic of the Italian family was bustling Manhattan. By the mid-1920s, Italians were closely associated with the power and passion of big cities—Fiorello La Guardia in New York City and Al Capone in Chicago. The star cast for *The Beautiful City* (1925), which included William Powell, Dorothy Gish, and Richard Barthelmess, suggests the marketable nature of stories about Italian crime and passion. Compared with the Irish-American films of the same period, Italian plots set in New York afforded a much greater range of family dynamics.

The landmark for Italian identity in early American film was Thomas Ince's *The Italian* (1915). Film historians such as William Everson have noted the film's striking realism, with its slum scenes of New York City (actually San Francisco, where the film was shot) (Everson 1978, 63–66). The film's Italian elements, however, have been ignored. Directed by Reginald Barker, it appealed mostly to non-Italian audiences who wanted clichéd Italian revenge touched up with familial sentimentality.

The film opens with Beppo Donnetti (George Beban) about to leave for America, where he must earn enough money in a year to send for Ann, his fiancée, or she will marry a local wealthy man. Beppo succeeds and, after Ann's arrival in America, marries her in a civil ceremony. A short time later their newborn son turns deathly sick from summer heat and lack of milk. Beppo tries to save his son's life by begging for help from an Irish politician. Ignored, Beppo watches his son die and then decides to take revenge. When he learns that the man's own child lies ill in bed, he sneaks into the Irishman's luxurious home and prepares to smother the child with a pillow. But suddenly, he thinks of his own dead son and breaks down in tears of repentance. Later, heavy with sorrow, he falls on his son's grave.

A lengthy prologue to Part 1 of this gripping melodrama introduces much ethnic lore and sets Italian values for later American films. In "Old Italy,"

> [at] the gray old monastery, flung like a rampart of the faith against the Italian sky, the bells were ringing the Angelus. A deep sweet silence had shrouded the vineyards, where the peasants stood with bowed heads. Even the shaggy burros seemed to understand as they gazed with calm, patient eyes over the scene they had grown to love; the sunshine, the mountains.

The idyllic landscape shows peasant life in a pervasively religious culture. Like the church bells in Griffith's *The Way of the World* (1910), the monastery's bells help create a sensuously sacramental Nature. The bells calm not only the common beast but also the bestial in Italian nature, an important sign for fearful nativist Americans. Similarly, the field workers show respect during the Angelus, the prayer honoring the annunciation of God's will to the Virgin Mary. To Anglo Americans, this quiet moment would also seem superstitious. But at least the bells and quaint religiosity would pacify illiterate workers.

The first trait of Italian culture to appeal to American moviegoers was a finely tuned aesthetic sensibility, which was most acceptable as the appreciation of pastoral beauty. Add the sacramental effect of tolling church bells, and this Italian naturalism struck a common cultural chord with American transcendentalism, especially with its love of Nature. The vibrant sense of scenery is strengthened further by a shot of flowing Venetian waters. Yet, there is also a dark fatalistic side to Nature, when the monastery stands "like a rampart of the faith *against* the Italian sky." The metaphor of a rampart further connotes the Catholic Church's confidence and separateness from a secular world, while remaining one with a divinely created Nature. For this reason Beppo, like D. W. Griffith's (Italian) Pippa, plays a guitar (here for wealthy American tourists). "One touch of nature makes the whole world kin," explains an intertitle. Thus, the prologue quietly assimilated Anglo-American audiences into Italian culture by proposing a sacramental sense of Nature and aesthetic sense of community.

Otherwise, an Anglo-American perspective dominates much of *The Italian*. First, the literary narrative frame (in the first and last shots) reveals a hand holding the book *The Italian* by "Thomas Ince and G. Gardner Sullivan." Second, Beppo's trip to the New World takes but a few seconds of screen time, as compared to the lengthy, more realistic trip in Chaplin's *The Immigrant* (1917). Third, Beppo somehow manages to save enough money in a New York slum to send for his bride. Any hardworking Italian immigrant can evidently make money quickly in America. But Beppo's success and his break with the Church (implied by his civil marriage) create a problem for nonethnic audiences: Who will control Italian immigrants, if they no longer respect religion? The assimilated Irish?

From either an Anglo or an Italian immigrant perspective, the Irish were self-serving politicians. This joint attitude accounts for the film's most harshly satirized figure. The city pol, Mr. Corrigan, gives Beppo a little money, telling him, "Have your wop friends vote for this guy." Later, when Beppo offers to buy drinks at a bar to celebrate his son's birth, the Irish bartender quickly signals to passersby to come in. Worst of all, when Beppo pleads desperately for help with his ailing son, Corrigan kicks him away. And the politician's neighborhood is no better: Beppo is mugged and beaten while on his way to buy pasteurized milk for his son. Thus, partly because of slum conditions but mostly because of the Irish, Beppo changes from an honest, hardworking citizen into a stereotypically vengeful Italian.

Surprisingly, Beppo's desire for revenge fails him because, true at least to Italian familism, he realizes the similarity between his own

son and the Irishman's infant; the helpless child is the prime analogue for the Italian family. In the film's closing shot, the bereaved
father throws himself across his own infant's grave. By opening himself to compassion for a loved one, he is able to reject passionate,
violent revenge.

In the 1920s, more than fifty American films presented Italian
characters from an even stronger Anglo Protestant perspective. These
ethnics typically are pawns in the hands of either Anglo-American
men and women or Irish Americans. They also serve as foils for
putting down others, usually Anglo-American women. If the Italian
shows violent passions, the plots are often set at some distance from
America, with over forty percent set in the old country.

These films also introduced Italian values as tied to the American
success ethic. *Society Snobs* (1921) satirizes wealthy socialite Vivian
Forrester who falls in a trap set by a rejected WASP suitor, with
an Italian immigrant as the bait. Lorenzo Carilo apparently deserves
to be used, for he has lost his job as a clerical worker. As the film
opens, wealthy Duane Thornton is resentful that Vivian has rejected
his amorous advances. For revenge, he pays Lorenzo to dress as a
wealthy Italian nobleman and arranges for Vivian to meet him. Later,
at the behest of her ambitious mother, Vivian marries Lorenzo, only
to flee on her wedding night when he confesses the truth. Still later,
she returns and forgives him.

The plot cleverly exploits Italian ethnic traits for purely Anglo-
American ends. Thornton's chicanery relies on two Italian stereotypes: the honest unskilled laborer and the slick nobleman. Curiously, the expected stereotype of the vengeful Italian lover is
displaced to Thornton, though still associated with Lorenzo. The displacement locates the power of revenge, which anchors the plot, with
the Anglo Protestant man. By contrast, the Italian Lorenzo remains
a weak, if kindhearted figure. More important, he is clearly a vehicle
for Anglo anger toward an independent woman. Thus, the immigrant figure expresses both WASP male anger at, yet desire for, the
haughty WASP woman.

Puppets of Fate, released a month later, also features an upstand-
ing Italian immigrant, this time manipulated by American women.
In Italy, Gabriel Palombra runs a *punchinello* or puppet show. Forced
to immigrate without his Italian wife, Gabriel becomes a helper in
a New York barber shop. One day, he acquires a reward after returning a lost pocketbook. The ambitious Babe Reynolds, the shop's
manicurist, advises Gabriel to bet on a winning horse and then helps

him build a fortune. Meanwhile, Gabriel's wife, Sorrentina, arrives in New York and works as a flower-peddler. Gabriel marries Babe, who soon charges him with bigamy to get his money. But the trial judge, perceiving Babe's ruse, sentences Gabriel to Sorrentina's care for life.

Puppets of Fate uses an honest immigrant to keep a shrewd Anglo-American working woman in her place. To begin with, Gabriel's bigamy defines him in the crudest terms as an Italian man of passion, as does his final confession. Here, positive ethnic values are secondary to an Anglo-American plot of anger and power, the full meaning of fate in the title. A similar sense of power is given to Vivian's mother in *Society Snobs*, though the later film concentrates on the fearful image of an ambitious, conniving woman, and the judge's final punishment falls mostly on her. Thus, the Anglo-American working woman and the Italian-American couple are both puppets in the hands of a law designed to safeguard WASP men from competition in love and business.

Italian culture in the 1920s also seemed to offer positive values. But before the public could openly acknowledge its desire for such values, including Marian love and large supportive families, Italian men had to be separated from the fearful stereotypes of the gangster and the forbidden lover; stories of exclusion were the first step toward ethnic assimilation. *Diane of Star Hollow* (March 1921) carefully separates the desired Italian woman from her gangster father. Diane openly rejects her father, a leader in a secret criminal organization called the Black Hand. When he later fails at crime and commits suicide, the separation is complete. An Irish police chief is partly responsible for driving Diane's father to desperation. The message to 1920s audiences was clear: If an Italian gangster is on the loose, the good Irish cop will smoke him out.

A similar narrative of exclusion is *When the Clock Struck Nine* (April 1921), in which an Italian man is sent to prison for admiring a young Irish woman. Still, the film leaves the final impression that an Italian may assimilate by associating with the Irish. As the film opens, Maggie Murphy is trying to decide between two admirers— Jim Grady and Tony Morrillo.

> Over her mother's objections, Maggie accepts a bracelet from Tony on the night of the big Kelly Club dance, but she discards it for a necklace from Jim. The events of the evening turn topsy-turvy the lives of all three: the necklace turns out to be stolen. Detective Jarvie catches Tony with the necklace in his possession, and Maggie's unwillingness to incriminate Jim results in

a 3-year prison term for Tony. By the time Tony is released, Maggie has married Jim and left him for wealthy gambler Dick Martin, and Jim has become a barroom lounger. Seeing an opportunity for revenge, Tony maneuvers Jim into burglarizing Martin's house, where he is shot by Martin. Maggie falls to Jim's side and . . . awakens from a bad dream. Arriving to escort Maggie to the dance, Jim assures her that the bracelet presents no problem and slips a ring on her finger. (Munden 1971, 836)

In this Irish-American context, the Italian American serves chiefly as a foil for the Irish belief that sexual passion is basically dangerous and should be punished. Maggie's dream expresses her guilt over the bracelet, a response induced by her Irish mother who objects to any association with a lusty Italian. Tony is punished in Maggie's dream because he represents her own displaced passion, a displacement clarified by Tony's actual innocence. Because Maggie believes she deserves to be punished, she imaginatively fails in marriage, and she is loosely, ironically tied to the killing of her true love at the hands of her own displaced desire. Once awake, Maggie quickly puts away her guilt about the bracelet and sex, since Jim says he will marry her; marriage, it seems, helps to repress Irish guilt about sexual passion.

Once Italian revenge, crime, and sexual passion had been admonished on screen, American films turned to the core of Italian-American culture, the family. If films about a large, extended family triggered a fear of papist masses, *Little Italy* (July 1921), with an Italian couple and one child, would better suit Anglo audiences. Moreover, the film points to the patriarchal center of Italian-American culture. Rosa Mascani's father banishes her because she will not marry the husband he has chosen. In revenge, the strong spirited young woman, played by Irish-American actress Alice Brady, vows to wed the first man she meets who, by chance, is Antonio Tumullo, a truck farmer. After the wedding, Antonio tries hard to win his wife's love but still cannot prevent her from leaving him. Later, Rosa, alone with a sick child, realizes that she loves Antonio and returns to ask his forgiveness.

This loving Italian couple challenges the patriarchal stereotypes of Griffith's Victorian family. Rosa is far stronger than a defensive, housebound wife, and Antonio humbles himself before his wife for the sake of their marriage. These ethnic characters were acceptable to general American audiences, and to men in particular, because they were carefully qualified by class: Antonio is, after all, a poor truck farmer. The Italian woman represents Anglo-American fantasy; in real life, immigrant wives rarely disobeyed their fathers or deserted their husbands. And unlike independent Irish heroines like Irene, the Italian Rosa must confess to the head of her household. These alternative working-class figures nevertheless introduced a limited sense of Italian culture. Antonio's love for his wife and child shows his firm commitment to family. And rather than the tragic death or the sudden rescue of Victorian melodrama, Rosa's contrite Italian confession closes the narrative. Compared to Irish confessions (such as the young beau to the Irish mother), this repentance occurs strictly within the family. In sum, American filmgoers could enjoy Italian passion and confession in exotic Little Italy, as long as Irish Father Kelly was there to protect them, and as long as sexual passion remained between husband and wife.

Films about Italians, like those about Irish Americans, tried to take the young ethnic woman out of her neighborhood. For instance, *Head over Heels* (April 1922) is a story of instant Italian assimilation into WASP society. Tina lives in Naples where she works as an acrobat, until Mr. Sterling, an American impresario played by Adolphe Menjou, discovers her and brings her to New York City. Sterling takes the plain, unkempt Tina to a beauty parlor from which she emerges an astounding beauty and quickly lands a film contract. Then Tina falls in love with Lawson, a member of a theatrical firm, but cannot decide between him and her career. In the end, she chooses neither and plans to return to Italy. But when she spies Lawson with another actress, she wavers, he repents, and she decides to stay.

If an established comedienne like Mabel Normand was willing to play Tina, public interest in Italian-American stereotypes was surely keen. Normand's Tina is allowed to have desires and choices over her life, provided in the end she abandons both her career and her mother country for a lowly American actor. Her decision to forsake her career seems inevitable once she enters the beauty parlor, that is, once she submits her natural Italian beauty to Anglo-American appearances. She nonetheless remains partly ethnic when, like the heroine of *Irene*, she requires her WASP suitor to confess. But she does not attract a wealthy socialite like Irene's suitor because her language and features cannot be so easily assimilated to Anglo-American norms.

The Italian woman entered mainstream film culture with the casting of Lillian Gish in *The White Sister* (September 1923), one of the first American films set entirely in Italy. Previously, Italian-based films like *The Love Light* (January 1921) had featured multiple romances and hokey sudden catastrophes, as if life were an Italian opera. But *The*

White Sister, directed by Henry King and based on the Francis Marion Crawford novel, captured the fatalism basic to Italian culture: Success in this life belongs to greedy, deceitful sinners who only reach heaven in a deathbed confession. The innocent victim, on the other hand, may only hope for better treatment in the next life.

The *White Sister* is the darkly fatalistic tale of Angela Chiaromonte, a young noblewoman cheated out of her inheritance by her sister. After Angela's fiancé, Giovanni Severini (Ronald Coleman), is supposedly killed at war, she grieves, begins to care for hospital patients, and finally takes vows to become a nun dedicated to the sick. Suddenly, Giovanni returns from war in Africa and tries to persuade Angela to renounce her vows. She refuses because, as her Mother Superior points out, to be a nun is to be already married to Christ. Vesuvius erupts and demolishes much of the town, and Giovanni dies helping local residents. At the same climactic moment, Angela tends to her dazed, injured sister who, thinking that Angela is a priest, confesses the theft of the family inheritance before she dies. Angela also learns of Giovanni's heroism and prays that God will keep him safe until she joins him in heaven.

The film's two plots of denied inheritance and romantic love create a distinctly Italian story of confession and romantic passion. Passion begins as Angela's love for one man until she learns, through her grief, to suffer gladly with others as a religious nurse. Confession as a statement of love occurs first when Angela takes her religious vows, emphasizing (for American audiences) freedom of will: When Angela approaches the Mother Superior in charge of admissions into the religious life, the older woman questions her motives, leaving no doubt the young woman is free to choose.

The visuals of Angela's vow ceremony transform romantic passion into service for others. The religious ritual helps Angela deal with the pain associated with Giovanni by turning to the *passio* or compassion for a suffering world. Dressed in a white wedding gown, she gazes on a large crucifix of the suffering Christ. The bishop then cuts her long hair with a pair of ceremonial scissors, symbolizing not just that she accepts chastity but that she willingly sublimates her erotic self to better serve others. She likewise places a crown of thorns over her bridal veil.

Giovanni similarly transforms his pain, if in a more complex fashion. The value of mediational self-sacrifice was much more difficult to present to Anglo-American audiences in a man. First, Giovanni must confront his stereotypes of women. When his request for Angela

is denied, he responds by challenging the "tyranny of the Church
—enslaving women who should be wives and mothers." But as a
monsignor points out to the tempestuous young lover, "Had Angela
married another man, would you expect her to break her vows? Marriage to the Holy Church is just as binding." In this love triangle with
the Church, Giovanni must give up Angela in order to discover a
similarly selfless love for others.

That is not to say the film is complacent about sublimated sexual
passion. Immediately following Giovanni's failure to recover Angela,
Vesuvius erupts. It seems only appropriate, then, that he take responsibility for the disaster and devote himself to its victims. Further,
Giovanni's thoroughly secular father, a scientist intent on harness-
ing the volcano's powers, has a breakdown just after Angela turns
down her lover. The father's death expresses the passing away of
Giovanni's secular and erotic self, and marks the beginning of his
new life of self-sacrifice to community.

The subplot of the treacherous but finally repentant sister reveals
the spiritual in an Italian feminine form. When the delirious sister
asks for forgiveness, she mistakes her sister for a priest: "Will she forgive me, Father?" And Angela immediately responds, "God is love.
She has forgiven you." The ambiguity of the nun as priest likewise
asserts the idea of a feminine God; Angela is here God's agent for
forgiveness, for she is the one who has suffered. So, the powerful
image of Angela with her dead sister in her arms is a summary, totally
female pietà.

It is precisely this Marian icon that illuminates Giovanni's subsequent conversion and eventual spiritual communion with Angela.
Immediately following the subplot's climax with the two sisters, Giovanni changes from a selfish lover to a selfless servant of the people.
He may initially be antireligious, but he is eventually transformed by
the caring, so-called feminine side of Italian culture. In later American
films, an important part of Italian immigrant men would be Marian
compassion, a quality especially attractive to WASP audiences raised
outside such a female-influenced religious culture.

The clearest statement of Italian community occurs at the end of
The White Sister, when Angela prays, "There is no death. Lord, keep
[Giovanni] safe until thou callest me." Her marriage to the Church
is to a community that includes the beloved dead. She is, moreover,
the nun as Italian Marian lover—one whose love is like the intense
passion of God's own love (Greeley 1984, 109).

Once a film star of Lillian Gish's stature had appeared as an Italian woman, the type began to appear in more independent, worldly roles. *The Wages of Virtue,* released a little over a year after *The White Sister,* is another story set at a safe distance from America—first in Italy and then in violent Algiers. It is a typically Italian and American story of jealousy, revenge, and success. In Italy, Carmelita, played by star Gloria Swanson, is saved from drowning by Luigi, a circus strongman. She then feels obliged to accompany him to Algiers, even after he kills his assistant in a jealous rage. In the end, Carmelita chooses the American Marvin over Luigi.

After the Italian woman in film had freely chosen an American, she could return to America, though no longer the quickly acculturated beauty in *Head Over Heals.* The impact of this new Italian woman was softened in *The Greatest Love of All* (February 1925) with the stereotype of the helpless Italian mother. Unlike the Irish mother, the Italian mother traditionally does not manipulate her children, and even approves of marriage for her son. The film opens with Joe, an Italian iceman, and his mother, who works secretly as a maid for the local district attorney to raise money for her son's marriage. At her job, she is accused of stealing a necklace and arrested as a common thief. Trina, Joe's Italian-American fiancé, proves the mother's innocence, but not before Joe takes revenge by helping to plant explosives in the district attorney's golf ball. After Trina absolves the mother of all wrongdoing, Joe relents and rescues the D.A. In the last scene, Trina, Joe, and his mother move to the country as one family.

The young Italian Trina mediated between Anglo-American audiences and the less savory side of Italian character, that is, thievery and murder. She is, in effect, the better side of Joe's two-sided nature; he is partly violent and partly loving, and he shows a passion for revenge but is also open to confession. In the end, the Italian sense of family is greater than the desire to avenge the mother, perhaps because Joe was never obsessively attached to her in the first place.

After the Italian mother's appearance in American film, the independent Italian woman was entirely acceptable, especially if she had an Irish beau. *The Man in Blue* (June 1925) is mostly about Tom, an Irish cop who patrols an Italian neighborhood where he meets Tita Sartori. Because she believes Tom to be married, she shuns his initial advances. But Tom wins her heart after saving her from a crooked politician, who has killed an Italian youth with a crush on Tita. *The Man in Blue* mostly shows how much Anglo-American audiences wanted an idealized balance of interethnic cultures. In real life, if an Irish family in a New York parish discovered that one of their sons planned to marry an Italian woman, the romance would have quickly been broken off (Herberg 1955, 157). Here, however, Italian and Irish figures bring together a sexually appealing ethnic woman (desired by no fewer than three men) and the model of ethnic self-control—an Irish immigrant. Thus, Anglo (male) audiences could fantasize about romance with an ethnic woman and still feel safely in control.

Sometimes, the filmic Italian woman had little relation to social reality, as when, for example, she saves a WASP marriage. In *The Manicure Girl* Maria Maretti loves a stingy electrician named Antonio Luca. She is also courted by Mr. Morgan, a wealthy hotel guest. When she learns that Morgan is married, she manages to reunite him with his wife, while she herself returns to a penitent Antonio. The idea that a manicurist could achieve either of these miracles is magical thinking. Maria reveals the early perception in American film that Italian young women, more than their Irish counterparts, would allow Anglo Americans both to explore sexual passion and to follow a family mediator. At the same time, these filmic women were used to reprimand the successful immigrant.

After the Italian-American woman had been partly assimilated on screen, audiences were ready for a much more complex treatment of the Italian immigrant man. He soon acquired a double-sided nature that was partly sexual passion and partly long-suffering com*passion*. *The Beautiful City* (October 1925) depicted these two sides as two Italian brothers in New York City. Italian flower vendor Tony Gillardi is less favored in his mother's eyes than his brother Carlo, who secretly receives money through mob connections with Nick Di Silva. Tony also loves Mollie O'Connor, although their chance to marry depends upon whether Tony can save Carlo from the influence of Nick; as in later American films like *Mean Streets* (1973) and *The Pope of Greenwich Village* (1984), the young Italian-American man's romance depends on his blood tie to the family's black sheep. When Tony finally fights Nick, Mrs. Gillardi is shot but not killed, and Nick falls to his death while trying to escape.

The Beautiful City clearly punishes not only the Italian gangster but also the mother who has raised a criminal son. As for the Italian man, he is accepted into society as long as he actively discourages the criminal element and marries the paragon of assimilation, the Irish young woman. While he fiercely fights for a strong sense of family, she has the Irish background to keep such spirit under control. Thus, the film strengthened the overall image of the family, especially in Tony's extreme sacrifices for his brother.

Soon, many 1920s films presented the two opposing Italian brothers as one double-sided character: the wealthy rake and the industrious immigrant. No film was more famous for this Italian type than *Cobra*, starring Rudolph Valentino. Released in November of 1925, *Cobra* is the story of Count Rodrigo Torriani, an impoverished but handsome nobleman who immigrates to New York, works for an antique dealer, and falls in love with secretary Mary Drake. Rodrigo also attracts Elise Van Zile (played by Nita Naldi, born Anita Dooley), a clever and worldly woman who pursues him but marries his employer. When she continues to chase Rodrigo, he agrees to meet her in a hotel room, where, stricken in conscience he leaves her. Then the hotel catches fire and she dies. A year later, Rodrigo returns to town to find Mary nursing her employer. Although he could have her for the asking, he puts on a casual face and sails for Europe.

This handsome Italian man with no apparent family has little sense of place in the New World. There he is chiefly a go-between for others, as he brings together a merchant and his secretary. He also sparks a fiery passion in Elise. But with no Irish character to cool her sexual appetite, she literally dies in the fire of passion; the Italian male cobra is deadly not so much for his sexual bite, as for eyes that create a desire never to be fulfilled. Rodrigo himself is saved by his critical conscience, a final essential aspect of Italian culture here.

When Valentino played the lead in *Cobra*, he was in the latter half of his career. In earlier films, his exotic face on screen had a mesmerizing effect with its openly Italian, expressive sign of masculinity. But under the influence of his wife Natasha Rambova (born Winifred Shaunessy), Valentino became increasingly effeminate in his roles. His Irish-American wife managed not only every detail of his career, but also emasculated his filmic image.

The Italian ethnic films that followed *Cobra* were immoderate and reactionary. As the degradation of Italian men and of Italy in general became the trend, film settings once again had to be in foreign locale. Alan Dwan's *Sea Horses* (1926), for example, is about Helen Salvia (Florence Vidor) and her four-year-old daughter in search of her fiendish husband, Lorenzo. Helen takes a ship bound for Panda, where she finds Lorenzo who promptly sells her and her daughter. After Captain Glanville (Jack Holt) buys them back, she still returns to shore where the half-crazed Lorenzo attacks her. But a typhoon breaks just as Glanville recovers Helen's daughter, and Lorenzo dies from a knife wound. In the end, Helen sails for England with Glanville.

The Italian man's lower passions here lead him to threaten even his own family, though the image of Lorenzo as a sot was less than credible. In real life, neither Italians nor Italian Americans had problems with alcohol (especially when compared with the Irish). This perverse portrait of a drunken Italian was a foil for Anglo Americans and the Irish, who enjoyed imagining an exotic land of endless drink. Still, there is a remnant of Italian culture in the importance accorded the family: If anyone, even a well-meaning captain, challenged it, nothing less than a typhoon would justify a change of fathers.

A more surprisingly varied and subtle treatment of the passionate Italian is *Puppets* (June 1926). The film's title suggests that Italian character is essentially pulled by the strings of passion. In New York's Little Italy, Nicki Riccobini is a domineering father and puppet master, while his cousin Bruno is a dreamer and a layabout. In this complicated romance, Nicki falls in love with Angela, a demure runaway whom he entrusts to Bruno before going off to war. Nicki instructs Bruno to protect Angela from the sinister Frank, the puppet accompanist. When Nicki is reported dead, Angela and Bruno fall fast in love. Even after a deaf Nicki returns from the front, the two lovers plan to leave together. But when Nicki later rescues Angela from Frank, his hearing returns. The ensuing struggle between Nicki and Bruno ends with a tremendous fire in the theater. Bruno's cowardice is revealed, and Angela is reunited with Nicki. The moral: An overbearing patriarch has suffered and learned to change his ways. In general Italian terms, when romantic passion includes suffering (deafness), it can lead to a new couple and a renewed sense of family.

The tumultuous plot of *Puppets* suggests the lack of good scripts with Italian characters in the 1920s. Producers began searching literary works about Italians to serve up violence and hot romance, perennial Hollywood solutions. The increased market for Italian figures led producer William Fox to adapt Joseph Conrad's *Nostromo*. In the actual adaptation—*The Silver Treasure* (June 1926)—George O'Brien's Nostromo might be treacherous and greedy but he does finally confess to Gould, the Englishman he has robbed. In later works by both Irish- and Italian-American directors, the Anglo-American fascination with the ethnic conscience would be essential for reciprocal assimilation.

Don Juan (August 1926) was an adaptation of Lord Byron's story of the notorious lover. Warner Brothers was so keen on the project that they signed up a big-name cast, with John Barrymore as Don Juan and Mary Astor as Adriana Della Vernese. The sensational plot included a duel, a stabbing, a fake suicide, and death by enclosure in a niche. And of course the film featured attractive Italian women, as framed by Don Juan's dominant attitude throughout the project: Take everything and leave nothing in return.

By 1926, audiences had come to expect that the Italian woman on screen would be fabulously beautiful and yet devoted to her husband and family. At the same time, she did not yet show an independent spirit of her own. In *Rose of the Tenements* (December 1926) the Jewish Kaminskys raise two orphans, Rose Rosetti, daughter of an Italian gangster, and Irish-American Danny Lewis. After the Kaminskys pass away, Danny and Rose continue to run the family business of artificial flowers, though Danny gets involved with Bolsheviks. In the end, Danny is exonerated from a charge of bomb-throwing and confesses his love for Rose.

Produced by Joseph Kennedy, directed by Phil Rosen, and adapted from the novel by John Moroso, *Rose of the Tenements* was very much a multiethnic production. Typical of the period, the Italian woman received less dramatic attention than the Irish young man and the Jewish couple. While awaiting Danny's return, Rose sells artificial flowers—a symbol of her (and his) artificial assimilation into American culture. Once again, an Italian isolated from family quickly loses all sense of identity. Separated from her gangster father, Rose has to hold onto the coattails of an Irish young man and a Jewish couple. If wide-ranging passions were to be expected in the Italian man, his sister had to lead a carefully restricted life.

Fighting Love (February 1927) is a sympathetic portrait of an active Italian woman, who tries to find happiness in a world ruled by marital laws. Born to a noble family, Donna Vittoria marries a friend, a military man, in order to prevent an arranged marriage. Then she falls in love with Gabriel, a soldier under her husband's command. When her husband is reported slain in Tripoli, she quickly marries Gabriel but then leaves him when her husband returns. In yet another reversal, she returns to Gabriel after her first husband commits suicide. The film's exotic setting and frequent noble names are further signs that Donna Vittoria's independent will is pure fantasy.

Once the filmic Italian woman could conceivably act on her own, the question arose as to what she might accomplish in America. The immediate answer was to let her substitute for the stereotype of the Italian man in pursuit of success. *The 3 Sisters* (April 1930) begins by spelling out the cruel patriarchy that Italian women without financial resources must face. The first sister prepares to enter an arranged marriage, but then stabs her rich fiancé and runs away with the second sister to America. The third sister dies in childbirth. In the end, the two Italian immigrants achieve moderate success, enough to send for their starving mother and her grandchild. Here storywriters George Brooks and Marion Orth concocted an unusual degree of independence for the two sisters. In real life, Italian women seldom immigrated before male family members. More to the point, Brooks and Orth have not only separated Italian women from oppressive male stereotypes, but also granted them completely independent fates and thus a chance at the American dream. The sisters run away from an oppressive patriarchy and set up a new life, one that Francis Coppola would resurrect five decades later for another Italian heroine.

The Italian woman reached a dead end in film when she was entirely cut off from her sense of family, the core of her cultural identity. *Oh, for a Man* (December 1930) is about Italian opera star Carlotta Manson, who discovers Barney McGann burglarizing her apartment. In an odd twist of plot, she recognizes in him a great potential as a singer and decides to coach him. Although he shows little musical aptitude, she marries him and gives him an Italian villa. The narrative cleverly inverts the immigrant success story, such that the foreigner offers both wealth and high culture to the WASP beau. But far from New York, Barney grows impatient for his American friends and deserts his wife. Months later, when Carlotta sings badly in a New York recital, Barney reappears, advises her on her singing, and agrees to remain with her.

Oh, for a Man was the end of Anglo attempts to assimilate the figure of the Italian-American woman. Carlotta is simply a wooden stereotype of the Italian opera singer at the service of Anglo desire. Like McGann, Anglo audiences evidently wanted to meet a woman from Italy's rich aesthetic tradition, especially classy opera: The filmic robbery symbolizes Anglo-American desire to acquire a rich Italian aesthetic sensibility, without getting invovled in lowly Italian ethnic life; McGann's final role as a voice critic is a disguise and translation of his earlier role as a burglar, someone who knows nothing about Italian opera but who believes that, through the magical assimilation of marriage, he can become an authority.

The contorted plot with the same man as both thief and husband, shows, as the film's title first suggests, the total focus of desire and power in the Anglo-American man. By comparison, Carlotta is nearly powerless as an Italian cut off from her family. Adrift in the world, she is vulnerable to burglary, that is, to the intrusion of Anglo-

American desire. Although it was this desire that in earlier films freed the Italian woman from Italian patriarchy, she only landed in another patriarchal culture. Her assimilation into America was indeed limited. Italian filmic figures in the 1920s served as extreme examples of moral corruption, revenge, sexual license, and wild jealousy. If the Irish were nearly paragons of virtue, Italians showed the worst side of the immigrant new masses. For this reason, the attractive Italian woman had to be taken out of her neighborhood. Lillian Gish's portrayal of a nun in Italy somewhat redeemed the Italian man, such that he turned away from rough passion to compassionate service to others. Later, the Italian man appeared in a better guise as both nobleman and dedicated worker, though there too lurked a human cobra who lured women with his sexual gaze. By the early 1930s, then, the Italian woman on screen had become an opera puppet pulled by the strings of Anglo-American desire, while the Italian gangsters of *Little Ceasar*, *Public Enemy*, and *Scarface* were all the rage.

Laurette Taylor, as Irish Peg in **Peg O' My Heart**
(1922), feels out of place in a British home of decorative
surfaces. (Museum of Modern Art/Film Stills Archive;
courtesy of Metro Pictures)

Lillian Gish, as an Italian nun in The White Sister
(1923), transforms erotic desire into religious devotion.
(Museum of Modern Art/Film Stills Archive)

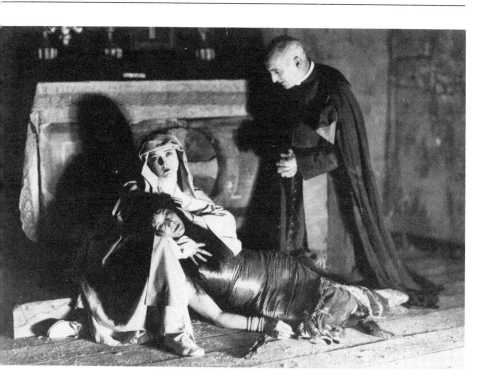

Rudolph Valentino, as an Italian immigrant in Cobra
(1925), sparks sexual desire but never fulfills it. (Mu-
seum of Modern Art/Film Stills Archive)

Colleen Moore, as a young Irish woman in Irene *(1926), achieves financial security by marrying into WASP society. (Museum of Modern Art/Film Stills Archive)*

The commandant in The Informer *(1935) speaks for Irish society when he corners Gypo Nola as an unforgivable Judas. (Museum of Modern Art/Film Stills Archive; courtesy of RKO Radio)*

CHAPTER 3

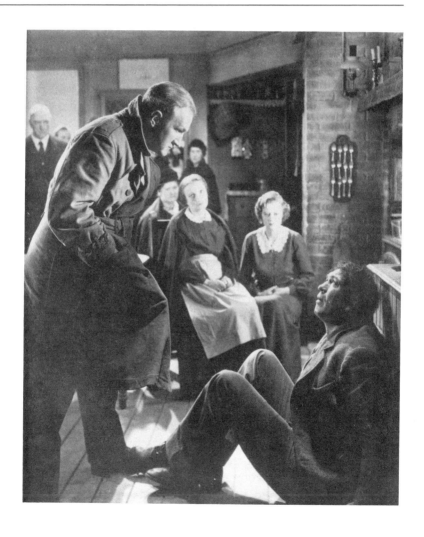

JOHN FORD

In *A Short History of the Movies*, Gerald Mast begins his discussion of John Ford's work with a shrewd cultural observation.

[Ford] is the spiritual descendant of D. W. Griffith. Like Griffith, Ford's values are traditional and sentimental: the pure woman, the home, the family, law, decency, democracy. Like Griffith— and like the two other important Roman Catholic directors of the studio era, Frank Capra and Leo McCarey—Ford was a populist who praised the little people and the institutions that protected the little people while he damned those who selfishly twisted the system to grab money and power. (1981, 240)

Griffith and Ford were both moralists and outsiders, one from the South and the other from Irish America. Mast's insight into their common cultural spirit encourages an ethnic reading of Ford's canon, in which he tried for forty years to express his Irish background. He explored this background in the foreign figures of Judas, Mary Magdalene, and the Virgin Mary. Then he brought his ethnic schema to the American West. This surface Anglo conformity revitalized American myth and history with basic Irish beliefs. Thus, as Ford gradually faced his Irish-American background over four decades, he discovered within it his major American themes of family, law, decency, and democracy.

Ford's critics have long recognized that his canon comprises films set in America, in Ireland, and in several foreign lands. To account for these differences of place as one canon, critics have searched for a central dynamic. Peter Wollen, for example, focuses on the wilderness and the garden as Ford's "master antinomy" (1972, 96). But the critics have completely overlooked the seminal impact of Ford's hyphenated ethnic identity on his canon, which clearly divides

and the Landscapes of Irish America

into four landscapes: Irish America, Ireland, foreign lands, and the wild West. Each landscape suggests a roughly chronological stage in Ford's career: First, early films set in ethnic America acknowledged and then improved on negative immigrant stereotypes; second, films set in the old country explored its violent social tensions; third, films set in imaginary foreign lands experimented with deeply conflicted Irish values; and fourth, the late westerns revitalized American history and myth by fine tuning earlier ethnic schemata. Each of these landscapes rests on an underlying tension in Ford's canon between the Irish and Anglo-American halves of his heritage.

Ford's style of working with writers, actors, and editors grew out of Irish-Catholic beliefs and attitudes acquired in childhood. In 1895, Sean Aloysius Feeney was born near Portland, Maine to an Irish-American family with thirteen children. In the busy Feeney household, mother Ford had final say in most matters, including her husband's allowance for betting at the races. Sean was her youngest child and her favorite, perhaps because he most closely resembled her in appearance. Ford's father spoke Gaelic and ran a saloon in town. With an Irish immigrant's sense of community, he regularly walked to the docks to greet new Irish emigrés, help them find jobs, and advise them how to vote. Portland at the time was home to many established Irish immigrants, as well as to Jews and Italians and Anglo Americans. There, the blend of multiethnic culture and Anglo-American history set Sean's self-image as a hyphenated American especially proud of his Irish roots. Years later, as a filmmaker renowned for westerns, Ford enjoyed telling friends that Sean was his "real name" (Tavernier 1967, 12 [translation mine]).

By the early 1920s, "Jack" Ford was directing westerns in Hollywood and still a practicing Catholic. He attended the Church of the

Blessed Sacrament on Cherokee Avenue, and went regularly to confession. On his first job as a stuntman, he would make the sign of the
cross just before each assignment. As a filmmaker, he often invited
a priest on location to bless a picture or say mass for the Catholic
crew members (Ford 1979, 31). And when his ketch the *Araner* was
returned to him after World War II, he had it blessed by a priest.
Blessings for any undertaking or possession were sacramental links
for Ford between the institutional Church and his workaday life.

Sometimes, however, Ford's idea of blessings bordered on the
superstitious. In the last weeks before his death in Palm Springs,
he regularly said his rosary, kept a statue of the Virgin Mary by his
bedside, and daily had a priest say mass (McBride and Wilmington 1974, 9; Sinclair 1979, 211). He also wore a necklace of talismans
from various faiths around his neck. Like many nonintellectual Irish
Americans, religion in his life was a great unexamined force.

Ford had a particularly Irish sense of community that kept him
close to the Church, the film industry, and other institutions such as
the military. During World War II, Ford's superior officer in the Navy
and friend, "Wild Bill" Donovan, gave him a free hand with film production, encouraging him to draw on his Hollywood resources for
Battle of the Midway (1942). Ford also became close friends with Father
Joseph Brady, a Navy chaplain who later proved a key liaison for
requests from Hollywood (Ford 1979, 50). After the war, Ford especially valued his friendship with James Kevin McGuinness, a writer
at Fox who was well connected in Catholic social circles (Ford 1979,
46). Mrs. Ford, a convert and a Southerner, also had the parish priest
to dinner each week (Sinclair 1979, 151). Eventually, Ford met New
York's Cardinal Spellman and even had a private audience with the
Pope (Sinclair 1979, 210).

Ford's Irish sense of community was mostly that of male camaraderie, especially with the Irish-American regulars in his company
—John Wayne, Thomas Mitchell, and George O'Brien. Two of Ford's
favorite scriptwriters, Frank Nugent and Dudley Nichols, were also
half or more Irish. In any case, Ford preferred to hire the same actors
and technicians for his films, forming a loyal list of one hundred with
a communal sense of themselves and their work (Sharpe 1936, 99).
"For the most part, the actors are good friends of mine," Ford said.
"I know their characters and their responsibilities" (Tavernier 1967,
14 [translation mine]). As long as he had a good collaborative work
situation, his methods meshed well with the studio system. In his
view, the role of the director was to help writers, actors, and cine-

matographers interpret a scene according to his own firm yet general guidelines. He was the Irish mediator between his company and the world of the filmic story.

As an Irish-American Catholic, he was accustomed to thinking of himself as a member of an institution with a clearly defined hierarchy and chain of command. Thus, the studio system suited his personal Irish style of collaboration and indirect authority, though he always had the last word. He had grown up, after all, with a religious liturgy in which a male authority figure presided each week over the communal ritual of the mass. In the American Catholic Church from the 1900s to the 1970s, the pastor, often of Irish extraction, had indirect but complete control of parish life—socially, financially, and liturgically. Ford took a similar approach to his responsibilities on set and off.

During Ford's lifetime, the Church's sacraments and liturgy were especially important to the legalistic and loyally institutional Irish. In large Irish families a child's first confession was second only to his first communion. In the liturgical calendar, Passion week was the most dramatic time, as youngsters and parents watched Christ's painful suffering and death on the road from Gethsemane to Calvary. Closer to a human scale in Irish-American culture were three related Passion figures: Mary Magdalene, the Mater Dolorosa, and the betrayer Judas. Each year parishes presented all three characters in liturgical pageants. In Ford's films, these characters also played key roles for an Irish confessional conscience.

The Virgin Mary in Irish-American parishes was a key figure of self-sacrifice, patient understanding, and forgiveness. Ford's own mother had a strong, if not unusually Irish hold on him: She sent him, he said, mental messages over long distances. In his films, images of strong Irish mothers and widows frequently appeared—women who always seemed to know intuitively when a son figure suffered and needed forgiveness. The Irish father, on the other hand, was an indirect figure of authority, partly because of his long work hours and partly because of the mother's strong presence in the home. It was with this sense of Irish fatherhood and vision of Irish community that Ford first walked on a movie set.

An Irish-American Idea of Film Production

Throughout Ford's canon, his role as a mediational director was inconsistent. Of course in Hollywood, all directors had to fight for control of their productions. Otherwise, writers, actors, and self-important producers would take over. Ford's answer was to make a virtue of the Irish father's background control of family affairs and to keep the same group together for future projects. The few times he was unable to work with his regular group of actors, or was not allowed to handle all details from a project's inception, the film looked a mess. The trick, Ford said, was "to turn out films which please the public, but which also reveal the personality of the director" (Mitry 1955, 306). Conversely, if the mostly WASP American public were directly told the director's personal vision, they would not be pleased—especially if he were of Irish Catholic heritage.

Ford's sense of Irish community both suited film production and encouraged filmic characters quite different from the clichés of popular genres or filmic figures created by Anglo-American directors like Orson Welles. While Welles's Anglo protagonists seemed estranged from the world and its objects, Ford's characters were members of a tight community and integrally related to the landscape.

In Ford's varied landscapes, the Irish issue of a scrupulous conscience often arose within mostly male groups. Typically, a small band of men is thrust by fate into a tragic life-or-death situation that allowed Ford to bring individuals "face to face with something bigger than themselves. The situation, the tragic moment forces men to reveal themselves, and to become aware of what they truly are." Ford points out here his underlying sacramental assumption that divine presence resides in mundane reality. "The device [of the tragic moment] allows me to find the exceptional in the commonplace," he said (Mitry 1955, 307).

Early in his career, Ford took control of all aspects of production, which was one way to establish a coherent atmosphere on set. As one newspaper critic noted, Ford was responsible for the choice of words in the script, the style of lighting, and even the design of the fireplace. Most directors in the late 1920s had to serve as guild workers in a fast production schedule. But Ford established a reputation among producers as an ornery cuss, and so they placated him rather than fight. As scriptwriter Nunnally Johnson recalls, "rarely, almost never, would a studio order [Ford] to do a picture he disliked" (Anderson 1981, 247). He even had a clause in his Fox contract that allowed him to accept outside assignments. Over the decades, however, the money men increasingly frustrated Ford. By the 1960s, he claimed he could no longer make pictures the way he used to (Ford 1979, 97). But in his best pictures, he had sufficient command to finesse the studio system with his own Irish style of managing people and directing shots.

Ford had definite ideas about every role, though he also believed he would defeat the collaborative spirit on set if he dictated his intentions. To avoid being authoritarian, he made certain that the story's world came before his own ego. Harry Carey, Jr. remembers "a very special feeling on every John Ford set. . . . It wasn't a feeling of reverence for John Ford; it was a feeling of reverence for art. It was like being in church" (Ford 1979, 222). With Ford's ego and those of his actors subordinated to the film's story, he was often able to capture the company's communal spirit on film. Because he usually allowed only one take, there was great pressure on the actors to focus their group spirit. James Stewart noted that "a lotta directors . . . y'know . . . it's a barrel a laughs on the set and ya have fun and . . . and then you see the picture and you say, 'Where is it? Where's the. . . .' But Ford *gets* it on the screen" (McBride 1974, 29).

At the center of Ford's communal world was the character, the focal point for the atmosphere of scenery and costumes. At the start of a new project, Ford often asked his writer to draw up a protagonist's biography so that the character's small habits and everyday behavior would be completely clear. Next, Ford required long story conferences in which he all but dictated the script. In the early days, for example, he gave his ideas to Harry Carey, who put them down on paper. In later years, as Frank Nugent remembers, "in story conferences—he's like a kid whistling a bar of music, and faltering; then if I come up with the next notes and they're what he wanted, he beams and says that's right, that's what he was trying to get over" (Anderson 1981, 244). With his fine Irish ear for the spoken word, Ford also frequently changed the script on set.

After story conferences, which sometimes took weeks, Ford began to set up an Irish work ethic on set. To begin with, he made certain that he was the head of his film family: Neither the producer nor the writer were welcome on set without his personal invitation. Ford once introduced a producer to his crew, "Get a good look at this fellow because he's the producer and you won't see him again." With his family on set, Ford went to great lengths to invest the smallest details of production with significance, that is, with an Irishman's sense of vibrant sacramental realism. To begin with, he gave the impression on set that he knew about everything, and that he expected everyone to pay close attention to their work. Every detail counted. As Harry Carey, Jr. recalls, "Ford had this tremendous control and he was total boss [of sets and costumes]. He was props-crazy and wardrobe-crazy. In fact he was everything-crazy" (Anderson 1981, 213). Ford invested every detail of his work with a sacramental significance.

Ford's Irish work ethic included his actors. Sometimes, he took an actor aside and talked about anything but the film, until the actor suddenly thought he heard Ford insinuate a particular direction for the role. Anna Lee recalls that he'd "get you in a corner and start talking—not about the scene—but about something entirely different —and instinctively you knew he was trying to tell you something . . . as if there was some kind of thought transference" (Ford 1979, 158).

Ford's style of playing the Irish-American father with actors varied according to their temperament and talent. With experienced performers like Thomas Mitchell and Mary Astor, he gently offered hints about a role, seldom spelling out his ideas. With actors less sensitive to his promptings, he used an altogether different style of Irish instruction. If an actor was to be a sergeant leading soldiers into a fort, Ford might give him no directions, letting him desperately try to divine where to go, with just the desired effect of fearful uncertainty.

One less appealing version of Ford's Irish work ethic involved verbal ridicule. The Irish are notorious for deriding a community member who wants to be different and, presumably, better than his peers. This use of ridicule limits full community, while it subtly, sometimes cruelly, retains individuals' allegiance to Irish political and religious institutions. Ford drew on this dark side of his Irish heritage when an actor was less gifted or less well trained than Mitchell. He would intentionally upset an actor to get a particular effect. The most famous instance is the Oscar-winning performance Ford bullied out of Victor McLaglen for *The Informer* (1935). Throughout the film McLaglen's face looks confused and wounded. Ford's male inner circle endured his occasionally degrading comments, and some actors even viewed the sarcasm as a male rite of initiation. A few, including John Wayne, were initiated repeatedly despite a close friendship with the director off the set.

In the tradition of the Catholic visual arts, Ford's world on screen was not based on the Anglo-Protestant Word but on a visible place that emanated a sacramental reality, mostly by focusing on communal actions and mediation. "I am a man of the silent cinema," Ford said. "That's when pictures and not words had to tell the story" (Sinclair 1979, 37). "The only thing I always had was an eye for composition" (Bogdanovich 1978, 108). Usually, Ford took the script and pared down paragraphs to sentences, and sentences to words. He kept only what contributed to the film's unity, and avoided both expository dialogue and camera movement, so that his narrative depends on physical action and especially gesture to reveal character type within a group (McBride and Wilmington 1974, 47; Mitry 1955, 306, 305). Ford guided his actors to find the expressive body language that would reveal inner character, paying close attention to telltale details like clothing, especially hats.

Lighting in particular served Ford's sense of ethnic community. He might wait hours for the right evening light, while expecting the actors to be ready at a moment's notice for the one take. One cinematographer said that Ford knew more about the craft of lighting than any director with whom he had ever worked. Thus, after carefully establishing characters in story conferences with writers and in talks with his actors, Ford devoted himself to the one remaining variable —the natural lighting that creates the characters' world.

> If you'll watch in any of my pictures, you'll see the trick I use for special effect: while the stars are running through their lines, a diffused glow settles over the background assemblage, which at the same time begins to murmur and then to talk intelligibly. And the louder the voices, the stronger the glow, until the main actors are merely part of a group and the general realism is achieved. (Sharpe 1936, 100)

Ford did not cut away to close-ups of individual characters but instead preferred groups in the context of landscape, the terrain serving as the context of a struggling community. While the characters talked, the landscape often told more about their conversation than the few overheard words (Anderson 1981, 213). Thus, Monument Valley, so often seen in Ford's westerns, was sacramental in part because it visually related Irish types and their self-sacrifice in the same frame.

Over the course of Ford's four landscapes, Anglo-American filmgoers might recognize nineteenth-century stereotypes of Irish immigrants, while Irish-American audiences discovered their religious and social values in all-American guises like the western. Ford's 1920s films often presented Irish-American stereotypes: the boxer, the drinker, the jockey, the devoted son, and of course the policeman. As opportunity allowed, Ford experimented with films set partly or entirely in Ireland; that is, he shifted from filling in the background of Irish-American stereotypes to introducing less familiar Irish types and their age-old conflict with Great Britain. He then tried to free himself from the realities of Irish culture—violence against the British and fear of informers—by working on Irish values in foreign places. These places of the mind also enabled him to experiment with religious allegory, especially Irish mother figures, Marian values, and the confessional conscience. In the West, he matched Irish types and principles to formulaic frontier stories. With American characters such as Ma Joad, Abraham Lincoln, and the Ringo Kid, Ford either satirized or praised Anglo Americans as mediators of community.

Urban Irish America: Ethnic Dangers and Virtues

The first stereotype of Irish America Ford explored was the common laborer. America in the nineteenth century had relied heavily on poor immigrants and especially the Irish to build its industrial infrastructure, which included rapid expansion of the nation's railroads. The Irish, the most easily assimilated of the newcomers, often assumed the job of straw boss or team leader.

The Iron Horse (1924) pictured a multiethnic group of men that in Ford's later films became simply an all-male group. His first Irish community comprised poor workers in an Anglo-Protestant society of rich landowners and industrialists. Here Ford carefully separated a crude Irish stereotype (the violent and self-centered Irish worker) from the Irish values embodied by a mainstream hero.

This landmark film clearly states Ford's major themes of law, decency, and democracy in the context of an immigrant labor that serves Anglo-American progress. In this rudimentary democracy, immigrants need protection both from wealthy Anglos and from their own, the Irish straw bosses who act in the interests of the railroad's owners. Ford's Irish-American slant was the hero's ability to act as a dual community mediator, saving laborers' jobs *and* protecting the interests of the eastern Anglos.

The Iron Horse (1924), like many of Ford's later films about mythic America, is based on an event in American history that places an Irishman in a firmly communal situation. On May 10, 1869, two crews of immigrant laborers joined the Central Pacific and Union Pacific railroads. Ford's epic story of national unity and ethnic assimilation shows Chinese, Italians, and other emigrés working together under an Irish straw boss, a figure Ford intentionally based on the nineteenth-century stereotype of the crude but useful Irishman: Slattery denigrates "foreigners" to his Anglo-eastern employer. This

Irishman's idea of assimilation is nationalistic Anglo conformity, pure and simple.

Ford's blend of American nationalism and immigrant stereotypes accounts for the film's broad appeal. The film opens with the myth of America's expanding frontier, as a young Abe Lincoln in Illinois envisions a West where the entire country can grow. But settled landowners like Mr. Bauman suppress the development of both the railroads and the new communities that spring up around them. Disguised as an Indian, Bauman sabotages railroad construction by leading war parties. In Ford's later films set in Ireland, he would clarify the Irish roots of Bauman's character: He is a Judas who betrays his own community.

Ford's sharp division between the landowners and migrating Easterners, represented here mostly by immigrant labor, requires an all-American mediator like Davy Brandon, a young scout raised next door to Lincoln in Illinois. Davy's father takes him West to explore the new territories and is scalped by Bauman. When Davy grows up, he avenges his father's death, while saving the railroad. The film closes with a scene of multiethnic communion serving Anglo progress: At the historic moment the golden spike—a symbol of male exploration, progress, and prosperity—is struck, the two work crews leap into one another's arms. Thus, Ford celebrates both Anglo progress and the multiracial sense of community it fosters.

Within Ford's Irish-American story of ethnic community and hard work, two characters suggest changes needed in Irish America if other immigrants are to emulate its success. Ford distinguished with precision between Davy and the stereotypical Irish immigrant, Sergeant Slattery. As crew foreman, the crude Slattery identifies with his eastern-bred boss, denigrating the non-Irish immigrants who work for him and sometimes using violence to control them. He complains at one point, "Say, boss, there's no gettin' on with these furriners— I knocked five of thim down—an' even then they wouldn't work." Just as stereotypically Irish is the later sentimental scene of Slattery, rosary in hand, mourning an Irish friend's death. Ford set up these Irish clichés in order to poke fun at them, while also separating them from the positive ethnic kernel in his tale.

Davy Brandon, played by the Irish-looking George O'Brien, is really Irish underneath his leather stockings, that is, in the context of Ford's story. The Irish issue of violence, already linked to the Irish foreman, also defines Davy's role. The Anglo Miriam begs him to swear he will never fight again. But when he recognizes Bauman from childhood as his father's murderer, he must avenge his father's death. Thus, the American myths in Davy's background (Lincoln and exploration of the frontier) lead both to his (Irish) role of violence and his function as a dual mediator.

The phallic ceremony of the golden spike symbolizes Davy's tie to Anglo patriarchal progress and his sexual reward: He gets to marry Miriam, the feminine figure of Anglo life. He is culturally acceptable as a husband because, like the Irish gang leaders in *The Blue Eagle* (1926), he has used force judiciously. Davy is, in effect, Ford's paradigm of the potentially violent but finally trustworthy ethnic. In the film's last scene, a Chinese worker boasts, "I Irish too, I marry Nora Hogan."

Ford's first representation of Irish values places them squarely in service to Anglo-American progress. Controlled labor and industrial development are finally more important than a multiethnic male community. Still, Ford has introduced the immigrant community of America's big cities in its most appealing form, as workers for progress. In later films he learned to substitute a socially mixed group for the multiethnic community, and smoother Irish figures for its leaders. In short, he learned to match an Irish-American narrative schema to Anglo-American stories.

After the buffoonish stereotype of the Irish straw boss, Ford drew closer to his immigrant roots. In 1926, the producers at Fox studio knew that Ford very much wanted scripts on the Irish, and so they gave him *The Shamrock Handicap*, a story about why an upper-class Irish family came to America and why, like the immigrants in *My Wild Irish Rose* (1922) and *Irish Luck* (1925), they also returned to their homeland. (In real life, only a small percentage of the immigrant Irish had any relation to the landed gentry. And they returned to their homeland, if at all, only for brief visits.)

The handicap of the title refers first to horse racing, which is often associated with the Irish. But it refers as well to the drawback of being Irish in America, where the Irish often felt unwanted. A sense of handicap or displacement was especially difficult for Irish immigrants, given Ireland's long history of British subjugation. First, the Irish lost their land to the British and then again in the nineteenth century to poverty, which forced thousands to immigrate to America. (In Ford's later films, the theme of losing one's land became a major [Irish] motif.) Because of this strong sense of displacement, the Irish, particularly the Irish in America, acquired an intensely nostalgic view of their heritage in general and of pastoral scenes in particular—including horses.

The Shamrock Handicap is about a well-to-do family in Ireland that gets out of financial difficulties by taking Dark Rosaleen, their best thoroughbred, to America. Sir Miles O'Hara has fallen on hard times, and Neil Ross, the O'Hara's best jockey, leaves Ireland with an American horse buyer. In America, O'Hara's new jockey, Bennie Ginsburg, is injured seconds before the big race, but Ross rides the horse to victory for his former employer and for the hand of Molly O'Shea, the daughter of the O'Hara's servants. Restored to his former prosperity, Sir Miles returns to Ireland with his family and the young lovers.

Secondary characters and scenes round out Ford's lively tableau of Irish culture. Besides the genteel Lady and Sir Miles, there is Mother O'Shea who, as the subtitle says, "ran the O'Hara household —and [her husband] Con!" Ford spells out the mother's sexual mores just after her daughter blows a good-bye kiss to Neil. As her mother's shadow appears in the frame, the young woman suddenly freezes in her romantic gesture.

In America, the Irishman uses his putative violence to defend the weak. Ross protects Bennie Ginsburg and his black helper Virus Cakes from a vicious locker-room bully, belting the fellow through a door. "Well, he sure made me feel at home!," Ross says. "It's just like the Old Country—always fightin'!" Evidently raised to use his fists, Ross channels his inbred passion by defending assumedly less capable minorities, a theme Ford would later often repeat. Ford also pointed out prevalent Irish-American stereotypes through the polite prism of Irish gentry. In America, Sir Miles, working briefly as a ditchdigger, is introduced both to a foreman named O'Flaherty and to a policeman named Pat.

It is, in fact, really no handicap to be Irish. Ford ends the picture with Neil reciting to Molly the four virtues of the shamrock: luck, faith, hope, and love. (The three cardinal virtues of Catholic American teaching in elementary school in the 1920s were faith, hope, and charity.) In *The Fugitive* (1948), Ford would carefully develop an Irish idea of self-sacrifice. But here he chiefly defined the Irish in the broad sentimental terms of their luck, their fine horses, and their genteel background—all reactionary images to the stereotype of the common Irish laborer.

The return to the homeland suggests both Ford's nostalgia for Ireland and an implicit Anglo-American rejection. Ford was slow to show moviegoers the Irish in America's big cities, where Anglo-

Americans knew them best. But once audiences had seen major Irish stereotypes worked into stories with positive social roles, with the Irish violent nature in check, then the time was right for an Irish story set in New York City. There the tight male camaraderie of the Irish was indeed threatening, unless harnessed by American labor or the military. It was time too to address Anglo-American fear of the Catholic Church, which seemed so foreign and hierarchical and thus unadaptable to American democracy.

If Irish immigrants were not wholly welcome in *The Shamrock Handicap*, in *The Blue Eagle* (1926) they proved themselves American as well as Irish. In World War I, two groups of Irish-American sailors, Darcy's Terriers and Ryan's Rats, plan to resume their street fights as soon as the war ends. The leader of the first group, George Darcy (George O'Brien), says, "when the war is over, all this patriotic stuff is OUT!" Evidently, military service barely keeps a rein on Irish-American violence. The social problem in the 1920s, then, was to find a suitable job for Irishmen after the war. Perhaps with such work the English-speaking, white Irish could even be a model of ethnic behavior.

As in *The Iron Horse*, Anglo America in this film needs Irish leaders to contain the worst elements of its own community, but now with the special mediational help of the Catholic Church. Ford's story also again brings together two male groups, although now the conflict is intra-Irish. Father Joe, the local priest, tells the two Irish gang leaders that if they help him end drug traffic on the waterfront, he will let them fight a grudge match in the parish gym. As so often in American film, the priest serves as a social worker among his blue-collar parishioners, and as a go-between for them and a fearful Anglo Protestant society. Father Joe appeals in particular to the religious discipline of the Irish: "Wars may end," he tells Ryan, "but a soldier of the Cross must carry on." (Behind these words on the intertitle is an acceptably plain Protestant cross.) Father Joe speaks to the so-called fighting spirit of the Irish and to their strong loyalty to the Church. Instead of destroying each other, these gangs should protect Anglo America from the criminal underworld with which they are assumedly already familiar.

The Blue Eagle opens with a visceral image of the hot-tempered Irishman: Stripped to the waist and glistening with sweat at the ship's furnace, he appears again as a brute laborer. He knows of course all about dynamite and the drug runners' submarine; the Irish are believed to harbor a dangerous illegal nature beneath surface conformity. Fortunately, some Irishmen are priests who referee fights and lead their flock against urban crime. After the gym bout, the victor George says, "Guess maybe there ain't nothing or nobody me an' Tim can't lick, together." Once the fighting Irish have been reminded of community, they can be used to combat social evil.

Ford's references to state and church in the film's last scene clarify his idea of the Catholic Church's role in American cities. George and Tim walk with Father Joe towards the new Rohan Post American Legion, with its Irish-American name spelled out in light bulbs. In the background to the left stands St. Matthew's Church, the institution that quietly maintains Irish-American patriotism. It is all right to be both Irish and American, the mise-en-scène suggests, as long as a priest (St. Matthew's Church) channels Irishmen's self-destructive violence (the two leaders on an urban street) into socially useful purposes (the American Legion).

Ford's next film introduced the essential Irish stereotypes of the widowed mother and her son, while raising the possibility of an Anglo American's marriage to an Irish immigrant. In Irish tradition the mother here is clearly modelled after Jesus's own Mother, which helps explain Ford's sentimental treatment of her and of families in general. He later often used some form of the Irish mother, including maternal figures in *Stagecoach* (1939), *Young Mr. Lincoln* (1939), and *3 Godfathers* (1949). Lack of the good mother, moreover, is the chief reason for the dissolution of families in films like *The Last Hurrah* (1958) and *The Grapes of Wrath* (1940).

Titled after a famous song, *Mother Machree* (1928) begins in Ireland where we see the extreme poverty of the rural villager, especially the mother who, in an abbreviated social history, suddenly loses her husband and leaves with her boy for America. In New York City, Ellen McHugh and Brian live in a poor tenement house. During the day she works in a circus sideshow as a "half-woman"—an ironic symbol of her social status as a hyphenated American. She enrolls Brian in a fashionable school but, when the principal learns about her work (and thus her poor Irish background), he forces her to surrender legal custody of her son. Years later, Ellen is the elderly, longtime servant of an Anglo-American upper-class family and has raised the family's daughter, Edith, from infancy. When a suitor, Brian Van Studdiford, calls on Edith, he sits at the piano to sing the popular tune "Mother Machree," and is reunited at last with his servant mother. The movie ends with Brian's departure to join the Army.*

Mother McHugh and Brian exemplify the Irish-American figures

*This plot summary represents three reels, all that remains today.

of the persecuted son and the all-sacrificing widow, an Irish translation of Mother Mary. Ford first introduces his Irish portrait of Ellen
McHugh as a woman on her knees in prayer. America might seem
to be an answer to those prayers, except that Anglo-American institutions like the school board treat immigrants harshly. On the other
hand, America provides employment and a miraculous opportunity
for wealth and success—provided mother and son separate. Thus,
Ford's ending is ambiguous about having both one's Irish family and
Anglo success, since mother and son must be separated again, this
time by military service, if he is to retain his identity as the successful (Anglo-American) Van Studdiford. This ambiguous or hyphenated immigrant identity addresses two audiences: Irish Americans
would likely relish the sentimental reunion of a self-sacrificing Marian
mother and her persecuted son, while Anglo Americans would approve of the young man's new name and dedication to country. Lin-
gering somewhere in the background is the promise that Brian will
some day marry the wealthy Anglo Edith.

Early in the film Ford also included strictly Irish material full
of superstition and magic, suggesting the famous Irish imagination.
After leaving her village, Ellen meets three traditional, almost imaginary Irish figures: the giant Terrence O'Dowd (Victor McLaglen), a
dwarf, and a harp player. Members of a traveling troupe, they perform sideshow roles that help relieve the misery of an impoverished
people. Ford stressed the close relation between poverty and the
Irish imagination, contrasting shots of gritty rural realism with filtered portraits of the three figures. But in America the division is
between poverty and wealth, which raises the question: When the
Irish assimilate to the American scene, do they lose their sense of
imagination and Catholic mystery?

For an Irish-American audience, any separation from the mother
strongly suggests just this loss, though Ford's loud notes of sentimental reunion and patriotic military service cover over the separation
anxiety. In any case, the promise of wealth and social standing seems
too appealing to worry about something as ephemeral as a cultural
imagination.

Ironically, Ford's own imagination seems to have run dry by late
1928 in his treatment of Irish immigrants. *Riley the Cop* is a slight piece
with a hokey plot and heavy-handed treatment of the Irish. Ford's
presentation of Riley is decidedly mixed, as if he had not decided on
a clear dramatic purpose for his Irish-American protagonist. On the
one hand, Riley is a good cop with a strong Irish sense of community.

He holds a young black girl in his arms; he turns on a fire hydrant for street kids; and he counsels a young couple in love. On the other hand, he acts like a bully when provoked: When another officer sits down in Riley's place for a free lunch in a woman's kitchen, the angry Irishman throws a brick through her upstairs window. Riley's salvation is a police assignment to trace a suspected young thief to Germany. In this comic side plot, the young man ironically must drag Riley away from beer and jolly German policemen. In sum, the contrived plot pictures Riley as an Irish American who is a fatherly officer, a sociable drinking companion, and a clumsy suitor. His type will always remain part of the working class because he enjoys his liquor too much to climb the WASP ladder of success. If early in the 1920s the Irish immigrant had been the ideal candidate for success in American film, by the decade's end he was suitable only for comic farce. In this context, Irish social values like Riley's sense of neighborhood and legal mediation look meagerly lower class.

In 1958, Ford attempted to return to the subject of Irish America. But, like the nation, he was not so much aware of Irish-American cultural identity as its social consequences. Adapted from Edwin O'Conner's novel of the same title, *The Last Hurrah* is a light-handed treatment of the last campaign of Boston's Irish-American incumbent mayor, Frank Skeffington. The film features superficial glimpses into Skeffington's life as a Catholic, including a funeral, a confession, and a deathbed scene. The film's most serious, if vaguely ethnic allusion is Skeffington's loving memory of his deceased wife, a highly idealized female figure and virtually a stand-in for the Virgin Mary. The mayor stresses his dead wife's continuing significance in his life when he pays for a funeral, telling the grateful widow that he is "just a messenger" for his dear wife. Skeffington's distinctively Irish trust in this Marian ideal of compassion and generosity gives him the confidence and innocence to go on waging his political battles.

In terms of the Irish-American family, Skeffington's weak relationship with his spoiled son typifies the strained rapport between father and son in general in Irish families.* Ford's story focused on this particular relationship much more than did O'Conner's novel, emphasizing the son's self-centered indulgence in popular music and thus the material success of the second-generation father. Meanwhile, core ethnic issues simmered in the background. The film's clear-

---

*For a more socially realistic view of the Irish father/son relationship, with an American slant, see the film *Da* (1988) starring the half-Irish Martin Sheen.

est sense of cultural differences arises when Skeffington confronts
Anglo town fathers about new housing for low-income families.*
Here again, to be Irish American means to be concerned about the
little people.

Ford did his best work on Irish-American subjects in the 1920s,
when he introduced general American audiences to immigrant
images of labor, patriotism, and law enforcement. He placed central
figures of Irish culture, such as the widowed mother and her persecuted son, in the service of Anglo society and its military. In the end,
the hyphenated Irish American was essentially a figure split in two,
like Ellen McHugh in her circus act. To get a better grip on the ethnic
half, Ford needed stories about Ireland, where political violence set
limits on Irish virtues and thus on the future of Irish-American culture
in film.

Ireland Remembered: The Holy Mother, Judas, and Mary Magdalene

In films set in Ireland, Ford reworked with new urgency his earlier
themes of law and decency, family and democracy. As he drew close
to the sources of conflict in Irish culture, the violent nature of Irish
character and history came clearly into focus. Betrayal, the Irish conscience, and the redemptive mother emerged at the center of Ford's
Irish-American identity. Filmic signs of conflict were the rain, fog,
and shadows that now appeared in his films.

Ford first learned about traditional Irish hatred for informers
when he attended school for several months in Ireland and read Irish
literature and history (Anderson 1981, 242). The Irish, he discovered,
have persecuted informers and their descendants for generations
(O'Flaherty 1961, 184–85). The Irish forgive no one who helps the
British; the informer is an unforgivable Judas. Consequently, the Irish
sense of community is restricted and, in Ford's films, often ruinous.

Hangman's House (1928), Ford's first film set entirely in Ireland,
depicts the violence at the heart of Irish society, focusing especially
on the traditional Irish figures of the informer and the judge. Visually, Ford expressed Irish repressed anger against the British in mist-
filled streets and soft close-ups, a filmic style he acquired from F. W.

---

*The accuracy of Ford's ethnic portrait of Skeffington was sufficiently biting to merit a libel
suit by Boston's former mayor, James Michael Curley, who settled for $15,000 in damages
(Gallagher 1986, 365).

Murnau and used earlier in *Four Sons* (1928). Baron O'Brien, known as "the hanging judge" because of his severe sentences, is father of the charming Connaught. Although she loves Dermott McDermott, the judge (Hobart Bosworth) decides she must marry John Darcy, a spendthrift gentleman whose father was an informer. Darcy himself turns Citizen Hogan (Victor McLaglen) over to the British authorities. But when Hogan escapes and confronts Darcy, the informer flees into the O'Brien's house and dies there in a sudden fire.

Ford aptly dramatized the informer's social standing when a bartender admits Darcy to his establishment, saying, "I'll have to go to confession for letting him in." Similarly, once Connaught has been forced to marry Darcy, she wears a large cross on her wedding night and closes a heavy oak door in her husband's face. Because she considers him to be a substitute for her authoritarian, Anglo-supported father, she cuts him off from her emotional and sexual feelings; Ford traced the violence of Irish culture to this self-destructive hatred of the British. The coldhearted judge also explains Irish women's suppression of their sexuality. The judge father is an unfeeling authority in a society that for centuries has lost husbands and fathers either to uprisings against the British or to exhausting manual labor and an early grave.

In 1935, Ford went against Irish tradition by taking the side of the informer in his adaptation of Liam O'Flaherty's novel *The Informer*. Before a line of script was adapted, Ford gathered together with his scriptwriter Dudley Nichols, his cameraman Joe August, his set designer Van Nest Polglase, and his music director Max Steiner (Anderson 1981, 239). Later, Ford rewrote most of Nichols' script himself, though Nichols also has claimed credit for every word (Ford 1979, 84; Anderson 1981, 239). After the script had been rejected all over Hollywood for four years, Ford finally secured the necessary finances and a back lot from RKO. (The picture turned out to be RKO's best-grossing picture of the decade and a turning point in Ford's career, with four Academy Awards.) In later years, Ford downplayed the film's importance, claiming it was not one of his favorites. But he was perhaps more honest in Paris when, away from the American press, he claimed it as one of the five triumphs of his career (Mitry 1955, 309).

Critics have panned the film as sentimental mush. Tag Gallagher, for example, gives the film short shrift, labeling Gypo a "troglodytic bore" (1986, 124). But to many American audiences, the film has always been deeply moving. At Ford's funeral mass, Cardinal

Manning alluded to the universal appeal of the film's Irish themes. "Deep in the recesses of every heart there will be the sense of guilt, the possibility of betrayal. A great director will take this theme of guilt, the intercession of an informer, and we will all see ourselves" (McBride and Wilmington 1974, 12).

Like *Hangman's House*, *The Informer* (1935) is a story of betrayal and guilt, featuring Irish Catholic figures such as Judas and the Holy Mother in a Passion story. Ford's protagonist, Gypo Nolan, is a simple-minded fellow with a guilty conscience. Offered the chance to escape poverty with his girlfriend Katie, he informs on a fugitive, his friend Frankie McPhillips, and collects £20 reward from the British authorities. But before he can sail for America with his girlfriend, he spends the money on fish and chips for a crowd, hoping his public munificence will relieve his private guilt. Played by a lumbering Victor McLaglen, Gypo is too ingenuous not to show his guilt in his face and his actions.

Gypo is not alone in his culpability, however. Ford uses the figure of the informer also to focus on community betrayal. When Gypo meets Frankie secretly in town, the supposed friend ignores Gypo's desperate situation of no food and no work. Frankie even scoffs at these problems and cruelly points out that the big fellow depends on him for brains. Frankie's mockery is one reason for Gypo's feeling of total isolation and thus for his subsequent betrayal. Similarly, Terry, another so-called friend, taunts Gypo with the sobriquet of "king," and then goads him into spending all his blood money.

The circle of communal guilt even includes Gypo's girlfriend. When he first sees Katie trying to pick up men on a street corner, he feels driven to take some kind of action. Later, she confesses she "drove him to [inform on his friend]." Hence, "he didn't know what he was doing," she says. When she later informs the I.R.A. of Gypo's whereabouts and then begs the hit men to show compassion, she proves that she too did not know what she was doing.

All of Dublin, it seems, is guilty, especially the I.R.A. Ford passes national judgment in visual signs, such as evening fog and newspaper scraps on the streets. When the moral atmosphere is rough going for Gypo, scraps of dirty newspaper wrap themselves around his leg on the windy streets. The same trash also blows down into the outside stairwell of I.R.A. headquarters, as the camera follows it to the center of Irish decay: the court where Gypo will be tried and surely found guilty. The I.R.A.'s idea of community is that of a small vulnerable group desperate to protect itself. Despite Gypo's heartfelt confession, Captain Gallagher explains that as far as the I.R.A. is concerned, "One man can destroy an army." This outlawed group is no more sensitive to Gypo's needs than was Frankie.

The pervasive fog on the streets of Dublin is more than an objective correlative of Gypo's guilt and confusion, and is more than a symbol of Ireland's repressed anger against the British. Sin, anger, and guilt together create the dimly lit conscience of the Irish community, which cannot recognize a simple man's suffering. This implicit sense of a restricted community, literally pictured here as underground, survives by unbendable laws and death sentences.

The film's most religious moment is Gypo's final confession, as first suggested by the film's opening biblical quotation (not in O'Flaherty's novel): "Then Judas repented—and cast down the thirty pieces of silver and departed." Also in the last scene, Gypo's entrance in church in effect begins a Passion liturgy. Because Gypo has committed the one unforgivable sin in Ireland, Ford turns to the Irish tradition of Marian compassion and intercession in the figure of Frankie McPhillip's mother: the Blessed Virgin Mary as Mother of Sorrow. This icon from the Passion narrative appears after Gypo has been fatally shot by I.R.A. gunmen and stumbles into a nearby church. In a front pew, Mother McPhillips kneels before a life-size crucifix; Gypo has sought out a Mother of Sorrow at Calvary. In Irish culture, the Holy Mother immediately feels others' suffering because of the pain she endured at her Son's death. In Ford's film, Gypo falls to his knees beside Mother McPhillips' and confesses that it was he who informed on her son. Her reply at first seems simplistic but in fact is religiously perceptive. "It's all right, Gypo. You didn't know what you were doing." In Irish Catholicism, a sinner who fully understands the implications of sin is not likely to choose evil; and all men become children on their knees before Jesus's Blessed Mother. So Mother McPhillips speaks to this simple man as to a little boy who didn't understand the consequences of his actions.

Though some critics have objected to Ford's sentimental ending, audiences have been deeply moved by his portrait of warm, consoling Marian intercession, especially when given to a sinner whom no one is willing to forgive. (Even the priest at the McPhillips' home puts Gypo off by talking disparagingly of the unknown informer.) In Irish religious culture, the Blessed Mother's mediation is often a crucial first step towards repentance and salvation. After speaking to Mother McPhillips, Gypo addresses the crucifix with his dying breath, "Frankie, Frankie, your mother forgives me." Here, Irish betrayal, guilt, repentance, and forgiveness all come together at the moment of confession to the Holy Mother.

Ford's sense of the Irish conscience was at the heart of his later work. "What interests me are the consequences of a *tragic* moment —how the individual acts before a crucial fact, or in an exceptional circumstance" (Mitry 1955, 308 [italics mine]). By emphatically repeating Mrs. McPhillips' line from O'Flaherty's novel ("You didn't know what you were doing"), Ford showed his distinctly Irish idea of sin as almost fatal tragedy, with a communal overtone. The implicit guilt shared among Frankie, Katie, and the I.R.A. is part of any moral judgment here; the community's tragic lack of both understanding and Marian compassion for Gypo is as bad as his one moment of betrayal.

In the summer of 1921, Ford returned to Dublin to help the freedom fighters. Although he had no active political role, he came back to Hollywood with a thoroughly righteous sense of the injustice suffered at the hands of the British (Sinclair 1979, 31). In 1936, Ford filmed *The Plough and the Stars*, his last 1930s film about political strife in Ireland. Set during the Easter uprising of 1916, the story featured Jack, a citizen soldier who barely has time for his girlfriend Nora because of his work for the cause. Nora's politically naive solution is to "forget everything but ourselves." The I.R.A. pursues a policy that defeats any sense of community and mediation, ignoring the needs of couples and, especially, women.

Troubles plagued *The Plough and the Stars* from the start. Dramatically, Ford failed to resolve the difference between the lovers' melodrama and wartime realism. First, he had been required to cast Barbara Stanwyck with actors from Dublin's Abbey Theater, leading to awkward differences in acting style. And the disjointed script by Dudley Nichols, adapted from Sean O'Casey's play, hardly helped matters, since it was riddled with clichés: "It's a woman's nature to love, as it's a man's nature to fight," says the hero. Ford later believed that the film was butchered by Hollywood editors (Ford 1969, 40). For all these reasons, the film lacks both a clear sense of Irish culture and Ford's own Irish-American vision.

The Quiet Man (1952), Ford's last film about Ireland, had almost as many difficulties. Despite fragmented surface allusions to Irish myths and customs, the plot depends chiefly on a donnybrook between Sean Thornton (John Wayne) and his brother-in-law Dan (Victor McLaglen). Ford made mistakes in casting as well. He chose family friends for small parts and eventually detested the female lead,

Maureen O'Hara (Mitry 1955, 309; Tavernier 1967, 19). Worst of all, Ford was unsure of his story. In the middle of production he came down with a cold and told John Wayne, by that time a close friend, that for once he did not know where the story should go. With no clear dramatic issue at stake, Irish pugilism took over. Mary Kate, the one character who could conceivably reveal positive Irish values, presents instead a narrow-minded legalism that encourages violence to solve private problems in public. (She also insists on defining herself as marital chattel.) Only the glossy sheen of Winton Hoch's photography helped matters by suggesting a lyrical Irish sense of pastoral beauty. In the end, the film was little more than sentimental Irish faces and stereotypical fisticuffs. While *The Informer* had come to terms with Irish identity through a Judas figure in a Passion narrative, *The Quiet Man* looked uncertain and unfocused. After this, Ford gave up setting his films in Ireland.

But at least the Irish films had allowed Ford to delve into the Irish psyche, where he found national problems with strong religious implications; sin, guilt, and forgiveness were very much part of the political struggle against British rule. The only sure reply to Ireland's "troubles" seemed to be Marian intercession in a Passion narrative. Ford's limited, eclectic development of religious values was to be expected in a country with so much unspoken anger, in a land where the possibility of unseen informers was a constant fear. Ford needed locales outside of Ireland to explore the positive side of his Irish heritage.

Faraway Places with Irish Types

In imaginary foreign lands Ford was able to work more freely with Irish values and, in one confessional film, tie together the Passion figures of Judas, Mary Magdalene, and a Mater Dolorsa. These filmic allegories of Irish culture and politics clarified the limits of Ford's fundamental ethnic themes.

The Lost Patrol (1934) delved into the terrible sense of vulnerability in Ireland, where anyone may be an informer. As an ironic, inverted allegory of the Irish-British conflict, the film places the British for once in the disastrous situation of being attacked by unseen enemies. Adapted from Philip MacDonald's story "Patrol," the film opens in 1917 in the Mesopotamian desert, where British soldiers fight Arabs. After the chief officer is shot, the patrol wanders to an oasis where they defend themselves, literally to the last man.

Ford highlighted several of the soldiers' philosophies of life in order to parody contemporary beliefs lacking Irish values. Lieutenant Hawkins, the ranking officer, explains his faith in an uncritical acceptance of life and ends in unintended self-parody. He believes, he says, in "a good horse, steak and kidney pudding, a fellow named George Brown [who later deserts], the asinine futility of this war, . . . the joy of women, the splendid joy of killing Arabs, . . . an old pair of shoes." To an Irish American like Ford, Hawkins wrongly believes that objects and events have only superficial meaning. For a contrast, Ford introduced the offbeat, fanatically religious character of Saunders. Played by a wild-eyed Boris Karloff, Saunders believes he has arrived in Eden where, dressed like a primitive, he walks into Arab bullets.

In another sense, *The Lost Patrol* is an allegory, perhaps unconscious on Ford's part, of the uncritical Irish desire to conform to Anglo values in America, the country represented here by a multiethnic patrol of men from England, Scotland, Italy, and Ireland. As in *The Iron Horse*, the film features a strong Irishman (the sergeant played by Victor McLaglen) who proves himself a leader, though also only a survivor. The patrol's terrible fate serves, then, as a warning to other American immigrants who might blindly follow Anglo conformity.

One traditional Irish answer to open vulnerability has been an unshakeable loyalty to their church. Ford thus concentrated in his next foreign film on a fiercely institutional faith. Like *The Lost Patrol*, *The Hurricane* (1937) used a stripped down, foreign locale to test personal character. Despite the film's reputation as a sensational studio stunt (the hurricane scene cost $250,000), Ford took the project seriously, worried about every detail of production, and had contractual control over scriptwriting and editing (Gallagher 1986, 138). Adapted from the Charles Nordhoff—James Norman Hall novel, *The Hurricane* is about a native community on a sandy South Seas island, with a romantic focus on the perfect love of Terangi and his girlfriend Marama. The film features three Irish stereotypes: the French Governor Delaage, played by the ramrod-straight Raymond Massey, who reasons by the letter of the law; Dr. Kersaint (Thomas Mitchell), a hard-drinking (Irish) physician who is also the governor's critical conscience; and the local priest, Father Paul, as rigid in his own clerical way as the Governor. Into this male triangle steps Terangi, a cheerful native who, when he cannot bear a thirty-day prison sentence, repeatedly tries to escape and quickly earns years of imprisonment from the inflexible Delaage. The film climaxes with a stupendous hurricane scene that erases law, religion, civilization, and the native population, although both Terangi and Delaage somehow survive.

Ford used Dr. Kersaint as a foil to suggest Delaage's lack of a critical conscience and to point out the folly of unbending justice. The governor's strict treatment of Terangi, observes (the Irish) Kersaint, alienates the entire native population. Only after a hurricane has wiped out every recognizable trait of civilization does Delaage finally acquire a sense of community with others. Unlike the novel's ending, in which Marama has died by the time Terangi is freed, Ford's last scene stresses the bending of the institutional conscience for the renewal of family and community.

Surprisingly, the well-meaning Father Paul is as legalistic as the governor, with his literal-minded (Irish) confidence in religious institutionalism. The good priest shows compassion to Terangi, but later values blind faith in the Church before innocent lives: When a hurricane threatens the island, the fanatical cleric orders his people inside the church where, he claims, the walls will keep out the water. When a wave finally crashes through the brick, Father Paul sits at the church organ resolutely playing for his terrified parishioners. As a mirror held up to Irish America, Ford's cleric suggests the worst side of the immigrant Irish priests who devoted their lives to grand building programs.

An institutional attitude, Ford knew, was still strong in the American Catholic hierarchy in 1938. Though the film was regarded by critics as a vehicle for a sarong-clad Dorothy Lamour (with a natural disaster as an added attraction), to Irish-American filmgoers the hurricane would likely have symbolized the Church's sense of disorientation at the passing of its rigidly institutional character.

Still, Ford had no intention of rejecting his faith on screen. In *Mary of Scotland* (1936), he made an impassioned and partly Catholic plea for religious liberty, rewriting political history to suit Stuart-Catholic sentiments: His Bothwell is entirely noble and his Mary has no schemes of her own. In typically Irish fashion, Ford began by stressing the similarities rather than the differences between his two historic protagonists, Elizabeth and Mary, picturing them side by side in their tombs in Westminster Abbey. Thereafter, Mary (Katharine Hepburn) seems to be from an entirely different culture: Upon arrival in Scotland, she wears a crucifix and keeps her priest (John Carradine) always by her side. Her cultural sense of difference in the English milieu is heightened when the Presbyterian reformer John Knox greets her with a virulent anti-Catholic attack. She responds, how-

ever, with an Irish-American claim for religious freedom: "Religion is
no garment to be put on and off with the winter. I shall worship as I
please and hope for all men to worship as they please in Scotland."

Queen Elizabeth's views, on the other hand, foreshadow the divi-
siveness of the Anglo-American success ethic in Ford's later American works. As soon as the two queens meet, Elizabeth immediately
shows her strong sense of difference: She observes that, unlike her
Catholic cousin, she rose from obscurity by building a secure political
base. Committed to the pursuit of power, Elizabeth goes on to explain
the WASP success ethic: She pursues power and defends her country
by sacrificing her personal relations with others. She scoffs at the pri-
ority Mary gives such relationships, especially her indiscreet liaison
with Bothwell (Frederic March). Like a committed American business
executive of the mid-1920s, Elizabeth rationalizes the sacrifice of her
emotional life. Mary, by contrast, says she sees no conflict between
the public political sphere and her private life. At her death, she hears
the sound of her deceased Bothwell's bagpipes, which gives her a
distinctly Irish confidence that her faith will soon be rewarded in an
eternal communion. Her love has, in fact, always been otherworldly
and communal, exactly what the practical, individualistic Elizabeth
does not understand.

The facts of English history limited Ford's experiment here with
Irish values. But in his next work about a powerful female figure in
a foreign country, he painted a magical portrait of the Irish mother,
imagining her as an effective mediational figure of childlike innocence, maternal warmth, and complete legal wisdom. Set in the
1890s and adapted from a tale by Rudyard Kipling, *Wee Willie Winkie*
(1937) is the story of an impoverished widow in India and her young
daughter Priscilla (Shirley Temple), who singlehandedly stops a war
between British soldiers and local rebels.

The figure of wee Priscilla becomes, in Ford's hands, a curious
version of the Irish widow. In a wink of the eye the rootless mother
is a naively confident wee person, a child–woman whose immigrant-
like innocence quickly settles a war. The child also appears as a Mater
Dolorosa, one who endures the death of a son figure; Priscilla's so-
called son is the man-child Sergeant McDuff (Victor McLaglen), who
shows his baby picture to the motherly eight-year-old and later virtually dies in her arms—a pietà. Only an Irish image of Mother Mary
could get the organized, powerful British to make peace with an army
of hot-headed natives (Ford's stand-ins for the Irish).

Ford had to give up the magical mediation of a child-woman after the brutality of World War II. So, he turned to a novel set in Mexico by the famous Anglo Catholic novelist Graham Greene. When Ford first suggested adapting Greene's *The Power and the Glory* into a feature film, all the major Hollywood studios turned him down. The figure of a priest as a political fugitive did not seem a marketable proposition. Ford himself admitted, in an exploratory letter to Darryl Zanuck, that the idea was "really not a sound commercial gamble, but my heart and my faith compel me to do it" (Gallagher 1986, 234). After production, Ford felt so strongly about the results that he donated a set of massive bronze doors to his local Hollywood parish, the Church of the Blessed Sacrament. When the film was finally released in 1947 under the title *The Fugitive*, it was a box-office success. It was also one of his personal favorites in his long career.

Ford's critics have either undervalued or roundly condemned the film, though all agree that Gabriel Figueroa's photography of Mexican landscape is superb. Greene, who never did see the film, claimed it was a "total travesty of my book, perhaps due to Ford's Irish type of Catholicism. The illegitimate child was given to the police officer instead of to the priest!" (Gallagher 1986, 234). But the brilliant novelist overlooked the limits imposed on Ford by American film censors, many of whom were of Irish-American stock. Ford could not have possibly portrayed a priest with an illegitimate child, let alone one who was living with a woman. Henry Fonda, the film's star and ever the stage actor, objected to the film because Ford drastically changed the initial Passion play he had worked out carefully with Dudley Nichols. But exactly what sort of Passion play did Ford finally produce? Or, to take Greene's grumblings as a lead, how did Ford's heritage shape his most explicitly religious film?

Greene's novel is about a priest-hunt during a Latin government's persecution to remove all clergy. Adapting his Anglo Catholic script, Ford highlighted the priest's return to his rural town, his refuge in a neighboring country, and his journey to hear a dying man's confession. Throughout his travels, the priest remains mostly in disguise, accompanied only by a peasant, a Judas figure who, once he discovers his employer's identity, sets a trap. A third man, a young lieutenant, pursues the priest with ruthless determination. At the priest's execution, all three male characters face critical moments of conscience. An added religious element was a mother who appears both as a Mary Magdalene and as a Mater Dolorosa.

From the opening scene, *The Fugitive* assumes the character of a religious allegory. Ford set the story "anywhere 1,000 miles north or south of the equator," and he limited the protagonist's name to "Father." The film's visual symbols, moreover, suggest a Passion allegory, especially the repeated shots of the priest's full-length shadow, with outstretched arms that fill the frame. The cross becomes a man again when the priest drops his arms; Ford's film reveals a crucified Christ in an isolated, modern Everyman.

Ford's opening section establishes the importance of the institutional Church, as the fugitive priest rings a bell to summon peasants to their deserted church. Suddenly, he is no longer a solitary man in ordinary clothes but a priest in a clerical stole, administering baptism. Throughout most of the film, however, he hides his Roman collar; he seems unwilling to take a stand and die for the sake of the church and what it means to these simple people.

The priest's Indian guide is the Judas in Ford's Passion narrative. Like Gypo in *The Informer*, the guide eventually regrets his betrayal, though he is not such a simpleton as the Irishman. This betrayer is, in fact, a more extreme version of the priest's character: He has moral scruples but hesitates to say he believes in God. Instead, he wears an illegal holy medal under his shirt and mocks the sacrament of Penance, even requesting confession from the disguised priest to ascertain his true identity. Although the Indian later repents, his intent remains ambiguous once he picks up the coins he himself threw at the priest's feet.

Another unwilling man of morals is the young lieutenant who, like the I.R.A. in *The Informer*, has a sensitive conscience that he suppresses out of loyalty to rigid justice. Although he shows the priest compassion when the two men are alone, he quickly reverts to his institutional role when his conscience is questioned.

Throughout the film Ford "celebrates openly cultural aspects that repel Anglo-Saxon sternness" (Gallagher 1986, 235). Ford's ending in particular develops facets of Irish tradition that WASP audiences surely would have missed. When the priest finally admits his cowardice to the lieutenant, he begins, in the Catholic phrase, an "examination of conscience." He first started this examination when he escaped to a sanctuary across the border and told a sympathetic doctor about his sin of pride at being the last priest in the country. Ford's climactic symbol of the priest's confession is a cool rain, visible only through a circular cell window that, in close-up, exactly repeats the church window in the film's first scene: The priest has finally returned to his Church.

Ford inserted here the traditional Catholic icon of the Mater

Dolorsa. Dolores appears at the cell window in a white shawl, looking just like the attentive unknown woman in the film's first scene.
As she passes the priest a simple wooden cross, Ford's close-up of
her rain-streaked face is an exact picture, as her name implies, of a
Mater Dolorosa or Mother of Sorrows at Calvary. She combines in
fact the two traditional Marys of the Passion story: Mother Mary has
been watching over this priest since the film's first shot and appears
finally in the figure of a Magdalene to console him by affirming his
priestly identity as a Christ who dies for his church.

Ford drove home his Irish institutional message in the film's last
scene, in which a new missionary arrives at a secret prayer meeting. The priest's name is Father Serra, the famous Spanish Franciscan who served in Mexico in the 1750s and later founded mission
churches along the California coast and near Hollywood. By adding
this well-known name to Greene's story, Ford drew Hollywood into
his religious history. From the perspective of Ford's canon, the last
scene testifies to his hopeful attitude toward the institution of the
Church outside Ireland.

Tag Gallagher may object to the film's "holy card images" and
"naive Catholicism" (1986, 235), but other critics have noted that
Ford's careful setup of religious myths creates a striking sense of
rural Mexican Catholicism, with a twist of British irony and self-
consciousness. Ford himself said of *The Fugitive*, "To me, it was perfect" (Bogdanovich 1978, 85). His treatment of the Passion blended
several national cultures. From Greene's Anglo Catholicism, the protagonist acquired an intellectual complexity and angst quite unusual
for Ford's heroes. In the Irish-American vein, the film was virtually a
big sell for religious institutionalism, while also asserting the equally
Irish and Mexican belief that a key intercessor for one's sins is Mother
Mary.

The Informer and *The Fugitive* were the two films most devoted
to Ford's religious past. Both based on major literary works, they
had a more complex, integrated view of religious values than Ford's
more extreme experiments, like *Hurricane* and *Wee Willie Winkie*. Each
featured, moreover, the confessional conscience and Marian intercession as the bases of faith, a fairly accurate reflection of Irish-American
religious attitudes in the 1930s and 1940s.

Ford directed two more films about foreign religious martyrs, *The
Bamboo Cross* (1955) and *7 Women* (1965). The former, a brief television
play for the *Fireside Theater*, was a staunchly pro-Catholic story about
persecuted nuns in communist China. A government official accuses

missionary nuns of poisoning babies with special bread called "communion wafers," though the nuns' servant attempts to rescue them before they are arrested. In the end, both the Chinese officials and the nuns die. The film not only champions missionary nuns but also addresses an anti-Catholic prejudice often found in America: Any woman who chooses a celibate life dedicated to God must also hate children and perhaps want to murder them.

Ten years later, Ford put behind him this clumsy moralistic plot to direct a major feature that critically portrays seven Protestant missionaries, twisted stereotypes of the mother, the wife, and the whore—all women without basic Catholic principles. His *7 Women* (1965) is the story of Protestant Americans, mostly women, who work for the Unified Christian Missions in China. A henpecked Charles Pether (Eddie Albert) represents the Protestant man as basically weak-kneed, while living mostly with women. In religion class, Pether teaches that according to Protestant tradition, religious authority depends on the Bible (not on mediational forms like an institutional church). And he instructs the children to sing, "Yes Jesus loves me—the Bible tells me so." The consequent individualism of Protestant culture proves ruinous here. Moreover, socially, these Protestant Americans show a surprising lack of unity for a missionary group cut off by themselves.

The other missing (Irish) element is a female intercessor. The arrival of Dr. Cartwright (Anne Bancroft), a pragmatic physician from America, only causes further dissension because she wears pants and boots, and smokes and drinks. She is in fact a secularist who believes that God has not seen the slums of Chicago and New York. Ironically, Cartwright in the end almost assumes the Irish role of self-sacrificing mediator, except that her final solution of a double death, for herself and a bullying Mongolian rebel, would be unthinkable for the Irish Catholic opposed to suicide.

Ford was attracted to the story of isolated Protestant missionaries because he had so often depicted isolated groups in life-threatening situations. But he was out of his depth when he took on both Protestant culture, presented here entirely in negative terms, and the social dynamics of a predominantly female community. The film's strongest Irish parallel was its Protestant sexual puritanism: Cartwright, in effect, deserves to die because she has slept with the native rebel; and Andrews must lead a hollow life because of her attraction to women. This extreme satire of Anglo-Protestant life signaled a dead end for Ford's experiments with religious values in foreign locales.

Unlike Ford's historical pieces set in Ireland, with their troubled history and tradition of violence, his films set in foreign locales let him allegorize more easily. He developed, sometimes in extreme form, key aspects of his Irish background, such as a determined faith in the church as an historic institution and in Mother Mary as a sinner's first mediator to God. Emotionally, these two commitments in fact balanced each other out: one the most impersonal aspect of religion, the other the most maternal and approachable. Moreover, Ford seems to have felt especially at ease portraying motherly Marian figures in relation to men who behave like unsure adolescents, such as the sergeant in *Wee Willie Winkie* and the good-hearted officer in *The Fugitive*. At the same time, Ford perpetuated the Irish distinction between Mater Dolorosa (the Virgin) and Mary Magdalene (the whore).

In summary, Ford's foreign allegories permitted him to further explore the violence and fundamental conflicts of his Irish background in an often fantastical style. Still, these foreign landscapes had a major limitation: They said little to American moviegoers about their country, and were widely regarded as either amusing fantasies or sentimental abstractions. Ford needed to include the American half of his hyphenated identity for a fully sacramental aesthetic, that is, for one with a richly incarnate sense of Irish tradition.

The Wild West: Irish Identity as American History

The western seemed ready made for Ford's Irish background. The plots were set in a locale where the East's dominant Anglo Protestant culture was weakest. There, as in his Irish films, Ford could depict a small group of men and women living on the fringe of accepted civil order. Among people struggling to survive, an Irish sense of self-sacrifice was also easy to establish. And Marian values matured quickly in Ford's heroes, even more so than in Ireland because there was less fear; Indians on the attack are easier to spot than native informers. The closest (Irish) sense of family was again a mostly male group, while women took on the roles of Virgin Mother (any mother giving birth under primitive circumstances) and Mary Magdalene (any saloon gal with a heart of gold).

The single greatest virtue of the West for Ford was its vast landscape, epitomized by Monument Valley, a place known and religiously respected among Hollywood directors as strictly Ford country. Ford's loving visual attention to western space showed his sacramental feeling for Nature as a place alive with spiritual presence. He also had more room out West to reconstruct American myths that might fit Irish-American values, helping him come to terms with Ireland's earlier political conflicts. In the West's immense open spaces, Ford relaxed his Irish, basically urban sense of vulnerability. As the American Catholic writer Mary Gordon has observed, "at the root of Irish puritanism is a profound fear of exposure. . . . I am convinced that this desire to hide for self-protection is at the core of a great deal of Irish behavior—behavior that was shipped successfully from Ireland to America" (1988, 36). In Ford's Irish films, the hidden informer in Dublin is always a threat, whereas the enemy in Monument Valley is the visible Indian; men and women who could defend themselves were finally responsible for Ford's ideals of civilization and decency.

By 1926, Ford had directed forty-two westerns and made the genre his métier. In the 1920s, the western had been a lowbrow movie, combining slapstick and camaraderie, bravery and daredevil deeds—all tied together by a breathless rescue. But western society, with its tradition of fierce individualism, also needed (Irish) men of community who could enforce the law. Such a decidedly Irish story is *3 Bad Men* (1926), which is about three fellows devoted to a mother and child. As Ford's western twist on the story of the three Magi, the film provided an unusual glimpse into his experiments with the western before he learned to sew nearly invisible threads of Irish culture into American history. Set during the Dakota gold rush in 1876, *3 Bad Men* is about Dan O'Malley, an immigrant who robs stagecoaches with two comrades. O'Malley and his pals, however, meet a helpless young woman who convinces them to return their stolen horses. When they discover that the woman has a baby, Ford's implicitly Irish Marian ideal is evident: To repent and dedicate oneself to the widowed mother brings one closer to the innocence of her son.

In 1939, the *annus mirabilis* of Ford's career, no studio would assign him a western. Still, he insisted on returning to his favorite genre, which he used to subtly interject Irish figures and values. *Stagecoach* was finally accepted by Walter Wanger at United Artists, with Dudley Nichols scripting from the story "Stage to Lordsburg." On set, Ford had no interference from either Wanger or Nichols, both of whom counted on Ford's name at the box office. *Stagecoach* was actually based on Ford's earlier idea in *The Iron Horse* of a multiethnic community led by an Irish straw boss and saved by an all-American hero. Ford's chief change was to substitute a socially diverse group for the earlier multiethnic workers, and to replace the crude stereotype of an Irish foreman with the partly redeemable Irish figure of an alcoholic doctor.

In an early scene, Ford pointed to his firm Irish sense of church and thus to the film's chief subtext: The coach briefly passes through a church's immense shadow that stretches across the road (and Ford's screen). Inside the coach is a cross-section of frontier types, an Irish-American emblem for a multiethnic church in transition. Ford's small, ad hoc group, moreover, suggests a church institution that is people-oriented, as might be expected in the undeveloped West or in a largely immigrant Catholic church.

Ford's coach holds a microcosm of western American society: an embezzler (banker Henry Gatewood), an alcoholic physician (Doc Josiah Boone), a travelling whiskey salesman (Samuel Peacock), a Southern aristocrat and cardshark (Hatfield), a saloon entertainer (Dallas), and a proper Eastern wife (Mrs. Lucy Mallory). Even before the travellers board, they begin to pair off and show telltale signs of community. Both the doctor and Dallas are despised by the ladies of the Law and Order League who see them off; the genteel cardplayer seeks out the well-bred Eastern wife; and the whiskey salesman becomes the doctor's shadow. Only the miserly banker, a truly unredeemable Judas, remains alone.*

The Irish-looking Thomas Mitchell (Bing Crosby in the 1966 remake) is the physician as a stereotypical Irish drinker. Yet, like the good doctor in *The Hurricane*, also played by Mitchell, this healer has a sharply critical conscience. It is mostly he who comments on his fellow passengers' moral limitations. But because of his dependence on liquor, he too needs an outside conscience. Ford turned thus to the whiskey salesman, whom Doc Boone quickly dubs "the Reverend" (a title later repeated by the gambler). A shy family man played by mousy Donald Meek, Mr. Peacock is at first merely a comic foil for Doc Boone. When Boone says they will all be scalped, for example, the nearly bald Peacock immediately covers his head with a cap.

In one key scene, however, Peacock's actions afford astute judgment and a sense of Irish conscience. Ford prepares for this scene with two more generally Christian ones. First, the gentlemanly Hatfield says how much he admires a true lady, by which he means partly to snub Dallas. Meanwhile, during the snobbish comment, Peacock walks off-frame in the background. Ford thus subtly regis-

---

*In the disappointing 1966 remake, a badly miscast Bob Cummings plays the banker and repents, which erases Ford's idea of an irredeemable Judas.

ters his disapproval. In Peacock's second moral scene, the scurrilous banker offers a drink to Doc Boone, who throws it into the fire where it blazes. In Ford's brief insert shot, Peacock, who has been standing beside the hearth, quietly notes the banker's deserved fate in the sudden hellfire. Finally, Ford uses explicitly Catholic material in a two-shot of Peacock with Boone, just after the affable doctor caps a whiskey bottle in order to deliver Mrs. Hatfield's baby. As Peacock stands against a background wall, he is dressed all in black with a dark scarf that looks exactly like a priest's confessional stole. The shot is, in effect, Ford's sign of confession, carefully qualified by an unlit wall lamp just behind Peacock's head: Boone may be a penitent drinker, but he still lacks sufficient resolve to reform for life.

Once Peacock's priestly presence is linked with the Doc's change of behavior, there is a general widening of conscience for the other main characters: The Ringo Kid decides not only to forget about Dallas's past but to return to prison, and Captain Simmons lets the Kid go free. In a later scene, Ford returns to his generally Christian presentation of Peacock. Just before an Indian's arrow hits the self-effacing fellow, he says, let's have "a little Christian charity, one for the other."

Ford's next explicitly religious scene focuses on Dallas as another Magdalene/Mother Mary figure, like Dolores in *The Fugitive*. After the delivery, Mrs. Mallory drops her stern tone towards Dallas and lets her hold her new infant. With a Mexican crucifix in the background, Ford clearly pictures a Madonna and child. The two women together, moreover, recall Ford's past references to Mother Mary and Mary Magdalene. In the final terrifying chase scene, the Anglo Protestant woman even becomes an ethnic figure, as she mumbles and works her fingers like a Mexican woman saying her rosary.

Unfortunately, Ford's tendency in *Stagecoach* to use special religious signs was at best secretive and at worst clumsy. He still needed a figure from America's past, an archetypal American in whom he might seemingly discover Irish values. The same year he directed *Stagecoach*, he purchased a story about yet another isolated outsider —Abe Lincoln. Ford tried to secure control over production of *Young Mr. Lincoln* by filming few inserts, though Darryl Zanuck still managed to cut a few scenes (Bogdanovich 1978, 73). The film turned out to be one of Ford's and the nation's favorites. Although his ethnic background was here nearly invisible, the film nonetheless reflected his Irish heritage in its basic shape and key dramatic points. Based on Lamar Trotti's script, it took America's assimilation of Irish values one step further: Irish communion, mediation, and sacramentality turned out to be in the American grain all along.

An Irish-American director would naturally be attracted to the life of Lincoln. Ford stressed a palpable mother-son relationship in Lincoln's rapport with Mrs. Clay, the mother of two young men accused of murder. According to a famous French essay (1970) on the film, "Lincoln fantasizes himself in the role of son of the [Clay] family" (Mast and Cohen, 1985, 814). Lincoln himself tells the boys that Mrs. Clay reminds him of his own deceased mother. When he finally proves that neither brother committed the murder, the (Irish) legal victory in effect saves the boys' mother as well.

Almost as important for the Irish is an idealized romantic love, usually expressed in pastoral images. Lincoln treats Anne Rutledge without a hint of sexual attraction, a neat match between the romantic reserve of the mythical American Lincoln and Irish-American puritanism. After Anne's death, Abe's love is perfectly platonic, expressed in his regard for the river along which he once walked with his sweetheart; he gazes at the river, we are told, "as if it were a woman." In light of Ford's ethnic subtext, Lincoln's sacramental regard for Nature and his enduring communion with Anne together fuel his later strength as the community's mediator and conscience.

The Grapes of Wrath (1940) focused even more intently on a mother-son relationship, this time to satirize the lack of Irish-American values in an Anglo-American family. The project was the climax of Ford's World War II period. "I bucked to do that picture, and put everything I had into it," Ford said (Mitchell 1964, 331). In July of 1939, Darryl Zanuck secretly assigned Nunnally Johnson to script the novel, while the film's art director, Richard Day, proposed the visual style of Thomas Hart Benton, the Missouri artist (Ford 1979, 143). But as soon as Ford began to shoot in the studio, he shaped the story to his own ideas. If 1920s immigrant films had usually pictured the Anglo family as wealthy and successful, Ford's treatment of the John Steinbeck novel would reveal the badly tarnished side of the Anglo coin.

Steinbeck's plot was in many ways strikingly similar to an Irish tale. It recalled a time in the old country, Ford said, "when they threw people off the land and left them wandering on the roads to starve" (Bogdanovich 1978, 76). Ford honed this parallel by drawing up close to a family circle. "It is the story of a family [and] the way it reacts, how it is shaken by a serious problem which overwhelms it," he said. "It is not a social film on this problem, it's a study of a family" (Tavernier 1967, 18 [translation mine]).

In *Young Mr. Lincoln*, Ford's idea of the family had essentially been the relation between a widowed mother and her sons. By comparison, *The Grapes of Wrath* heavily satirizes Anglo America according to Irish family values. For instance, Ma Joad (Jane Darwell) is virtually a lone mother. In Ford's original ending, she bids a final farewell to her son Tom, which is the crushing blow to family unity. Zanuck, objecting strongly, decided that Ford's stark Irish ending would never sell and stuck in Ma's final upbeat words about the common people's endurance.

Despite Zanuck, the Joads display little sense of cultural identity, family tradition, or relation to their land—all important values for Irish America and in sharp contrast to the secure self-confidence of Ford's immigrants in *The Shamrock Handicap*, a confidence he later translated into stalwart frontiersmen in *Drums along the Mohawk* (1939). The Joads, on the other hand, seem the exact opposite of an Irish family because the two leaders, Ma and Tom, lack a concrete sense of communion with others; consequently, they are unable to negotiate the terrible demands of poverty that force them out on the open road. Worst of all, they both lack an Irish critical conscience. Whereas Irish immigrants are understandably ignorant about the ways of a new world, Tom seems willfully naive when he explains his murder in the film's penultimate scene. "I'm sorry, Ma. I didn't know what I was doing anymore than when you take a breath. I didn't even know I was gonna do it." Although Ford lifted the phrase "didn't know what I was doing" directly from Steinbeck, the words also allude to Gypo Nolan's failure in *The Informer*. The comparison is instructive. In the Irish story, it is Frankie's mother, not Gypo, who puts forward the explanation (You didn't know what you were doing), which reflects Ford's Irish understanding of sin and intentionality. Here, Tom, while talking of natural reflexes, offers a similar excuse. He thus has no better understanding of himself in the last scene than in the first.

Ford's Tom also fails as a mediator for his family in a tough new world because of his mother's weak sense of community and family. Whereas an Irish mother would firmly uphold cultural tradition, Ma Joad has little idea how to preserve her family's past. Leaving the small house that the Joads have used for decades, she burns the few remaining mementos. Yet, when she finds a worn paperback book in a camp shelter, she miserly saves it because, she says, one never knows when it will come in handy. Worse, she later resorts to a stultifying sense of familial self-protection: When Tom wants to scout

out a new work camp, Ma curtly advises him, "Don't you go stick-
ing your nose into anything." But perhaps the greatest contrast with
Ford's past Marian mother figures is Ma Joad's inclination to violence. Angered at the thought of her deserted pregnant daughter,
she brandishes an ax handle—the film's most repeated symbol of
violence.

Tom adopts a vaguely Emersonian view of his situation after
Casey's death. He replies to his mother's concern, saying there is
"one big soul, then, it don't matter. I'll be everywhere . . . wherever
there's a fight so hungry people can eat—I'll be there." But his Anglo
idealism seems hollow when he exits across an empty dance floor,
the film's strongest sign of communal life. As in the film's opening
scene, he acts again like an unconfessed criminal. Still, Ford ended
his satire on an Irish-American note, stressing Tom's willingness to
fight and his need of an Irish Marian mother, that is, one who will
help him confess his sins and be forgiven.

Ford's last hurrah for religious values in the western was *3 Godfathers* (1949), a throwback to *3 Bad Men* (1926). Ford's critics have
noticed the film's forced mixture of religion and western clichés,
not to mention its sentimental religiosity (Sinclair 1979, 152). But
from an Irish viewpoint, Ford's tender story is a religious allegory
about Christmas in an American setting, an idea Frank Capra would
later employ in his most successful post-War hit. As the story begins, Robert Hightower (John Wayne) and several outlaws escape
into the desert where they discover a mother and child, just before
the woman passes away. Later, after the death of his two comrades,
Hightower goes on alone with the baby. Ford's Marian story champions, in essence, the Christ Child's innocence in grown men. The
power of Irish self-denial, moreover, stems from complete dedication
to the Virgin Mary and the Infant Jesus, supported by an unshakeable
male communion with the dead.* When the two deceased comrades
appear in the end as ghostly figures, they serve, to use a Catholic
phrase, as Hightower's own Communion of Saints.

The Christmas-like births in Ford's films were limited, if hopeful,
signs of healing in community. Ford was not up to stronger communal symbols, given the conflicted nature of the Irish family—with
its silent anger towards absent fathers and manipulative mothers.
At times, Ford treated violence as if it were a social sacrament, an

*The scene of Hightower's desert trek ranks, along with the ending of Erich Von Stroheim's
Greed, as one of the great desert scenes in American cinema.

idea Martin Scorsese would later explore in depth. Yet compared to the strife-torn, foggy streets of Dublin, Ford's Monument Valley was an improvement; the West, with its expansive openness and clearly limned rock formations, was a relief to Ford's troubled Irish soul. His greatest achievement there was to revitalize nineteenth-century tales of America, such as Lincoln's early manhood and a stagecoach's survival, with a nostalgic Irish schema: a sinful Judas, a repentant Mary Magdalene, and a forgiving Mother Mary.

Still, Ford's small, mostly male groups handicapped his ability to live in the present and treat contemporary national issues. Lacking a broadly based sense of community, he never seriously considered American populism in film; his conflicted Irish heritage limited his empathy for the country's little people. It would take an ethnic Catholic director far removed from Ford's bitter Anglo-Irish tradition to enliven mainstream populism with a vital sense of the ethnic family.

The fully assimilated Irish son in Mother Machree
*(1928) finally discovers and acknowledges his mother, the
person responsible for his mainstream success. (Museum
of Modern Art/Film Stills Archive)*

Victor McLaglen, as the Irish Judas in The Informer
(1935), stands before a Marian mother (Una O'Connor).
(Museum of Modern Art/Film Stills Archive; courtesy of
RKO Radio)

Donald Meek, as Mr. Peacock in Stagecoach (1939),
serves as a comical Irish conscience for the hard-drinking
Doc Boone (Thomas Mitchell). (Museum of Modern Art/
Film Stills Archive; courtesy of Wanger United Artists)

The three Wise Men in John Ford's Irish/western Christmas tale, 3 Godfathers (1949). (Museum of Modern Art/Film Stills Archive; courtesy of Argosy Pictures–Metro-Goldwyn-Meyer)

Small-town America in It's a Wonderful Life *(1946) as the (Italian/Irish) family. (Museum of Modern Art/Film Stills Archive; courtesy of Liberty Films/RKO)*

CHAPTER 4

FRANK CAPRA

Frank Capra hails from the same social tradition in American film as D. W. Griffith and John Ford. Like them, he explored issues of family, law, decency, and democracy. Yet, Capra's distinctive ethnic background also made a difference. Though as much a social moralist as Griffith, Capra brought to his characters an Italian sense of gentle compassion; his familial concern for others was an ethnic world apart from Griffith's Anglo view of greedy human nature. As for a resemblance to Ford's work, Capra's films often relied on communal values and family scenes. But whereas Ford wrestled with age-old Irish conflicts or their multiethnic equivalents in America, Capra asserted positive Italian virtues to revitalize Anglo America; his big mild-mannered men, typified by James Stewart and Gary Cooper, encourage a subtly Italian familial vision based on immediate compassion and a long-suffering nature. Perhaps Capra's greatest insight was to show that a fellow's (Italian) virtues could attract and even redeem a success-obsessed Anglo heroine.

Because of Capra's pragmatic focus on the present, he did not share Ford's Irish sense of the past and was free to criticize contemporary America. At his most critical, Capra roundly satirized the success ethic as a great danger to the little people, whose (ethnic) familial vision could be a model for America's social and political institutions. On the other hand, he knew, too, that perhaps the little people might not live up to his Italian family ideal. Perhaps in the final analysis they were no better than a selfish, violent mob whom national bosses could direct to suit their own ambitions. This dark side to Capra's pragmatic vision thrilled contemporary filmgoers but has puzzled his critics. But they have only to turn to *It's A Wonderful Life* to find Capra's most incisive summary of WASP greed versus (Italian) familial values in social action.

and His Italian Vision of America

Capra's filmic canon falls in two parts. The films before 1936 worked out the essential figures of a narrative schema that would later emerge in his mature social comedies: a mild-mannered fellow, a blonde woman driven by her desire for success, a wealthy and powerful figure from the ruling class, and the common folk. The early films approach this schema by first satirizing a rich WASP society, while trying to match positive ethnic traits with mainstream counterparts. Following an experience of religious conversion, Capra grouped his key figures in 1936 to define the core conflict of his hyphenated immigrant identity, a conflict between a young couple with implicitly Italian values and avaricious members of the WASP ruling class. Once Capra discovered that this core conflict would appeal to filmgoers across the nation, he fully explored its potential for social comedy, starting with optimistic family endings and gradually shifting to the darkly fatalistic side of Italian culture. After the war, Capra showed renewed optimism in the efficacy of his ethnic vision.

Capra's critics in general pay scant attention to his Italian background and treat his political comedies largely as sentimental, dated images of America. Without the paradigm of the Italian family, they typically praise Capra's work in Anglo-American terms. For instance, Raymond Carney (1986) situates Capra in the Anglo-American Romantic tradition as an idealist and visionary, along with Emerson, Whitman, Faulkner and Mailer, but says nothing about Capra's ethnic heritage.

Capra's critics have badly underestimated the complexity of surface assimilation in his works. This clever immigrant director used blonde, nonethnic women and all-American men to put across his intensely Italian vision of the country. Avoiding ethnic stereotypes, Capra first satirized conspicuous consumption and then experi-

mented with Italian family values. Eventually, he featured mainstream couples with Italian ideals. Public response to his work was a
sure sign of reciprocal assimilation: Anglo Protestant and ethnic audiences alike cheered when Capra's all-American couple triumphed
over a grasping Anglo patriarch.

The closest Capra came to explaining his ethnic social vision were
his ideas of production and comedy. Traced to their origins in the
Italian family, these ideas were the basis of Capra's filmmaking.

The Italian Success Ethic in Capra's Films

The story of Capra's immigrant life begins in 1903 when, as a six-year-
old, he emigrated with his family from Palermo, Sicily. In Los Angeles, little Frankie soon discovered that the American dream meant
long hours of factory labor. Standing by his mother's side in a can-
nery, he learned first hand about social conditions in America. At
home, his father ran family affairs by staying in the background and
encouraging others to discuss their ideas and career plans, though he
always had the final word. When the inevitable conflict arose between
one person's future and the family's, Capra's father was the key mediator. A similar Italian family dynamic would appear in all Capra's
later work, where father figures mediate for family-like groups, that
is, for America's little people and sometimes even for rich Anglo
Americans. Likewise, Capra's innocent young men are quick to show
Italian values that settle political conflicts and foster a social ethic
in which Italian-Marian values like compassion, patience, and complete self-sacrifice are at the heart of the family. Whereas 1920s films
featured an Italian immigrant ruled by lust, greed, and vengeance,
Capra's father figure immediately shows compassion to his extended
families, especially to children, the poor, and the little people. This
father will endure even social crucifixion in order to mediate for his
family or a family-like institution.

Just as Italian in Capra's films was his focus on the joyful side of
communal city life. In his hands, urban banks and parks and federal
buildings turn into special places, where family-like groups work out
their differences. Moreover, in the Italian tradition of a strong aesthetic sensibility, these places of celebration often include the arts,
usually music. Whereas John Ford was deeply nostalgic about the
untamed outdoors, Capra was a thoroughly urban immigrant filmmaker.

In a sense, Capra's rise as a Hollywood director began in childhood with lessons in survival. In his later autobiography he vividly recalled the hardship of immigration. "Thirteen days of stench and misery in steerage; two more days of panic and pandemonium at Ellis Island; then eight more days of cramped, itchy, hardship in an overcrowded chair car; crying to sleep in each other's laps, eating only bread and fruit Papa bought at train stops" (1971, 5).

Two realities prevailed in what Capra called his "peasant" childhood. "I was born into a family that worshipped, first the Crucifix, and second, a coffee can stuffed with cash, preferably gold" (1971, 112). As soon as Capra's family arrived at the Los Angeles depot, they headed for the Plaza Mission where everyone knelt to offer a prayer of thanksgiving. Within the week, however, the celebratory spirit turned into the grim reality of factory labor. Capra's father worked in a bottle plant, twelve hours a day, six days a week, and his mother labeled olive cans. Later, as a teenager, Capra stuffed newspapers, sang in various lunch spots, and waited on tables to pay for high school and help support his family. His dual faith in religion and a regular job carried over into his later social portraits of the 1930s and 1940s: If Americans had faith in God, their neighbor, employment, and a new social ethics, then the country would be secure.

Capra's immigrant childhood helps account for the happy families and particularly the positive father figures in his films. For example, when he wanted a high school education, the family consensus was that he should go to work like everyone else. But then his father "put his foot down," Capra recalled. "If Frankie no ask for money —he go to school" (1971, 6). Capra's father thus took a background position in family discussions until the final decision, and then countered short-term judgments with long-range plans. This Italian style of decision-making taught Capra to appreciate the respect due each family member.

Regarding religion, Capra has said that as a young adult he was a "Christmas Catholic" and a "Christian humanist." But after a conversion experience in the early 1930s, he took religion more seriously, identifying with an Anglo Catholic who discovered within himself a dormant spirituality: "When Eric Gill (one of my heroes), the English illustrator and sculptor . . . said after his conversion, 'I invented the Roman Catholic Church,' I think I understood him. He discovered values already discovered within himself" (1971, xii). The Italian Capra, too, was an individualist who needed to find his religious heritage on his own. In his later films, he deftly matched the individualism of Italian America with that of the country's Anglo Protestant ethos.

Once Capra had approached religion in his own way he was ready, he said, to surrender his rugged individualism.

> It may happen to you only once in a hundred Masses, but it will happen. You walk back from Communion with the Host on your tongue—a nobody. You kneel, drop your head in your hands. Slowly the wonder of it fills you with joy—the dissolving Host in your mouth is the living Christ! . . . Your mind empties itself of all thought, your body of all substance. You are a spirit suffused in a glorious Light. (1971, 130)

Although Capra here unwittingly uses gnostic phrases (the body as pure spirit), he nonetheless articulates his deeply personal experience of emptying himself of his usual ambitious drive. It is this *kenosis* —an emptying of the self in a Christ-like sacrifice—that on screen marks Capra's fatherly heroes. When dramatized as a humble leader who sacrifices himself for a social cause, this religious act strongly appealed to Anglo America.

There was another side as well to Capra's individualistic spirit: It fostered a critical conscience. In sharp contrast to an obedient laity, Capra has characterized himself as

> not even a good [Irish-American] Catholic, . . . not one that tailors his actions to the verbotens of Popes, bishops, and priests. I'm worse, I'm a Catholic in spirit; one who firmly believes that the anti-moral, the intellectual bigots, and the Mafias of ill will may destroy religion, but they will never conquer the cross. (1971, 443)

Capra quickly dissociated himself from the legalistic mentality encouraged by Irish-American clergy. And to show he was not an Italian chauvinist, he mentioned as well the Mafia. In his later satires of political demigods, he dramatized his deep resentment of autocratic rule. While this typically Italian skepticism pertained to large political groups, Capra's positive religious vision was rooted in his childhood experience of family, the basis of Italian-American community.

Capra's celebratory sense of American community comprised other ethnic groups. He was proud, as he put it, of attending high school with "Dagos, Shines, Cholos, and Japs" (1971, 6). To broaden his immigrant Italian views, he read widely, took a college degree in engineering, and cultivated friendships with European intellectuals. In Hollywood, he appeared a distinctly cultured man, so much so that to one actor friend he seemed more like a gentleman from Genoa than a Sicilian-born immigrant (Scherle and Levy 1977, 73).

With his Italian identity firmly based in the family, Capra on set quickly established himself as the head of a film family. He had to be the guiding figure, he believed, if the movie was to be any good.

> I could not understand how anybody else could write the material for you and then you'd shoot it; and then you'd give it to an editor, and the editor would put it together the way he wanted; and then the producer would do it up. I just didn't understand how all of this could happen and yet produce an art form. This was a committee. Everybody would give their own interpretation to that film. And naturally, when a committee dabbles in art, they don't come up with much. . . . And the first thing I asked for [at Columbia Studios] was to have complete control of what I was doing. (1981, 200)

Although Capra was unaware of his Italian familial assumptions, he knew that one person had to bear the responsibility for a film's basic unity. Artistic squabbles had to be minimized so that the actors could concentrate on their craft, and, just as important, so that the communal atmosphere could be felt on screen.

Capra learned quickly what happens when a director turns autocratic. After *The Miracle Woman* (1931) pushed religious ideas, the critics roasted Capra for lecturing the public. Worse, the film bombed at the box office. Capra later admitted, with more than a touch of religious self-irony, that they "burn you at the stake for spouting ideas" (1971, 131). If you want to send a message, "you have Western Union for that" (1981, 203). By 1932, Capra had learned to appreciate that the director was decisive but only in "collaboration with thousands of people." It is in this context that "one man has to make the decisions, one man says yes or no. That man should be the director. And if it isn't, then you get unevenness" (1971, 21).

Capra's film family started with his scriptwriter. Recalling his long professional relationship with writer Robert Riskin, Capra said, we "vibrated to the same tuning fork . . . we'd write everything together. . . . He'd go off and write and then he'd come back and we'd go over it, then he'd go off and write. We'd change a script often during the making of the picture" (1971, 11).

Capra had an equally close regard for his actors, whom he treated like "blood brothers" (Scherle and Levy 1977, 14). "I never told an actor or actress how to act," Capra said. "I was only involved in whether they were thinking right; then they could do no wrong. . . . I could talk to them about what the scene involved, what the relationships were, the emotions, and particularly how to think right" (1977, 43). Barbara Stanwyck confirmed this opinion. "Capra discussed the character and its relation to the story and other characters with the performer," she said. "He recognized and respected what you [as an actor or actress] were trying to do—your interpretation" (Scherele and Levy 1977, 1).

On set, Capra seemed indistinguishable from his crew and actors, just as his father had not asserted his authority during discussions. "You'd never pick Frank as the director," Gary Cooper recalled. There was, Ralph Bellamy said, a special "rapport with each other—cast and crew, writers, director, and producer. It was a companionship relation that I believe even photographed in some mystic way" (Scherle and Levy 1977, 103).

Rooted in this Italian sense of community, Capra's post-Depression films translate the camaraderie of his crew and actors to the screen. This was at a time when the nation was struggling to keep its populist image of itself as a good-hearted, sharing people. Capra's image of the country as a cooperative family conflicted with the dominant civil myth of fiercely competitive individualism; the Italian director was in effect challenging the Anglo-American paradigm of the rugged individual. In his films, Capra often satirized the nation's uncritical belief in this myth by championing supportive families and family-like institutions.

From the perspective of the Italian family, the little people and the "little guy" are uniquely good. Capra spelled out this idea in a late interview.

> I like people, I think people are just wonderful. I also think that people are all equal in the sense of their dignity, their *divinity*; there's no such thing as a common man or an uncommon man. . . . Each one is actually unique. Never before has there been anyone like you. Never again will there be anyone like you. One mold, one young lady. So you're a very unique person, so is he, so is she. You are something that never existed before and will never exist again. Isn't that wonderful? Isn't that something pretty exciting? So I look at you as something that plays a part of a great whole, an equal part of everything, or else you wouldn't

be here. . . . The biggest thing is that I want [audiences] to care about these people. (1981, 201 [italics mine])

In his own stumbling way, Capra articulates here the divine nature of individuals, closing with their strong communal relation to others. His final words picture him as an artistic mediator between screen characters and audiences.

Capra created a unique sense of family characters by frequently using what he called a "reactive character," a figure that directs the audience's attention. The figure's observant eyes point up the comic side of several nearby characters during a frivolous argument or other potentially comic scene. At the same time, this gaze distances audiences from sadness and misfortune. In this way, human troubles appear in the light of a brotherly or sisterly gaze (Capra 1971, 17).

Capra used crowds, too, for an overall sense of family. They were, moreover, essential backdrops for the main characters' mediational decisions (Capra 1977, 43). "I tried to make a film believable," he said, "and that starts, of course, with getting very good actors for all the small parts; because if you believe the small people, you're more liable to believe the derring-do of the stars" (1981, 200). The small parts helped moviegoers see strong major characters as part of a larger community; in a familial sense, all actors are equal. This is what Capra meant when he asserted, "I don't think there are stars and bit players or extras" (1971, 10). He brought out minor characters by giving each "an attitude." For example, he told the actress playing a bank teller in *American Madness* to imagine her mother sick in a hospital.

Capra applied the same sense of individual worth and dramatic plausibility to Nature, so that an object's or scene's human spirit is evident: "Such things as snow that looks like snow, and cold that looks like cold are made more credible when we see the breath of *people* that are working in the scene" (1981, 200 [italics mine]). When scientists asked Capra in the 1950s to film a documentary about the sun, he first warned them that he had a thoroughly Italian attitude towards Nature as something filled with God's divine presence (1971, 442). Similarly, the unobtrusive camera work of Capra's favorite cinematographers—Joe Walker, William Daniels, and George Barnes—focuses attention on the unique nature of characters and sets.

Capra, as already mentioned, relied on believable minor parts and evocative details to create a spirited and spiritually alive world. Major characters would reveal a sharply critical conscience. For this, actors had to get across the "people who are to make these decisions," Capra said (1981, 198). Major roles had to be both convincing and clearly "in relief" (1971, 24). Capra began each work day by asking his actors to read a scene together. Then he experimented with different setups and movements to "get the whole thing worked out in long shot." It was especially important to get the effect of "natural moves": "You work it out so you begin to feel they're real people talking really, talking over each other" (1971, 2). The acting always had to look "natural and effortless," recalled Gavin Gordon (Scherle and Levy 1977, 108).

In the editing room, Capra became the decisive head of his film family. Unlike John Ford, who shot as little as possible by so-called editing in the camera, Capra used multiple takes and a master shot that together left him much leeway in the editing room. There he thought of himself as a mediator between the audience and the people on screen. No longer would he try to send messages. Movies are "a people-to-people thing, not a director-to-people, not a cameraman-to-people, not a writer-to-people thing," he said. "The illusion takes place in watching people's faces" (1977, 43).

Capra in general thought of his directorial role in carefully couched religious terms. When asked why God was on the side of so many of his characters, he replied,

> In It's A Wonderful Life, I showed a little angel who hadn't won his wings because he was such a lousy angel. But the characters themselves had an idealism within them that eventually won out. They reached for something they had inside, and they came up with a handful of courage, . . . and they beat their adversaries with it. Not with prayer. The only prayer you'll find is when Jimmy Stewart goes into that saloon and he says, "Show me the way, God. I'm at the end of my rope." He just barely says it when he gets punched in the nose. Then he says, "That's what I get for praying." I'm wise enough to know that you can't make a religious tract or a political tract out of a film. People go into a theater to be entertained, titillated, inspired. But they don't go in to hear a tract. (1978, 41)

Capra was rightfully wary of magical angels and desperate prayers, signs of the prevailing Irish-American Catholicism. He was, after all, an immigrant who had worked hard for every break he got.

Capra knew that change, inner change, begins not with fairies and words but with difficult action. For this reason, Capra was leery of films based on a verbal aesthetic.

> You have to dramatize [your idea] with people, not through sermons. Audiences will not buy it. But they will buy a human being who's trying to do the right thing for his fellow man, and they'll cheer like hell for him if he's got odds to win out. . . . They'll cheer for the good guy, for the guy who's got compassion, forgiveness in his heart, for that good Samaritan. Those kinds of people counteract all the meanness there is in the world. They're idealists. They will go down fighting for a lost cause, and you cheer for them. That's the closest I can get to heaven. (1978a, 41).

As an Italian-American, Capra focused on social action that includes others as family members. Capra's heroes discover their unique worth by helping others. For instance, George Bailey (James Stewart) shows the traditional Marian virtues of compassion, patience, and mediation. Like the Bible's good Samaritan, mentioned above, and like a film director, the Capra hero acts regardless of religious affiliation. Thus, Capra intended the Italian ideals imbedded in characters' actions to speak to Anglo-American as well as Italian audiences.

Capra's clearest summary statement about religion in film is his theory of comedy. Once again, he began by relating the film's purpose to its audience.

> Comedy is good news—"How beautiful . . . are the feet of him that bringeth good tidings. . . ." The Gospels are comedies: a triumph of spirit over matter. The Resurrection is the happiest of all endings: man's triumph over death. The Mass is a "celebration" of that event. Priests and parishioners "celebrate" a Mass. It is a divine comedy.
> In social terms, comedy is a complete surrender of one's defenses. . . .
> Therefore, before you can laugh you must surrender yourself—let your defenses down. Enemies, strangers, snobs, the sarcastic, the haters, the brutal, the fearful, the ugly, the dangerous, the unknown—no laughs.
> But—you laugh easily among friends; you love them; you let down your defenses. And you laugh easily among the innocent; babies, for instance, whether human, animal, or bird. (1971, 453)

Capra discovered comedy in the Gospels, in the mass, and in his own Italian heritage, with the offhand allusion to Dante's *Divine Comedy*. He was trying to link his religious heritage to general audiences. As in any audience-based theory of comedy, he argued for a particular psychological effect. The experience of attending mass, described earlier as an emptying of the self, was like the pleasure of watching a good comedy: Both moments encourage self-surrender. Moreover, moviegoers laugh at a comedy as if among friends, as if part of an open family that quickly feels concern for the innocent and helpless; again, an emptying of the self allows for greater compassion. Laughter, the Italian Capra concluded, reveals "the God within" each of us.

The Early Years: Irish Types and WASP Women

Capra spent his early years as a filmmaker crafting the basic characters of a narrative schema that would later fit his mature social comedies. These characters together suggested the core conflict of his hyphenated immigrant identity: an Italian familial vision versus WASP individualism and its success ethic. Capra slowly learned how to configure characters, as he sharply satirized Anglo high culture and searched for mainstream counterparts to his ethnic values. To begin with, Capra turned to the accepted Irish ethnic, to young blonde women, and to street-wise young men. From these materials he gradually invented a flexible narrative schema in which the all-American fellow with Italian familial values rescues the WASP young woman.

Because Italians in 1920s ethnic films had been erotic and vengeful figures, Capra initially expressed ethnic identity in the accepted figure of the Irish-American woman who pursues WASP men and wealth. Next, Capra, in a clever cultural twist, substituted a WASP heroine and prepared for her conversion to Italian values by pairing her with a fellow who exemplifies Marian traits. To intensify the young woman's struggle, Capra personified her worst side in the figure of an older, successful boss, who tempts her with success; she must choose between that WASP promise of power and her fatherly young man's belief in Italian family values. Thus, Capra's street-smart heroine typically stands half-way between Anglo and ethnic father figures. Once she picks the young man and his (ethnic) ideals, the couple became in effect concerned parents for the country's little people. In this way, Capra's Italian familism revitalized nineteenth-century American populism.

In comparison to John Ford's films, Capra's canon points up distinctive contemporary tensions within an ethnic culture and WASP America. Whereas Ford was concerned with old stories of Irish bravery and British injustice, Capra, a pragmatist of the present, criticized both his church and his country. Capra shared neither Ford's religious legalism and unswerving loyalty to the faith, nor his nostalgic nineteenth-century view of Nature. Raised in Los Angeles, the urban Italian-American thought first of America as big cities with cheerful parks, and then of small towns with tree-lined streets. In this setting, Capra valued the (Italian) family and broadly analogous social groups. While the Irish-American Ford held to a restricted social vision of small, threatened male groups, Capra repeatedly featured extended families to dramatize his upbeat social ethics. College-educated and well-read, he worked out a particular social ethics based on the (Italian) family.

Capra's social ethics led him to explore the immigrant art of surface assimilation, in which he reshaped American civil myths to his Italian background and, for a time, even restored Anglo-American idealism. He especially valued Italian-American immigrant virtues, lauding

> idealists [who are] non-conformers [because they] walk alone and live alone and swim up the stream from some kind of jungle, and we're better off now than when we were in the jungles. Some of us have a little more compassion within us and forgiveness within us, and make a kind of an evolution. (Capra 1981, 201)

Capra refers here to a new version of the success ethic, in which the Darwinian image of a struggling fish excludes Anglo competitive individualism; that is, he did not pit one American against another in a fight for survival. This allowed him to introduce the Italian values of compassion and forgiveness for a new and basically Italian evolution.

Critics have long recognized the heavily moral nature, if not the ethnic roots, of Capra's work. According to the film historian Gerald Mast, the

> Capra-Riskin film was generally a witty contemporary morality play that pitted a good man—invariably a "little guy" who is

naïve, sincere, folksy, unaffected, unintellectual, apolitical—
against evil social forces: money, politics, affectation, social
status, human insensitivity. The "little guy" converts the social
heretics to the human truth, usually by making the film's heroine, who embodies the false societal assumptions, fall in love
with him. The "little guy" emerges from the struggle not only
victorious but also wiser about the ways of the world. (1981, 232)

Filmgoers took Capra's moral and social values to heart, as long as
he did not preach, and as long as he avoided ethnic types that might
trigger anti-immigrant feelings. At first Capra, like most young directors in 1920s Hollywood, had little control over a new project. In one
of his first films with a Catholic immigrant, he carefully separated
himself from ignorant, superstitious Catholicism by picturing it on
screen. In *Fultah Fisher's Boarding House* (1922) he adapted Rudyard
Kipling's ballad about a naive Dutch Catholic sailor who is murdered
after he falls for an unscrupulous barmaid. This superstitious young
man wears a "silver crucifix that keeps a man from harm." Although
Capra deleted much from Kipling's story, he retained criticism of the
uneducated ethnic. Years later, he returned to this criticism in *It's A
Wonderful Life*.

In 1926, Capra used the Irish-American success story to show a
timid ethnic finding a new life in America. *The Strong Man* featured
childlike Harry Langdon as a Belgian captured during World War I
and later brought to the United States. Written by Irish-American
Frank Ripley, the story ended with the young man conforming to an
Irish-American image of success: He becomes a policeman.

In 1927, Capra, like Ford, resorted to the popular genre of multiethnic stories about the Irish and Jews. He accepted sight unseen the
script *For the Love of Mike* and soon regretted the decision (Poague
1975, 46). He found himself forced to work with crudely drawn
stereotypes of the Irishman, the Jew, and the German in a predictably
formulaic story about three men raising an orphan boy. As a young
college man, the orphan disgraces himself at Yale by getting drunk,
but finally redeems himself with a victory on the crew team. Capra
tried hard thereafter to avoid ethnic clichés altogether.

In 1928, Capra directed his first feature film for Columbia and
had his first chance to rework a script (1971, 83). *That Certain Thing* is
a social fantasy about Molly (Viola Dana), an Irish-American young
woman who marries a millionaire's son; the story is an immigrant's
dream-come-true (Scherle and Levy 1977, 51). Because the young

man's father, however, is convinced that Molly wants only the family fortune, he disinherits the couple. But when the hardworking pair successfully compete with the father in the restaurant business, he accepts them into his WASP family. A supposed golddigger, Molly turns out to be an industrious wife and a suitable mate for a rich Anglo husband. Many of Capra's later social comedies would likewise focus on a young couple's decision to confront a capitalist father figure.

Capra's plot resembled the popular immigrant formula in films like *Irene* (1926). A wealthy Anglo-American young man badly needs an Irish-American woman to revitalize his family's success ethic. Unlike the young man in *Irene*, however, this fellow does not confess to his fiancée's Irish mother. Even more unusual for an Irish-American story, Molly leaves her neighborhood, including the stereotypical controlling mother, without so much as a backward glance. To an Italian-American like Capra, Irish preoccupations like confession to the powerful mother or guilt for leaving one's neighborhood were of little importance. Molly, despite her name, is not really an Irish-American, for neither in real life nor in 1920s films did the Irish-American woman show an acumen for business. Molly's ability to bargain, in fact, more closely resembles that of an immigrant Italian merchant or street-vendor. Even more striking, she competes with the capitalist father in his business world. Capra's later social films switched to Anglo-American women who would learn to assimilate Italian-American values.

Capra was struggling at the time to fit together three separate pieces from his ethnic background: the Italian ethnic, the independent young woman, and the success ethic. *Say It with Sables* (1928) took an especially dim view of the ambitious Irish woman with no talent besides that of swindling a well-to-do Anglo-American lover. Bowing to popular taste, Capra cast the ethnic in the villain's role: Irene Gordon blackmails the wife of her beau, a wealthy banker, by getting the couple's guileless son to propose marriage. Luckily for the husband, his righteous wife shoots Irene, and afterwards the police look the other way. Written by Capra and Peter Milne, the story cashed in on the prevalent fear of the rising ethnic. The scurrilous Irene is a double ethnic threat: She jeopardizes both the career and the marriage of the successful banker.

Ladies of Leisure (1930) broached the generally taboo topic of streetwalkers, taking an open-minded attitude typical of Italian sensuality and aesthetics, and quite unlike John Ford's Irish puritan mores. In one of Capra's scenes, when a man and woman undress in adjacent rooms, she clearly expects the fellow to sleep with her.

Following a string of hits at Columbia, Capra directed *The Miracle Woman* (1931). The story was, in his words, "one woman's life in three acts: disillusion, venality, conversion" (1971, 131). Critics have noticed only overtly Anglo-Protestant material, overlooking Capra's subtle references to his own Italian background. Adapted from the play by John Meehan and Robert Riskin, *The Miracle Woman* is the story of the increasingly successful and sensationalist evangelist Florence Fallon (Barbara Stanwyck), who as a girl was devoted to her father, a selfless minister. As the film opens, the quiet kindly minister dies without recognition from his congregation, which deeply disillusions his daughter. In revenge, she becomes a traveling evangelist who deceives the public with phony miracles and circus tricks. But one night at a revivalist gathering, she meets John Carson, a blind man who has heard her radio broadcast and regained his hope to live. Later, in an ironic plot twist, she is saved by the good-hearted Carson. By the last scene, Fallon works for the Salvation Army, while her former manager laments, "she gave up a million bucks for that."

The Miracle Woman was a seminal story for Capra's later political films, in which a young man changes a WASP girlfriend's cynicism to effective social action. Carson is a Capra hero with the closely related Marian traits of patience, compassion, and forgiveness. At the same time, Capra criticizes the hucksterism of tent revivalism: Fallon is a con artist, and her religious service a circus of trumpets, lions, and ceiling entrances. In Capra's later films, Fallon's businesslike attitude to religion would be reflected in the fervid political campaigns of rich industrialists. Capra came to believe there was a definite moral choice to be made between a civil religion of success and one of social action.

Fallon's journey to conversion teaches her commitment to the Protestant social gospel, with an Italian slant. First, she condemns her father's Protestant congregation for its hard-heartedness and implicit lack of community. The blind Carson, on the other hand, is associated with a religion of suffering, self-sacrifice, and images. Whereas Fallon refuses to accept crucifixion in this life ("You crucified [my father]," she angrily tells his congregation"), Carson accepts the cross of disability. He is thus able to show Italian Marian patience and compassion.

Capra specifically commented on the film's Marian vision by placing on the wall of Fallon's room an Italian Renaissance painting of the Blessed Mother and the Infant Jesus. Like Carson, the icon's religious values are visible every day to Fallon but go unnoticed. Fallon's subsequent conversion begins with her recognition of the people's faith in her; the family of believers spurs her hope and her strong religious principles. At the same time, a large fire breaks out in the church tent, a final sign of Anglo hucksterism in collapse.

In 1931, Capra took on the WASP upper crust he would so often castigate in later films. To make money after his first loss at Columbia with *The Miracle Woman*, he filmed a fast-paced satire of a young rich woman who uses an ordinary journalist to restore her American sense of success. Written by Harry Chandler and Douglas Churchill, *Platinum Blonde* satirizes the wealthy Schuyler family, especially blonde Anne Schuyler (Jean Harlow) who decides to reform a spunky news reporter named Stew Smith (Robert Williams) by marrying him. She does not take into account, however, that Smith will feel caged in the pseudofamily atmosphere of the Schuyler's mansion, where he quickly loses all sense of himself as a respected individual. In the end, he rejects WASP wealth and high society to marry an Irish-American friend, his newspaper pal Gallagher (the well-known and Catholic actress Loretta Young). The idea of divorce from a WASP wife was something that a liberal Italian American like Capra could consider, whereas a religious legalist like John Ford could not.

Capra's romantic plot was a new twist on a popular 1920s ethnic formula: the rise of an Irish-American woman into high society through marriage. Capra's special twist was to place the nonethnic newspaper man in the role of the upwardly mobile Irish young woman, while the visibly Irish-American role goes to his pal/girlfriend. When Smith finally realizes that neither his WASP wife nor her wealthy social circle suits him, he turns to the long-suffering Gallagher for compassionate understanding; thus, the feisty Anglo-American working stiff gets together with the Irish-American woman. Along the way, Capra devoted many scenes to satire of the Schuyler's opulent life-style—the success ethic gone bad.

Despite the film's popularity at the box office, Capra never cared for it. He was dissatisfied with the awkward mix of cultural identities in his romantic couple. Moreover, by weighing social comedy heavily towards satire, he was unable to express positive moral values. So, in *American Madness* (1932) he proved the power of the little people— as investors who turn the tide on a bank run. And in the Academy award-winning *It Happened One Night*, he acquainted a spoiled rich girl with the little people of America.

Capra had yet to discover the core dramatic opposition of his mature social comedies: the (Italian) young man and converted blonde woman joined together against a greedy rich patriarch from the WASP ruling class.

The Mature Years: Italian Social Ethics in Anglo America

By 1936, Capra had filmed enough social satire to put together all the pieces of a new narrative schema for familial social comedy. Having sharply satirized the wealthy WASP woman, he continued his social criticism but shifted to a white-collar heroine, whom he paired with a fellow as gentle and compassionate as an Italian. And he no longer needed a blind man to make his point; Jimmy Stewart or Gary Cooper in the role sufficed. With an (ethnic) familial couple in place, Capra drew closer to serious social problems, safe in the knowledge that his comedy would end with a familial union in which his idealized couple stood as substitute parents for America's little people.

Capra's mature period began when he discovered how to arrange his narrative schema to highlight the core conflict of his hyphenated immigrant identity: He pitted a pragmatic (Italian) familial couple against a WASP patriarch from the ruling class. Capra's idealized couple was sure to follow after the Anglo individualism in *That Certain Thing* and *Platinum Blonde* began to crumble; he needed an upbeat ethnic alternative to biting social satire. Later, towards the end of this period, Capra turned to the darkly fatalistic, anarchic side of his ethnic background. Perhaps the little people were not so much childlike concerned citizens as an easily swayed mob.

The social values of Capra's mature, ethnic-based period were virtually a blueprint for the Catholic principle of subsidiarity. As explained by Andrew Greeley:

> Simply and bluntly stated, subsidiarity means a bias in favor of the maximization of participation in decision making in every sector of society. The Catholic social theory tends to believe that "small is beautiful" (nothing should be bigger than necessary), not merely for aesthetic reasons (though these are not to be automatically rejected), but because it believes that participation is more likely to be maximized in smaller organizations than in larger. (1985, 292)

If Capra's social ideals were neither Democratic nor Republican, and strike some critics as fuzzy and sentimental, they nevertheless reflect a fully coherent religious view of society (Maland 1980, 114).

Catholic social theory, in this view, begins with the smallest social unit. A "planner who does not take into account village, neighborhood, tribal or familial loyalties may impose his reforms," Greeley continues, "but he will find them stoutly resisted and stubbornly frustrated. You cannot fight intimate, decentralized networks" (1985, 292–93). Or, as the newspaper man says to the wealthy capitalist in *Mr. Deeds Goes to Town*, you can't fight "the people."

Capra picked up his social ethics as a boy, standing at his mother's knee in an olive plant. He learned that without political representation, a worker can easily be exploited. In his films, his sense of subsidiarity seems close to anarchist politics, which has long been associated with Italian Americans. The impression that subsidiarity equals anarchy is particularly strong, Greeley says, "when compared with the centralizing tendencies of both capitalism and socialism" (293). American films about Italian immigrants raised Anglo-American fears of anarchy as early as *At the Altar* (1909). Capra triggered a similar fear with the mob scenes in *Mr. Deeds Goes to Town* and *Meet John Doe*. Here subsidiarity was not only an answer to social anarchy, but also turned large institutions into family-like places of business.

The warm, personal nature of Capra's Italian familism gave subsidiarity a strong appeal. Capra couched social problems in terms of family-like relationships: boy rangers and U.S. Senators, a wealthy fatherly heir and starving farmers, an Irish-American angel and a frustrated, depressed man. As for the institutional, hierarchical character of Roman Catholicism, it had little appeal to or impact on an Italian layman like Capra. Capra's romantic couple usually leads in the effort to maximize the American people's participation in institutions. The couple might found a nationwide network of small-town clubs, or run a building and loan, or lead boys' clubs. Capra's romantic couple not only formed the basis of a future family but also stood up to autocratic demigods for the sake of a childlike people. Thus, Capra's Italian social ethics began by celebrating the familial individual and led to an increasingly inclusive idea for community.

Capra's critics often deride his political themes as sentimental fluff and as out of touch with the times. Nick Browne believes that the demise of Capra's comedies was inevitable, due to increasingly irrelevant, nineteenth-century (Anglo-) American myths (1980, 11). Richard Glatzer considers Capra's political myth-making, at best, a dated response to world fascism (1975, 148). But none of the critics has examined the social comedies, especially the later darker comedies, from Capra's own Italian-American perspective.

In 1936, Capra finally found the narrative schema of the (Italian Marian) man who suffers for others and converts the streetwise young woman of the (newspaper) Word. If the Protestant Fallon was too cynical and the WASP-ish Anne Schuyler too snobbish for Capra's commoner hero, then a savvy, articulate working woman was just what the fellow needed. This couple became the basis for Capra's later family-like groups, as he repeatedly criticized the WASP business establishment.

Mr. Deeds Goes to Town (1936) has divided critics over the years into two camps: those who dislike the cheery sentimental values of its political message, and those, more recently, who read it as Capra's dark vision of America. Victor Scherle and William Levy have straddled the two positions, describing the film as "goodness and simplicity manhandled in a deeply selfish and brutal world" (1977, 139). Italian America's religious values and images clarify Capra's double-sided vision: his strong, sometimes fatalistic satire of WASP society alongside positive social action. Especially important to this Italian view are the traditional figures already pictured in the icon of *The Miracle Woman*—the Blessed Mother and the infant Jesus.

Mr. Deeds Goes to Town is Capra's story of a young man from the country (Gary Cooper) who suddenly inherits a fortune from a distant uncle. After Deeds moves into the uncle's New York mansion, he faces a list of new responsibilities, from chairing the elitist opera board to talking with greedy relatives. Babe Bennett, a sharp newspaperwoman played by a bright-eyed Jean Arthur, arranges an accidental meeting with Deeds in order to start a column on the "Cinderella Man." Later, against her better judgment, she falls in love with him and needs his commonsense idealism. After Deeds stakes unemployed farmers to new land, his lawyer has him declared insane. Worst of all, Deeds learns that Bennett has been responsible for the newspaper ridicule. Falling into a depression, he refuses to defend himself at a public hearing about his mental state. But when Bennett confesses her mistake and her love, he rouses himself and outsmarts his opponents.

Capra's typing of main characters in *Mr. Deeds Goes to Town* neatly contrasts civil and Italian values in America. The story was split between a family man of swift social action, hence the name Deeds, and a slick reporter who personifies a civil faith in the cynical Word. Although Deeds at first seems to be an all-American folk type, his character gradually adds up to much more. He possesses in fact all the virtues of the Italian icon of Madonna and Christ Child: the patience, long-suffering forgiveness, and compassion of the Mother, combined with the Child's innocence and sense of easy celebration; Deeds celebrates life (in his new mansion), shows compassion (for the unemployed), and is quick to forgive (a desperate man who threatens to shoot him). In a final ironic statement of ethnicity, Deeds joins Babe Bennett in the courtroom, where she assumes an infant's or babe's (ethnic) innocence in relation to this Marian man.

Deeds himself looks especially innocent earlier when he plays his tuba and shows his country ways. More important, his tuba lets him work over critical matters of conscience; as in Italian Marian tradition, innocence and wisdom go hand in hand. Although he lacks experience in the sophisticated ways of opera boards and literary luncheons, his family attitude towards servants and farmers gives him the strength to take confident action: He punches a sarcastic author, and he dismisses a haughty opera board for ignoring the common people.

Bennett's life story is almost that of an immigrant: the young woman raised in rural America who moves to New York City. It is not Deeds but she who has the divided personality referred to later by the courtroom psychologist. On the one hand, she is a streetwise, shallow woman, just like the smart-looking, two-dimensional woman's figure sketched by her roommate. On the other hand, she has been raised in a small town by a newspaperman dedicated to social action.

Deeds is able to rescue Bennett because, unlike her, he is not absorbed in big-city life. His problem is how best to dispose of his sudden windfall in a startlingly new urban setting. (Capra himself faced a similar situation in the early 1930s, after his initial string of hits.) Deeds's task of transplanting his basically Italian idea of an open, sharing family is especially difficult, given tabloid cynics and crooked lawyers.

Yet, Deeds only loses his optimism and sense of reality when the "family," the people and Bennett, appear to turn against him. What he does not realize in his depression is that he has virtually won both Bennett's heart and the fight against greed. When this WASP woman finally confesses her love in court, as in earlier 1920s Irish-American romances with confessions, she clears the way both for marriage and greater social harmony: Capra's last shots show Deeds and Bennett in the crowd's familial embrace.

Capra further dramatized his belief in the family as respect for the individual in the memorable "echo scene." In the huge marble foyer, Deeds commands his servants to experiment with their voices, hoping to change their obsequious manners. After each fellow has made a successful attempt, they join together in one harmonious chord, a playful boyish exercise that introduces innocence and communal celebration to the cold surfaces of Anglo-American wealth. Capra later said about the film, an "honest man" will "reach deep down into his *God-given resources* and come up with the necessary handfuls of courage, wit, and love to triumph over his environment" (1971, 186 [italics mine]).

But there was also a dark side to Capra's vision of America. The common people can turn into an uncontrollable mob. The first sign of this for Deeds was the angry farmers who stormed his mansion, and the second, the final courtroom scene where Deeds is barely able to close the courtroom doors on a jostling crowd of well-wishers, after earlier ordering them to rise and sit. Thus, a shrewd Capra transformed America's fear of ethnic mobs into a general national problem. Later films like *Meet John Doe* linked the common mob to the fascist underside of political organizations run by rich industrialists.

Lost Horizon (1937) and *You Can't Take It with You* (1938) explored popular literary works that stress the responsibilities of strong father figures who keep a low profile, like Capra's own father. James Hilton's novel, *Lost Horizon*, let Capra film a family-like utopia called Shangri-La. Despite the film's pie-in-the-sky unreality, the familial subplot is effective—especially the conflict between two brothers. Robert Conway, the British Foreign Secretary, barely escapes from war-torn China with his brother George and a handful of Americans. But the group soon discovers that they have been kidnapped to the mountain paradise of Shangri-La, where for more than a century Father Perrault, a Belgian missionary, has ruled in peace as High Lama. Here Capra matches Hilton's idea of utopia with his own belief in a family-like community: the paternal/clerical Father Perrault (the priest addresses Conway eight times as "my son") and the two Conway brothers, one an idealized hero and the other a self-centered coward.

Critics have claimed that Capra's visionary tableau was "all solution and no problem." True, Çapra does glamorize the Valley of the Blue Moon, where the best of humanity's culture is preserved in a tranquil agricultural society. But the critics choose to ignore that Capra, after the film's poorly received preview showing, destroyed the film's opening two reels, thus deleting the film's (Italian) fatalism. In those crucial missing reels, wild Chinese crowds attempt to tear Conway's plane to pieces, a violent image of mob rule that recalls similar scenes in later Capra films such as *Meet John Doe*. It was against this backdrop of extreme (ethnic) anarchy that Capra adapted Hilton's story to his own Italian family vision.

The remainder of the film couches Shangri-La in the clichés of American civil religion: Perrault's golden rule is to "be kind" and show "brotherly love" towards all so that, after the greedy and wicked have destroyed themselves, "the meek will inherit the earth." As even the film's printed introduction points out, Capra's abstracted story is part utopia and part dream.

But a key familial thread remains in the relationship between the two brothers. Robert Conway (Ronald Colman) temporarily sacrifices his belief in a Far East utopia and his personal interests for the sake of his demanding and dependent younger brother; Robert's fatherly concern for his brother is so strong that he is willing to sacrifice social concepts for blood ties, even in evident folly. Self-sacrifice for a self-destructive male relative would reappear four decades later in Italian-American films like *Mean Streets* and *The Pope of Greenwich Village*. For Capra, the family relationship is the core of the older's brother's character, giving him the strength to later return. Had Robert not left Shangri-La for his brother's sake, he probably would not have been the right father figure for a Tibetan haven.

Lost Horizon also had specifically religious resonances for Capra. Shangri-La resembles the Catholic Church of the 1940s in its isolation from the modern world, its admirable social planning, and its male hierarchical structure (from servant Chang to the High Lama). More generally, visual symbols like the exotic buildings, Perrault's funeral rite, and tolling bells create an overall impression of a non-WASP religious culture. The exotic locale, like John Ford's faraway lands, allowed Capra to experiment with his social, religious beliefs.

The Pulitzer Prize-winning play *You Can't Take It With You* let Capra portray Italian-American values in two New York families, one led by an (Italian) grandfather open to change and the other by an autocratic wealthy WASP banker (a stockbroker in the play). To Capra, the original Broadway play by George S. Kaufman and Moss Hart, had a distinctly religious angle. "What the world's churches were preaching to apathetic congregations," he later wrote, "my universal language of film might say more entertainingly to movie audiences—*if* it could prove, in theatrical conflict, that Christ's spiritual law [Love thy neighbor] can be the most powerful sustaining force in anyone's life" (1971, 241). Capra dramatized this communal law in a family led by an emotionally strong, gentle-mannered grandfather. Grandpa Vanderhof (Lionel Barrymore) lets each family member grow as he or she thinks best—as a novelist, a dancer, a xylophone player, or even a fireworks-maker. The warm, fatherly fellow even opens up the family to include strangers, provided they get along with the others and work to define their talents. When he meets Mr. Poppins, a frustrated bank employee, he invites the timid man (Donald Meek) to come home with him and pursue his lifelong dream.

Grandpa Vanderhof is above all the ideal Italian mediator for community. With dispatch, he deals with Kirby's heartless plan to buy up the neighborhood; he smooths out the romance between his granddaughter Alice (Jean Arthur) and Kirby's son (James Stewart); and he fixes Kirby's estrangement from his son. Unlike the figure in the play, Capra's Kirby is a ruthless financier with munitions factories, which further highlights the film's underlying ethnic/WASP conflict. Vanderhof, on the other hand, approaches problems in a direct, familial way: He is able to strike up a harmonica duet and a friendship with the brusque Kirby by treating him like a brother. The music, like the soothing sounds of Longfellow Deeds's tuba, serves an Italian communal end; it clears Kirby's mind and refocuses his values on family life. After the fraternal duet, Kirby finally learns to put paternal affection before business. In the closing supper scene, the Kirbys and the Vanderhofs sup together as one family. At the head of the table sits the kindly grandfather, whose low-key mediation has struck a warm note of common fatherhood between himself and a stubbornly autocratic Anglo-American.

Capra was encouraged by the popular success of the fatherly Vanderhof. In *Mr. Smith Goes to Washington* (1939) he felt ready to explore the dark side of his Italian heritage. He sketched in a greedy WASP father to play the "heavy" opposite yet another blonde street-wise woman; this was *Mr. Deeds Goes to Town* with a cynical patriarch. The ensuing political struggle between an idealistic rural young senator and a fascist political boss had strong religious implications for Capra. Senator Smith was "Daniel in the lion's den," a man "crucified" by a political machine. This religious undercurrent surfaces in the present when Catholic boys in the Senate gallery applaud their hero.

Capra packed the film with father-son relationships. In an early scene at a family dinner table, the proper balance of wisdom between America's fathers and sons seems to be reversed. School-age boys badger their father, Governor Cooper (Guy Kibbee), since they know more than he about political reality. At the national level, by contrast, boss Jim Taylor runs his political machine with a velvet-gloved fist. As for the boyish Smith, he tries to redress the balance by blocking Taylor in the Senate and by reminding senators that, like their pages, they too once were boys.

The film's most complex father-son dynamic is Smith's own character. As the leader of the Boy Rangers, he seems the ideal father, though in Washington his political naiveté makes him appear a callow youth. But when Paine shows a fatherly regard for Smith, who recalls in him his own dead father, Smith becomes the good son ready to step into his father's shoes.

Paine, played by a smart, tense Claude Rains, is torn apart by his fatherly feelings. He finally draws the line when he must surrender substantial power in order to help Smith with his national boys' camp. Capra visualized Paine's conclusive rejection of fatherhood in the final mise-en-scène. First, Paine and Smith chat in the senator's home, with a small sculpture of a black infant behind the former's head, a symbol of Paine's negative attitude toward his new political son. Second, Paine explains his sellout to Boss Jim Taylor with a large photograph of Taylor directly behind his head; Taylor is the all-controlling political patriarch. From these two perspectives, Paine tells Smith to stop "living in a boys' world," and later he cannot reconcile his feelings of fatherly compassion with his hard-hearted need for power: After witnessing Smith's carefully arranged political crucifixion in the Senate, he falls apart. He has served in Washington so long and become so distant from his family-like constituency that he has lost his critical conscience for family and community.

While Taylor's fascistic Anglo-American patriarchy has consumed Paine, there remains one Anglo capable of crossing over to Smith's familial vision. The big city has not jaded Clarissa Saunders so much that Smith does not touch her basic maternal, small-town instincts. He triggers in her the Italian Marian relation of a mother to an innocent baby. First, he draws her into a familial context with (Italian) personalism: Sitting casually on her desk, he sidetracks her analysis of his political options by repeatedly asking for her first name. Soon enough, she discovers herself taking a strong maternal interest in this innocent young man headed for his political Calvary. After he leaves for his first day in the Senate, she even says she feels like a mother sending her son off to school. As part of her ethnic association, she shows no erotic relation to Smith in the climactic Senate scene and is closer, in fact, to the Italian role of a Mater Dolorosa or suffering mother. Later, she suffers with him at his crucifixion; she endures compassionate suffering and becomes a truly Marian mother.

Instinctively, Saunders realizes that compassion is the real issue in the power struggle between the Anglo-American establishment and Smith's familial vision. Soon after her first meeting with Smith, she excoriates him, "So you want to be a senator? Go ahead. Try and mess up Mr. Taylor's little graft. But if you can't—and you can't in nine million years—go home! Don't stay around here making people feel sorry for you." Because Saunders realizes the heavy price of compassion, she struggles here against her better instinct. By the time she rallies the boys back home to support Smith with letters and honest newspaper coverage, she has opted for Capra's Italian-American ideal of the open family.

Jefferson Smith has an emigré's assimilative name and eager patriotic inquisitiveness. Similarly, he ignores the written instructions of his Anglo-American hosts in favor of national monuments. And his filibuster is not important so much for what he says as for what he does—his decision to follow his ideals to the point of physical exhaustion. As a fatherly (Italian) mediator, he has the support of a Marian mother and of the children in his home state. So, he chooses to take up his cross like a suffering innocent son.

Given the Anglo-American civil religion of the constitutional Word, as dramatized by Senator Paine, it is no surprise that instead of the country (ethnic) boy adapting to the big city, the city folk learn from him. In the film's last moments, Capra carefully matches Italian and Anglo-American traditions. The closing shot neatly juxtaposes Smith's triumphant Italian fatherhood with the Anglo-American tradition of the wise rural father: The Vice President, played by an easygoing "Yankee" (Harry Carey), leans back in his chair and rocks just like a country sage on his front porch (Capra 1971, 263). Anglo-American tradition and government have been restored by the Italian values of Capra's all-American hero.

By 1941, the country's mood had blackened with reports of fascism in Germany, Japan, and Italy. Capra realized that America had begun to lose faith in its national myths; fascism was a threat to the country's civil religion as well as to its political power. Capra, fed up with articles criticizing his ideas as wild-eyed idealism, decided to film a political tragedy that would shock Americans into recognizing the fascist threat at home. He did not realize, however, that tragedy is not easily compatible with Italian ideals. In a telling piece of characterization, the heroine changes from sunny Jean Arthur to the mercurial Barbara Stanwyck.

Meet John Doe (1941) at first seems typical of an Anglo-American film culture that isolates central figures and often cites the newspaper Word. Here Ann Mitchell (Barbara Stanwyck) invents the tale of John Doe to keep her job as a columnist. Supposedly, the disillusioned fellow will jump from the roof of City Hall on Christmas Eve to protest the dismal state of humanity. Mitchell backs up her desperate fiction by finding a hobo to impersonate Doe: a down-and-out baseball player named Long John Willoughby (Gary Cooper). For Willoughby's speaking engagements, she writes public speeches based on her father's diary, and then to her surprise falls in love with him. Meanwhile, her fiction becomes a national myth controlled by D. B. Norton, a newspaper owner and industrial tycoon who regards the grass-roots movement as his chance to become president of the United States.

The film's biggest problem, Capra realized, was Willoughby's shift from a homeless drifter to a noble man of self-sacrifice. Initially, Capra had intended a tragic story about unfettered political ambition. In pre-production the project was titled The Life and Death of John Doe and was to end with Doe's suicide. Like Citizen Kane, the classic American tragedy released the same year, Capra's film was to show political power in the hands of a ruthless newspaper owner. In both stories the populist hero is eventually exposed as a sham and forced to retreat into political obscurity. As satires of an Anglo Protestant culture based on the printed word, both films focus on an ambiguous spoken name—"John Doe" and "Rosebud." At the last moment, Capra pulled back from dark satire, leaving his work in a political limbo between fascism and national renewal.

Capra first tried to end Doe with Willoughby's suicide leap. But preview audiences rejected tragedy, along with five other endings. As he did later in Arsenic and Old Lace (1944), Capra changed events and lightened the mood. (When filmgoers at a preview screening of Arsenic saw Edward Everett Horton die, they threw objects at the screen.) Thus, preview audiences redirected Capra's innate Italian fatalism towards a cheerful populism. Similarly, after a showing of Meet John Doe, Capra said, a moviegoer wrote him a letter recommending that Mitchell, Norton, and his small-town friends persuade Willoughby not to jump. This was the ending Capra finally chose: The diehards of the Doe movement walk away with Willoughby, promising to reestablish the movement on Christmas eve. Evidently, it took an unknown moviegoer to point out to Capra that he should return to his own Italian tradition with a proper Christmas ending, in which both Willoughby and the Doe movement are reborn. The Christmas story, after all, is the archetypal Catholic narrative.*

Still, the film's social satire reveals little sense of Italian identity. From the start, Willoughby's decision to impersonate Doe undermines any possible Italian values. Although scenes of small-town community and mediation at first fuel the Doe movement, Willoughby's fakery leaves him powerless against the ruthless Norton. Likewise, even the climactic national rally has a hollow ring, for without a secure father figure there can be no lasting sense of family.

The divided character of Doe/Willoughby epitomizes as well the ambivalence of Capra's crowds: Sometimes they behave like a caring Italian family, and sometimes like a destructive mob. As a concerned father figure, Willoughby wonders what the boys of America will think of a baseball player who agrees to fool the public. Mitchell quickly recognizes this potential paternity, and just as quickly associates Doe with memories of her own father. But Willoughby is also a man without a family who lacks the hope necessary for a father's strong critical conscience. And so he returns to his hobo life. Even when his friends surround him in the film's last scene, he seems barely convinced of a larger, familial community. The bad father in *Mr. Smith Goes to Washington* was not crippling for the young hero because, like an Italian with an established church, he could turn to the (paternal) institution of the U.S. Senate.

With neither a political base nor a supportive Italian family, Willoughby is no match for D. B. Norton. Once in power, the big boss says he will show America "an iron hand." Capra needed a break before he would be ready to direct his most uplifting and America's most famous (ethnic) Christmas story.

The Follow-Through: An All-American Ethnic Story

After the war, Capra returned as quickly as possible to filmmaking. If in 1941 he had been consumed by a serious Anglo-American tragedy, he returned to Hollywood with a light spirit and renewed energy,

---

*Unlike the varying biblical passages chosen for many Protestant services, the annual schedule of readings for Catholic liturgy builds towards Christmas as the chief event of Catholic culture.

ready to assert his ethnic roots in America's most famous Christmas movie. *It's A Wonderful Life* (1946) pitted postwar materialism against Italian social ethics. It also summed up ethnic assimilation in American film, acknowledging both Irish and Italian stereotypes and then pushing past them to the fundamental socioreligious values of each ethnic culture.

Critics such as Robin Wood have critiqued the film in sweepingly broad terms as "fed by the fears and aspirations" of America (Maland 1980, 152). But for Capra, the project was both personal and pointedly cultural. It was, he said, "my kind of film for my kind of people" (1971, 383). For many years at Christmas, he screened the print for friends (Scherle, 230). More important, the key dates in George Bailey's life exactly parallel periods in Capra's own (Maland 1980, 151).

The development of the film script is a tangled history that began when a friend sent Capra a short story, by Philip Van Doren Stern, on a Christmas card. Many months and contributors later, the script was a "Goodrich-Hackett-Capra version," supplemented with scenes by Clifford Odets and advice from Jo Swerling (Maland 1980, 135). In Capra's autobiography, he said in the end he had to rewrite the entire script because none of the amended versions suited his gut feelings (1971, 377).

Capra's story line clearly distinguishes between several ethnic identities and mainstream Anglo society. He first set up clichés about three ethnic groups in order later to develop Italian familial values. He linked the stereotype of the greedy Anglo-American banker with newspapers, when Potter discovers the Building and Loan's available cash in a misplaced newspaper. Thus, the culture of the Anglo printed word cares once again only about money.

Next, Irish and Italian stereotypes introduce the general topic of ethnic identity. The Martini family, says the banker Potter, is a bunch of "garlic-eaters," even after they acquire their own home in Bailey Park. Clarence, George's second-class angel, personifies Irish superstition about angels as well as the Irish habit of tipping the bottle. (Capra again linked the Irish with drink when Uncle Billy has one too many and sings "My Wild Irish Rose.")

George, initially an all-American small-town boy, acquires a distinctly ethnic color by the company he keeps—Clarence, the Martinis, and Uncle Billy. Capra also tied George's cultural identity in small ways to immigrant life. George's hearing problem, for example, separates him symbolically from a WASP culture based on the Word.

Likewise, he excels not in the newspaper business but at the Building and Loan, here a model of Catholic subsidiarity and of the extended familial community. George's chief problem is that he does not appreciate the (ethnic) worth of his hard work. But by the time he runs through Bedford Falls and past a movie marquee advertising *The Bells of St. Mary's* (1945), one of the most popular Catholic movies of the 1940s, he has learned to fully appreciate Italian familial identity—in social ethics, in sacrificial mediation, and in the film's final communal celebration.

At first, George grapples with the dilemma of how to work for the community's good, while also finding time for his own family. The dilemma is especially difficult in a town rooted in Anglo-American individualism and the success ethic; Italian-style subsidiarity is hard to practice in a society built on autocratic management and individual success. In George's case, he must face this problem prematurely. Whereas Jefferson Smith and John Willoughby freely choose to enter big-city affairs, George has his father's duties foisted on him, just when he planned to travel the world and go to college.

George's situation is symbolic in general of America just after the war years, when a national sense of being overwhelmed by sudden new responsibilities helped unify Anglo Americans and immigrants already familiar with that experience. Even though good-hearted George willingly sacrifices his plans for the sake of his father's institution, he still resents his choice. In his proposal scene to Mary, he angrily blurts out that marriage will tie him forever to his hometown. "I want to do what I want to do," he says in protest. To underscore this moment of critical conscience, Capra made it the film's longest take. The narrative pace thereafter also conveyed George's sense of having grown up too fast: The shot shifts abruptly to his wedding and then just as quickly to his wife's pregnancy.

George has not yet thought through his own noble acts of familial self-sacrifice. So, when Potter suggests the young man would be worth more dead than alive, George feels overwhelmed and isolated and cuts himself off from his family, just when he needs them most. He also badly needs a critical conscience. The angel Clarence is a conscience personified, that is, the one who helps George turn away from magical ideas of the success ethic and religion. Critics such as Nick Browne have quickly dismissed Clarence as a symptom of Capra's weakening ability to shape American myths (1980, 11). But Browne overlooks not just the film's longstanding national popularity but also Clarence's psychospiritual role. As soon as Clarence appears, he literally describes himself as a conscience, as someone "who knows everything about [George]" and never gets discouraged. He seems, for instance, already to understand that George has not worked out the conflict between his boyhood desire to have "a million dollars," as he says, and his commitment to poor families. In the end, Clarence fosters a social, moral viewpoint to rebut Potter's greed.

George begins his (Italian) journey accompanied by Clarence, who adds a cleverly ironic twist on the confessional conscience: George is the (Italian) community man who gets to see what his town would have become without him. First, George must learn that the Virgin Mary has nothing to do with magical help on request. Entering Martini's bar, he mutters a prayer to the "Mother of God" and immediately gets slugged.* This is Capra's sly way of saying that a sudden miracle would only short circuit the value of community self-sacrifice. Once George fully appreciates the difference his past sacrifices have made for Bedford Falls, he is ready to receive the more mundane but real miracle of friends' help.

George's tour of his exploited home town also helps him re-assimilate into Capra's (Italian) town. At home again with his wife and children, George greets the townspeople as if they were one caring family. He finally realizes, he says, that "each man touches so many lives, and leaves a hole"—a visual metaphor of absence that symbolizes the effect of Italian suffering in community. To bolster George's assimilation into a town that is both ethnic and mainstream, Capra linked the American classic, *The Adventures of Tom Sawyer*, to Clarence and a Christmas tree. A bell's chime on the tree, moreover, signifies that an angel has finally earned its wings, that George has at last internalized the critical conscience and communal vision of his fatherly angel. He has learned to see himself in Italian terms, that is, analogous familial relationships instead of competitive, individualis-tic differences.

Capra's last shot stresses the vitality of his ethnic vision for America in general. He turns from religious allusions such as the angel Clarence (the bell) and a Christmas story (the carols) to the sights and sounds of American civil religion: the Liberty Bell and "Auld Lang Syne." The shift to an inclusive, civil religion further sup-

---

*Although the immediate dramatic reason for the belt in the mouth is the angry husband of a schoolteacher whom George earlier insulted on the phone, Capra's shot sequence clearly establishes a cause-and-effect relation between George's prayer and the slug.

ports Capra's idea of an open, familial society. Thus, Italian culture and American popular culture can serve the same social end.

It's A Wonderful Life was the apex of Capra's career as far as encouraging the country to assimilate his ethnic background. Its timely success depended on Capra's guarded recognition of Irish and Italian stereotypes, on his shrewd use of social values in a Christmas story, and on brilliant acting all around. Within two years, Capra lost control of production at Liberty Films in a co-venture with William Wyler and Robert Riskin. Capra blamed himself for a failure of nerve and never fully recovered the artistic control essential, he said, for good filmmaking.

Still, Capra continued to assert his Italian-American identity on screen. In 1948, Spencer Tracy asked to work with Capra on the Pulitzer Prize–winning play State of the Union. Adapted by Anthony Veiller and Myles Connolly, the film includes a stereotypical, working-class Italian and a reformed idealist politician, but lacks a firm sense of community as Italian family. Grant Matthews (Tracy) is a wealthy airplane manufacturer who decides to run for president. His powerful friend, newspaper publisher Kay Thorndyke (Angela Lansbury), fans his ambitions and tries to take the place of his estranged wife (Katharine Hepburn). Shrewd and manipulative, Thorndyke is a female version of Capra's usual capitalist/newspaper figure.

As a sequel to Meet John Doe, this Tracy-Hepburn vehicle allowed Capra to again address the problem of national powerbrokers. He used a mainstream play to portray WASP authority and self-criticism, and then he developed Grant's character to imply ethnic values. To start with, his script severely criticizes Anglo-American patriarchy for corrupting women with the success ethic. At the same time, Capra tried to resolve the problematic ending of Meet John Doe by aligning a wealthy industrialist with little people like an immigrant Italian barber and a television grip.

The opening reveals the terrible effects here of WASP patriarchy on women. Just before Kay Thorndyke's father dies, he hands over his print empire to his daughter. She has, he says, "a woman's body with a man's brains," an image she evidently relishes. Taking the place of the son her father never had, she gladly conforms to his autocratic patriarchy.

So, Capra interjected an Italian immigrant's values. Mrs. Matthews agrees to accompany her husband on a national speaking tour to give the public the impression of a happily married couple. But to their mutual surprise, they fall in love again and she encourages him to speak up for the little man, rather than use the double-talk prepared by Thorndyke's friends. At this crucial juncture, Capra inserted an Italian hotel barber and added the names Garibaldi and St. Francis of Assisi to a list of the world's great men associated with the White House.

The Italian barber's small part brings both comic relief and, indirectly, a woman's point of view to the couple's discussion of love and politics. The scene begins with Grant ordering a barber to his hotel suite, only to begin a serious marital discussion. Worse, political aides enter and leave the room, completely ignoring Grant's attempts to talk with his wife, while his barber stands patiently nearby. At one point, the barber even reminds Grant where he left off in his pillow talk. Finally, left alone with the candidate, the barber explains in broken English his own wife's idea of politics: The White House needs not another fighting rooster but a hen. He then proposes Mrs. Matthews, who in fact is the Capra character with the most presidential qualities.

Capra's closing scene pulls together the Italian Marian virtues of patience, compassion, and a willingness to confess. After Mary Matthews learns that Thorndyke influenced a pivotal earlier speech, she gets drunk before an important political broadcast. But she rallies at the last moment and reads prepared lines before the television cameras. Seeing his wife's sacrifice of pride, Grant turns to the cameras and confesses his gradual loss of integrity to a national audience. His wife, in effect, has awakened his social conscience.

Capra also used the scene to suggest the importance of subsidiarity in grass-roots politics. As Grant waits to deliver his televised speech, he stands beside two television grips, one of whom stares at him. Because Grant's conscience bothers him about the lack of candor in his speech, he cannot look either grip in the eye; he is ready once again to betray the little man. But instead he confesses his self-deluded ambition to a country of ordinary citizens like the immigrant barber.

Yet, Tracy's change of heart is not convincing by half because of his status as an Irish-American star. If Long John Willoughby was penniless and shy about confessing to thousands, Tracy's Matthews has a boldness rooted in financial security; he is, after all, paying for the broadcast. By the 1950s, this image of security was paramount for a country in a postwar economy, just as it had once been for a newly arrived immigrant family named Capra. The Capras, however, held onto their core ethnic values. After the war, the country was determined to get ahead and so lost interest in both subsidiarity and Italian Marian traits like patience, suffering, and self-sacrifice.

Once Capra relinquished control of production, he lost along with it the chance to further assimilate his Italian-American background into the movie mainstream. Stars and middle management were making too many decisions for him to continue matching and expanding on the common values between his own ethnic background and Anglo America. He could only spin a saccharine father/son story in *A Hole in the Head* (1959) and a thoroughly sentimental mother/daughter tale in *Pocketful of Miracles* (1961). In the end, his Italian vision of society as an extended supportive family could not, he said, compete with the trend toward "bitter realism" (1971, 460).

David Manners, as gentle John Carson in The Mira-
cle Woman *(1931), is linked visually to Capra's Italian
Marian heritage. (Museum of Modern Art/Film Stills
Archive; courtesy of Columbia Pictures)*

Jean Arthur, as Anglo Babe Bennett in Mr. Deeds
Goes to Town *(1936), debates whether to remain a*
two-dimensional urban woman like the sketch in the back-
ground. (Museum of Modern Art/Film Stills Archive;
courtesy of Columbia Pictures)

An (Italian) familial society literally run by little people in Mr. Smith Goes to Washington *(1939). (Museum of Modern Art/Film Stills Archive; courtesy of Columbia Pictures)*

Jefferson Smith (James Stewart) at his political crucifixion in Mr. Smith Goes to Washington *(1939). (Museum of Modern Art/Film Stills Archive; courtesy of Columbia Pictures)*

Gary Cooper, in Meet John Doe *(1941), poses grudgingly in a travesty of family and "little people." (Museum of Modern Art/Film Stills Archive; courtesy of Warner Bros.)*

George Bailey (James Stewart) in It's A Wonderful Life
*(1946) hopes to improve his organization's finances in
Capra's familial model for American success. (Museum
of Modern Art/Film Stills Archive; courtesy of Liberty
Films/RKO)*

George Bailey's angel of conscience in It's A Wonderful Life *(1946) gently shakes him out of his depression
and isolation by reminding him of his (Italian) sense of
familial community. (Museum of Modern Art/Film Stills
Archive; courtesy of Liberty Films/RKO)*

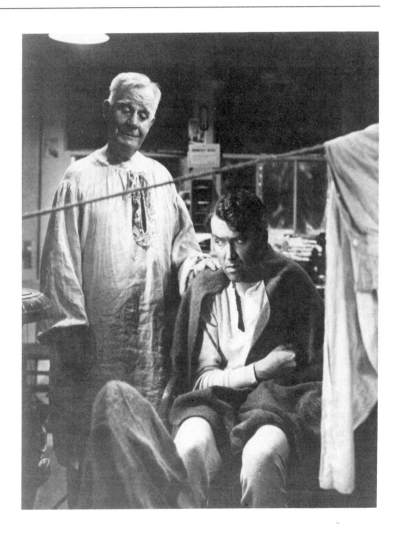

The Godfather *(1972) contrasts two, very different gen-erations of Italian-American patriarchy (Al Pacino and Marlon Brando). (Museum of Modern Art/Film Stills Archive; courtesy of Paramount Pictures)*

CHAPTER 5

FRANCIS COPPOLA

As a child, Francis Coppola often changed schools to keep pace with his father's musical career. Growing up in various suburbs, he experienced ethnicity not as a way of life on the streets but as a way of relating within a middle-class family. Coppola the filmmaker constantly mirrors both this close-up familial vision of the self and anger towards the symbolic absent father. Although this conflicted familial vision might seem to negate the social values of John Ford and Frank Capra, Coppola does assert similar themes of family and home, law and decency and democracy in seemingly self-contradictory narratives: In *The Godfather, Part II* there is not the family so much as the familial individual; in *Apocalypse Now*, not established law, so much as the right to define the law; and in *Rain People*, not decency so much as fundamental social responsibility. In short, Coppola reaffirms his inherited ethnicity in the very act of rejecting it.

This personal paradox, not uncommon in third-generation Italian Americans, helps account for the complex and thoroughly psychological dynamic of Coppola's films. There Coppola seldom asserts overtly ethnic values because they are intimately tied to anger about his own family history, in particular with regard to his father. Because Coppola shares a sense of anger with Ford, his ensembles resemble not only Capra's familial gatherings but also Ford's small conflicted groups. Yet, as a critical third-generation ethnic, Coppola is much quicker than Ford to find fault with his ethnic past, his religious heritage, and Anglo America.

Ethnicity, to a third-generation American, means not so much consciously choosing between one's heritage and mainstream culture as living with the contradictions entailed in double identity. For Coppola, to be Italian/American means to be both an Italian familial individual and a WASP individualist. It means to believe in success both

and Ethnic Double Vision

as immigrant survival and as a mainstream status already achieved by assimilated parents.

Not surprisingly, then, Coppola's images of both ethnicity and America are deeply ambivalent. While the immigrant Capra championed Italian virtues for a greedy, profit-driven America, Coppola seems equally attracted to both Italian and Anglo cultures; the hyphen that separates the ethnic and mainstream parts of immigrant identity is for Coppola an ambiguous slash—Italian/American. In this divided spirit, Coppola blurs distinctions between ethnic and mainstream cultures, often employing one as a metaphor for the other. If he has frequently succeeded in his parallel satires and double cultural metaphors, that is largely because he has skillfully matched the underlying success ethic in both cultures. At the same time, he holds on tightly to core Italian values that, like old glue, somehow still hold together his third-generation sense of ethnicity.

The need to live with internal (ethnic) contradictions is readily apparent in Coppola's protagonists: in *Rain People*, the mother who deserts a child-like disabled man; in *The Godfather*, the gangster as respectable citizen; in *The Godfather, Part II*, the good citizen as gangster; in *One from the Heart*, the true lovers who cannot live together; and in *Tucker: The Man and His Dream*, the automobile manufacturer who cannot manage finances. At the core of these contradictory filmic lives is Coppola's own desire to be at peace with a childhood issue: the success-oriented father who was emotionally absent from the Italian family.

The double-sided, sometimes hypocritical character of a small Italian/American family strongly shapes Coppola's canon. The films comprise three life stages, as Coppola's narrator matures from angry boyhood to acceptance and attempted replacement of the absent father. Spurring Coppola on from one all-consuming project to the next has been his Italian/American belief in the sacrament of technology. First, there are figures of troubled teenage boys or a frustrated Italian young woman, each trying to escape an oppressive patriarchy. (Partly because of Coppola's Italian Marian background, ethnic identity issues surface in female and male protagonists alike.) Second, there are figures of adult men who initially face society on their own and later confront an internalized image of the destructive father. And third, there are either figures of self-assured older brothers, often acting as substitute fathers, or figures in flight from an openly violent patriarchy. As for conventionally ethnic issues, Coppola featured first Irish and then Italian stereotypes, followed by a long filmic struggle with the self-destructive Italian/American father.

Growing Up with the Success Ethic

Coppola did not grow up in a poor immigrant family like Frank Capra. Nor did he spend his teenage years on the streets of Little Italy like Martin Scorsese. Coppola's father, a successful symphony flutist, moved the family frequently and enrolled Francis, the younger of his two sons, in more than twenty-four schools (Coppola 1983, 67). Despite the constant change, Francis was able to attend family weddings and baptisms, mostly in the Italian-American tradition. As a result, the ethnic values of the adult Coppola are far less self-conscious than those of Martin Scorsese because they are so deeply embedded in a particular family dynamics.

The Coppola children—August, Francis, and Talia—enjoyed a home life that was both artistic and troubled. Their father had always wanted recognition as a composer, but his big break never came. His disappointment had an immediate effect at home. Years later, Coppola recalled, "My childhood was very warm, very tempestuous, full of controversy and a lot of passion and shouting. My father, who is an enormously talented man, was the focus of all our lives. . . . Our lives centered on what we all felt was the tragedy of his career" (1975, 185). Every night as a child Coppola prayed, "Let Daddy get his break" (1983a, 67). Although all three children later enjoyed successful careers in the arts, the constant early worry about his father's success undercut Coppola's sense of the Italian-American father as someone closely atuned to a child's interests and talent.

Coppola sorely missed this sense of individual worth, the basis of

Italian family and community. If during adolescence he was unaware of this lack, his actions at the time betrayed his true feelings.

> I worked for Western Union one summer when I was 14 and, for some unknown reason—I still don't know *why*—I wrote a phony telegram to my father telling him he'd landed a job writing the musical score for such and such a film. I signed it with the name of the guy who was in charge of music at Paramount Pictures. My father was overjoyed and yelled, "It's my break!" And I had to tell him it wasn't true. He was heartbroken. Is that a terrible story? (1975, 185)

The adolescent Coppola was extremely conscious of his father's total focus on his own career. Coppola's own new job provided him with the perfect opportunity to make up for his father's so-called failure. Years later, he would hire his father for a walk-on part in "Life Without Zoe."

The young Coppola turned for attention to his older brother August, with whom he shared a room until he was eleven. But even as he idolized August, he never believed, he said years later, he could be so handsome or so athletic. In one of Coppola's childhood nightmares, he knocks frantically on neighborhood doors to phone for the police because a street gang is forcing August under a manhole (Coppola 1983a, 66). But the dream's fearful projection suggests it was the younger brother, not his popular sibling, who felt forced out of the public light. The dream's third identity, the cruel gang, images Coppola's anger about the lack of recognition he felt within his family. Thus, the frequent brother-figures in Coppola's films have an autobiographical and psychologically complex source.

During college years at Hofstra University, Coppola quickly learned to channel his anger and talents into musicals. Years later, the American musical was repeatedly to provide him with a match for the celebratory side of his Italian aesthetic; the musical became for him a special, ritualistic world of childlike innocence. As for Coppola's later tender-hearted films about social problems, such as *Rumble Fish*, they also were Italian and autobiographical: He replaces a symbolic, success-oriented father with an Italian model of brotherly compassion.

For many years, Coppola felt troubled by an Italian/American success ethic. From his family he had inherited an immigrant drive to succeed in terms of money and public recognition. After the phenomenally popular and critically acclaimed *The Godfather*, Coppola reflected,

> Ever since I was a little kid, I was raised to be successful and rich. If you were raised as I was, everything you do is to make your family proud of you. It relates to the immigrant thing. Get an education, have a reputation, have your picture in the paper in a suit, and have lots of money and security. It's hard for me to decide to do anything that doesn't have that as a possible end. (1972, 223)

Like his father, Coppola felt unsatisfied with the success he had achieved. "Yet I know that's over," he continued. "I now am as successful as I ever want to be, and I'm pretty rich, so I've got to change all my motivations. I've found that I really do not wear well being famous or successful" (1972, 223). After *The Godfather*, Coppola used his dissatisfaction with current success to constantly strive for new narrative forms. This strong personal motivation helps explain why his later films often seem to be radical departures from earlier work.

The family is a special source of ideas and creative energy for any Italian-American filmmaker. When Coppola was interviewed in Paris in 1982 about his idea of the family, he reacted defensively.

> Too much has been made of this theme. People organize as best they can. The staff of *Cahiers du Cinéma* is also a family. Those who work together, have similar interests, and play together side by side through life naturally organize themselves like a family. It is not just because I am a little Italian that I like to cook. . . . IBM is also a family. (1982, 44 [translation mine])

Coppola tries to downplay his ethnic background, while, ironically enough, asserting a thoroughly familial perspective of society. But in an earlier, more relaxed interview, he said, "I'm fascinated with the whole idea of a family. In the things I'm writing that is constant" (1972, 222).

The familial value that Coppola mentions most often is what he calls "the personal." His films have carefully developed a family-based personalism, for which Italian-American culture is well known. For instance, the intimate focus of *The Conversation* shows, Coppola said, that "right from the beginning I wanted it to be something personal, not political [like the Watergate tapes], because somehow that is even more terrible to me" (1974, 33). To Coppola, the most important values are personal and familial and they transcend politics. The personal, moreover, shows up in both large and small film projects. "What I hope to do in the future is make only personal films—but in such a way that even my big projects will be what you would call personal films" (1974, 30). Then Coppola clarified his Italian idea by citing the films of Federico Fellini: "Something like *8½* or *La Dolce Vita* where you really launch into an enormous personal vision of things" (1974, 34).

As Coppola elaborated on his idea, he showed a penchant for metaphor that is essential to Italian realism. "I believe that the emotional makeup of people is a system not unlike the circulatory system or the muscular system. And if you can make a film that not only lays bare that system but is itself constructed out of those things, it would be an incredible thing to witness and to feel" (1974, 34). This flesh-and-blood symbolism shows that the emotions (and the spiritual) are as much a part of human reality as the body. Coppola assumes a basic similarity between a filmmaker and his audience. In his visceral Italian way, he learned to develop a filmic narrator that uses metaphor to draw close to characters' deepest emotions.

Coppola was more articulate about "the personal" when he applied the term to filmmaking and the autobiographical unity of his canon. First, he wants his films to be signs of his own growth.

> I want to make movies I give a damn about. And that means the script must come from me and not from some novel or play. I just want to try and do my work. The key word is growth. It doesn't happen very often, but if you really look at a film someone wrote and directed you should get an impression of where he's at, of what he believes in, of how he feels about the world. If you see a film some director did from a novel or play, even a great director, then it's very rare to find anything *personal* in it. . . . (1969, 10 [italics mine])

The key words here are "personal" and "growth," which together suggest an overall coherence in Coppola's canon. Even though each film, as Coppola said, is "a new beginning," his works are all of a piece. "Why do we continue to think that in cinema one makes a film, then another? . . . I prefer to think that my films are the same film. You know, if you take all my films from first to last, it is all the same film" (1982a, 45 [translation mine]).

Coppola typically begins every project out of "an emotional thing" rather than a concept (1974, 30). He often adds details from his life, like references to family history or to moments in childhood. Filmgoers sense this personal touch mostly in his frequent metaphors, a family based language of analogous imagery that draws audiences into a character's viewpoint and distinctive emotional life. Critics who dislike Coppola's work for its sentimentality are often actually objecting to his Italian penchant for metaphor. But it is precisely this use of metaphor, for both characterization and narrative structure, that reveals his personal, Italian-American touch and analogical imagination at work.

Coppola's personal approach begins in the studio, where he expects his staff to see themselves as members of an open family. He insists on a family atmosphere: He once fired officeworkers who objected to his daughter and her friends trying to help out (Coppola 1983a, 61).

A Coppola script is largely an intuitive affair in which characters, not words, dominate. Typically, his first drafts are disorganized, jumbling together many subjective ideas. But his final rewrites straighten out the lines of character development. "My films are raw and shapeless and lack focus and really seem like a disaster," he has said. "Only with editing and repositioning and a real last rewrite do they start to shape up" (1974, 32).

On set, Coppola adopts a decidedly personal, familial tack with actors. Actor Martin Sheen, also raised Catholic, summed up Coppola's traits as a director by describing the Italian-American father in his friend. Coppola is "compassionate, sweet, [and] protective" with actors, Sheen observed. "Francis is so good when he deals in family, when he deals with tradition." It is just this key Italian value—a parental compassion rooted in family—that Coppola has developed over the years.

Coppola's commitment to Italian family values and figures, especially to caring older brothers, runs very much against the Anglo-American grain. He often undermines an impersonal Anglo-American patriarchy by acknowledging the so-called feminine traits in male (ethnic) behavior. In a 1975 wide-ranging interview with *Playboy*, Coppola asserted,

I'm convinced that men and women are basically very similar in many more respects than we've been brought up to believe. We've been taught so-called masculine roles, just as women have been programmed into so-called feminine ones. But the lines aren't so clearly drawn any more, partly because of the women's movement. . . . I know a great many heterosexual women who are very masculine in many ways, and many heterosexual men who are very feminine. I include myself among the latter and always have. (1975, 184–85)

Coppola first remembered empathizing with a woman's viewpoint when he learned about the Virgin Mary. During his childhood there was "a kind of feminine, magical quality, dating back to the Virgin Mary or something I picked up in Catechism classes, that fascinates me," he recalled. "I think I've always been empathetic enough to put myself in a woman's place, although they say it's impossible" (1972, 221). Having recognized the so-called feminine or Marian side of the Italian-American man, Coppola experiments with the narrator in his films in order to rethink and reform his success-oriented father-figures.

From Angry Irish Son to Italian-American Mother

Like Frank Capra, Coppola first expressed his sense of ethnicity in Irish characters. But Coppola, a filmmaker of the 1960s, was far more directly, if unintentionally autobiographical, as evidenced by youths on screen rebelling against both an Irish family's success ethic (*Dementia 13*) and a distant Anglo father (*You're a Big Boy Now*). When further Irish stereotypes proved a dead end in *Finian's Rainbow*, Coppola turned in *The Rain People* to an Italian/American young woman in order to again rebel against patriarchy and to articulate an Italian/American need for protective mothers. During this early period, when Coppola had his most hands-on experience of filmmaking, his work subtly revealed key identity themes. In summary, Coppola's early narrator shows a pervasive conflict between warm Italian Marian values and an insensitive success ethic inherited from ethnic and WASP cultures alike.

In 1963, Coppola's narrator in *Dementia 13* adopted the autobiographical and initially background role of an angry younger brother, albeit a filmic Irishman. The seminal plot idea first occurred to Coppola in a desperate attempt to get funding from producer Roger Corman. That year, Coppola was working in Europe for Corman as a scriptwriter. After the film crew had finished the work at hand, Coppola proposed a cheap film in Ireland before everyone headed home to America.

I sold the picture to Roger on the basis of one scene. The time is late at night. The place is Dublin. A woman comes out of a castle. She is carrying a bag. She stops, opens the bag, and takes out five dolls. She ties strings around the necks of the dolls, then attaches the strings to a weight. Then the woman takes off all her clothes and dives into a pond. She places the weight on the bottom of the pond, and the dolls start to float up toward the surface. The woman starts to turn in the water, and there she finds the perfectly preserved body of a seven-year-old girl with her hair floating in the current. The woman rushes to the surface and screams the words: "Axed to death!" (Johnson 1976, 31–32)

Although Coppola, in his own words, "had no idea what the woman was doing there," he quickly fleshed out the script and worked intensively on every visual detail (Johnson 1976, 32). Professionally, his work on staging, framing, and editing proved he was a young director of great promise. But more important for his later work, the story established the identity themes of two artistic brothers, an absent father, and a repressed feminine self. Coppola's Irish brainstorm was actually an Italian-American fantasy about a quietly angry younger brother who murders out of anger at the death of his "feminine" or creative self.

Ostensibly, *Dementia 13* is the story of three brothers and a mother who reunite each year for a graveside service in Ireland. Mother Haloran wants her boys (John, Richard, and Billy) never to forget their blonde sister Kathleen, who died as a youth in a mysterious drowning. Coppola's film opens with the accidental death of John, the oldest brother and an extremely successful American businessman. The plot heats up when John's wife, Louise, first hides her husband's body and then tries to make her mother-in-law dependent on her by planting several of Kathleen's nursery dolls in the pond, so that they will float to the surface. As Louise lingers on the pond's bottom, she discovers to her horror a wax replica of Kathleen and in a panic swims for the shore, where a dark figure brutally bashes her with an axe. This scene is the kernel of Coppola's story.

Further tragedy is averted by a wise country doctor who, during Richard's wedding celebration, exposes Billy as the murderer by placing a wax figure on a fountain. When the bridegroom finds the figure, Billy attacks him, and the doctor is forced to kill the psychotic young man. The doctor then explains that, as a child, Billy accidentally pushed his sister into the water and "made a wax doll, something he could protect to relieve his guilt." The family mystery at last solved, Richard, a professional sculptor, begins his creative life anew with an attractive all-American wife.

Dementia 13 is about the difference between two brothers in a deeply troubled (ethnic) family. Coppola's script dwelt on the second and third brothers, the ones most affected by the gloom that still hangs over the family after the sister's untimely death. The second brother, Richard (William Campbell), is a sculptor like his father and high strung, moody, and quick-tempered, whereas the school-aged Billy (Burt Patton) seems mild-mannered and still lives with his mother. In reality, Billy suffers from severely repressed guilt and only expresses the anger associated with that guilt, which has ruined his childhood, when his idealized wax substitution for his sister is finally uncovered. Guilt is not just Billy's problem, however, for Kathleen's death has set a dark pall over the entire family.

The opening scene accounts for Billy's lost childhood and stifled creativity, symbolized here by the female wax figure: By hiding John's body, Louise reveals a coldhearted, greedy nature that personifies the worst aspects of her husband, a heartless man devoted to American success. Furthermore, Louise sheds direct light on Kathleen's death because, like Kathleen, she has blonde hair. In summary, the death or denial of the feminine (creative) self for the sake of the family's success ethic explains why the two brothers who sculpt hold so much anger. (Richard behaves irritably throughout much of the film.)

Coppola's narrator, like Billy with his secretive murders, essentially stays hidden until the good doctor's explanation, which finally expresses Billy's anger and overwhelming guilt. With Billy's true feelings uncovered, he dies and Richard, who had been stymied in his sculpting, regains full control of his creativity. This recovery leads immediately to sex and success: Richard happily begins his marriage to an American woman already associated with success. It is thus possible for a male sculptor, or a male filmmaker, to live with the so-called feminine side of his personality and still strive for success.

The autobiographical overtones of Coppola's film about two brothers—one talented and publicly recognized, the other quiet and repressed—are unmistakable. The film ends with the narrator's desire that Richard replace Billy, one answer to the younger brother's anger. But fraternal substitution, not to mention the projection onto an Irish family, is at best an awkward solution. In Italian terms, little sense of family remains with two brothers dead. And the sudden interjection of a wise family doctor is a clumsy narrative device. But at least submerged issues of family identity have risen to the surface.

Coppola's next autobiographical project drew closer to the American scene where a teenage son judges his patriarchal father for living according to a WASP success ethic. *You're a Big Boy Now* (1967) was the first of Coppola's films about a father-son relationship and the first of many romances. In this genre he covertly developed an Italian-American aesthetic, celebrating youthful romance and culturally feminine traits in men.

You're a Big Boy Now is a love story with a cheerful tone and a predictable boy-gets-girl plot. Coppola himself wrote the script, though he later included aspects of David Benedictus' novel, after first purchasing the rights to the work. Under contract to Paramount at the time, Coppola used this ruse to retain the legal rights to his own writing. His protagonist, Bernard Chanticleer, is a thoroughly innocent, suburban nineteen-year-old who enjoys working as a page on roller skates in the New York Public Library. He only resents that his father, the library's chief administrator, oversees his every move. This successful, self-righteous father becomes so dissatisfied with his son's work and habitual tardiness that he decides the boy should live on his own in Manhattan. So, the naive Bernard eagerly moves into his first apartment and meets both Amy Partlett, an amiable co-worker, and Barbara Darling, a self-centered go-go dancer. Although Bernard quickly falls for the sexy, sadistic Barbara, he eventually learns to distinguish between sexual attraction and suitable romance.

In essence, Coppola's film is about a young man rebelling against a distant father in order to explore sex and romance. The first tracking shot joyfully depicts a young man's sexual desire, as Barbara (Elizabeth Hartman) walks the length of the library's main aisle in her short skirt. For Coppola, this camera view is (Italian-American) passion at its most innocent and lighthearted, especially when accompanied by the sweet adolescent lyrics of "Beautiful Girl." Raef, a library co-worker, plays the part of the worldly older brother who encourages the timid Bernard in romance.

Bernard must first learn to stop behaving like a dependent child. Initially, he apologizes to his parents for his poor performance at work, as if he were a scolded ten-year-old: "I'm sorry I embarrass you, Daddy and Mummy. I'm sorry I embarrass myself." But once he has his own apartment, he discovers that his almighty father (Rip Torn) has broken conventional sexual moves. (The old man makes sexual advances towards Amy [Karen Black] and keeps a secret collection of rare erotic art.) Although Bernard cannot overthrow this comical fantasy father or the Anglo-American patriarchy he represents, he can at least reject both and claim his independence. So, he steals from his father's office a prized Gutenberg Bible, a cultural sign of written WASP authority.

Despite the many WASP allusions in Coppola's narrative, there remains an ethnic aesthetic to this superficially Anglo comedy. Coppola's Italian penchant for clever metaphors throughout the film brings his audience in line with each character's perspective. (This use of metaphor as similarity in difference stems from a basically Italian aesthetic.) For instance, the true character of Barbara Darling becomes clear chiefly through technological metaphors. After she entices Bernard into her bed while a recordplayer churns in the background, she turns away with a sudden headache. Bernard asks if she would like him to turn off the machine and she replies, "It turns off by itself"—a wry phrase that sums up her own sexual game. A similar machine metaphor expresses Bernard's feelings. In a slapstick cafeteria scene, the anxious fellow talks to girlfriend Amy, while trying to fill a glass from a milk machine. As the glass overflows, Bernard's sexual inexperience is comically evident.

Coppola turns to a summary metaphor in the final scene, when a reunited Bernard and Amy romp through a pretzel factory. The scene serves, in fact, as Coppola's paradigm for similarities between the sexes. Two bins catch identical two-hole pretzels off an assembly line, a cheerful symbol of these youths: Despite the factory-like nature of their middle-class upbringing, the end result is wholesome, innocent, and good-natured. The two bins further suggest an underlying similarity between men and women, which is Bernard's main discovery after his awkward first attempts at romance with Barbara Darling. The pretzel's image of doubling, two circles joined by a twist, signifies not only the lovers' togetherness but also the similarity of the masculine and the feminine. This similarity is spelled out even more clearly in the subsequent scene: Swept up by the giddy feelings of adolescent love, Bernard hands flowers to passersby. That is, he attains full manhood by realizing that, according to the situation, he can adopt so-called feminine behavior. He discovers this principle only after rejecting his father's stern patriarchal model, that of the institutional man who treats women either as a passive wife or an erotic art object.

After this light romantic satire of the Anglo-American father, Coppola began in 1968 to work in earnest on the musical, hoping to please his own father (Johnson 1976, 61). But *Finian's Rainbow* proved to be an embarrassingly dated mixture of Irish leprechauns and white liberal attitudes about Southern racism. Coppola's attempt to stuff big social ideas in a threadbare Irish formula failed.

The script for *Rainbow* stressed the Irish immigrant's belief in the success ethic, starting with the immigrant song "Look to the Rainbow." Because the newly arrived immigrant Finian (Fred Astaire) believes "everyone in America is rich," he declares himself a millionaire. For a white, English-speaking newcomer, "When you're on Park Avenue, Cornelius [Vanderbilt] and Mike [the Irishman] look alike." Since quick riches are essential for easy assimilation, Finian plans to bury his gold in the ground near Fort Knox, where he believes it will quickly grow. But when the racist Senator Rawkins turns black, the idea of a facile assimilation is turned upside-down. Coppola's satire and use of analogy are at odds with each other here. On the one hand, his satire maintains a critical distance between his social subject and his audience, while on the other hand clumsy analogies encourage community spirit.

Coppola nonetheless reveals richly autobiographical material. He originally intended that the introverted Og gradually acquire a forceful personality, just as did Bernard Chanticleer. But to Coppola's dismay, actor Tommy Steel played Og with barely a hint of shyness. Coppola also later regretted the film's dated Irish stereotype of cultural assimilation.

In 1969, Coppola reined in his social ideas to direct a small, touching film that again features rebellion, although this time with an Italian/American woman as protagonist. After talking with actress Shirley Knight, Coppola decided to revise an old college script, "Echoes." *Rain People* became his personal favorite in his canon. As the films opens one morning, Natalie Ravenna, a pregnant housewife, is fleeing her Italian-American husband and home on a long-distance trip to anywhere, a journey that gradually forces her to confront her maternal self and her responsibility to care for others. On the road, Natalie picks up Jimmy Kilgannon (James Caan), a good-natured, beefy hitchhiker who is mentally handicapped after a severe head injury in college football. The rest of Coppola's film depicts Natalie's struggle whether or not to accept some responsibility for this child–man.

In the film's last sequence, Natalie tries out sex with a motorcycle cop (Robert Duvall), after leaving Jimmy with a cruel, exploitative employer. The film ends in an abrupt, violent confrontation that forces Natalie to recognize her feelings of (Marian) compassion.

Rain People is about a woman discovering her maternal identity,

Coppola said. Natalie "comes to the conclusion that somehow her destiny is to be a mother" because she has a "compassionate side" (Coppola 1972, 221). This Italian-American belief in maternal Marian compassion is the film's central metaphor and the basis for Coppola's later ideal of an open, caring family.

> Ultimately, I became fascinated by the idea of the responsibility that we have to one another. And it seemed like a beautiful metaphor to me: a woman decides she doesn't want this thing that's been parcelled out to her—she doesn't want to be a wife and mother. She goes on this symbolic trip to avoid that, and in the course of it picks up this guy who's a metaphor for her baby that she's pregnant with. (1972, 221)

Natalie's tragedy is that she acknowledges too late her own maternal compassion. Similarly, Gordon the cop puts both his daughter out of his trailer and his dead baby out of his mind. Thus, an Italian Marian heart is as appropriate for men as for women because it binds the family together, fostering a sense of community with the poor, the disabled, and the homeless.

After the film's release, Coppola was not entirely satisfied with the way he had told Natalie's story. He noticed that halfway through he had shifted the plot focus to Jimmy, instead of staying with the issue of Natalie's conscience; he realized he had not sufficiently developed the central conflict between Natalie's maternal attachment to Jimmy and her desire to be free (Coppola 1972, 221). Natalie's flight from patriarchy was but a temporary answer to a major struggle within Italian-American patriarchy itself.

Facing the Self-Destructive Successful Father

The Godfather triggered a second life stage in Coppola's films, revealing his deep symbolic anger against his immigrant identity, his childhood religion, and especially the successful ethnic father. Coppola then filmed a mainstream parallel in *The Conversation*, picturing yet another breakdown of familial identity and childhood religious values for the (Italian/American) man who has achieved success through technology. But Coppola saved his deepest sense of ethnic loss and betrayal for *The Godfather, Part II*. In that famous sequel, he intently traced the fall of the familial individual who succumbs to Anglo conformity and an unbridled Italian/American success ethic. Finally, in *Apocalypse Now*, Coppola directly confronted the symbolic self-destructive father in a painful and deeply personal (Italian) confession. Following these major films, with their prolonged degeneration into violence, Coppola held out the hope of a new fatherhood on screen.

In 1972, Coppola adapted Mario Puzo's popular novel about a patriarchal Mafia family. Although both men initially worked together on the script, Coppola completely reshaped the project on set. (Later, *The Godfather, Part II* was entirely Coppola's creation.) Puzo had wanted to tell a romanticized story about a distinctly Sicilian gangster. But Coppola cut out much of the novel's violence and stressed instead the mobsters' ethnic family life. To begin with, the Mafia is an ethnic metaphor for America, says Coppola.

> I feel that the Mafia is an incredible metaphor for this country. Both the Mafia and America have roots in Europe. America is a European phenomenon. Basically, both the Mafia and America feel they are benevolent organizations. Both the Mafia and America have their hands stained with blood from what it is necessary to do to protect their power and interests. Both are totally capitalistic phenomena and basically have a profit motive. (1972, 223)

But *The Godfather* came across as a morally ambiguous portrait. Coppola had intended above all for ethnic and religious hypocrisy to stand out. As he would later say of Harry Caul in *The Conversation*, "that also seemed very Catholic to me: to do one thing and yet believe another" (1974, 31). Coppola's satiric thrust, however, was diffused among a rapid series of attractive family scenes. For instance, after the married Sonny coaxes a bridesmaid upstairs for energetic sex, the camera quickly returns to an innocent joyful wedding. So, our reaction here, as throughout the film, is mixed. Even the climactic, brutally violent tour de force of the Corleone baptism paired with multiple assassinations, does not stop us from enjoying Michael's triumph over his ruthless enemies.

Coppola had intended the violent baptismal montage, which he added to Puzo's story, to point only to hypocrisy. To his surprise, movie audiences cheered for the gutsy Michael (Al Pacino) and his family (1972, 223). Filmgoers clearly liked the beleaguered Michael, who first proved his WASP worth by separating himself from his disreputable family. They were repulsed only by the hypocrisy of institutional Catholicism and Italian ethnics, while they savored the justifiable violence of a man defending his family and achieving success in a brutal business world. Thus, the Corleone family was accepted in America's movie houses at the expense of its ethnic identity. As for Coppola, he realized he had badly underestimated the power of the Capra formula: An audience will always root for the underdog who fights hard to overcome the odds and marry the WASP woman (Diane Keaton).

In 1974, Coppola released *The Conversation*, a more intimate yet basically parallel look at the breakdown of ethnic and religious values for a familial individual who achieves success via male technology (whether as Mafia guns or as microphones slipped into walls). Although Coppola had grown accustomed to shooting with an unfinished script, for once he was fully prepared. The new project was also the only time, he said, when he attempted to begin with a "logical premise," instead of working from gut emotions: His inventive idea was to start with a surveillance expert instead of the criminals he records (Coppola 1972, 221; Coppola 1974, 30). Ironically, Coppola was more personal in this maverick experiment than with more overtly ethnic material.

The Conversation is about a man who, like Coppola, records other people for a living. The film's protagonist tragically puts job success before love and friendship. Harry Caul (Gene Hackman) is a surveillance expert in San Francisco who for the second time in his life finds himself implicated in murder. Like Natalie Ravenna, Caul refers to himself as a Catholic and feels torn between his feeling of responsibility for others and his desire to be independent, which for him means an amoral devotion to his job. But when someone is murdered because of his work, he realizes there is no escape from the bizarrely interconnected family that is modern society.

Coppola spent the first half of the film setting up Caul's isolation from his co-worker, his girlfriend, and his fellow professionals. Caul's family name refers in fact to a fetal membrane at birth, an image that suggests his naive innocence, a painful struggle, and afterwards a completely new life. Once Caul has lost all ability to trust others out of fear of betrayal, this sensitive and basically compassionate man cannot develop a critical conscience. He cannot discriminate between his caring girlfriend and his lowlife peers in wire-tapping. He may have achieved the pinnacle of professional success, but at the emotional cost of distrusting everyone.

By 1974, the topic of privacy, so important in *The Conversation*, was a major problem for the director of the phenomenally successful *The Godfather*. "All the people who tell me nice things I tend to distrust,"

Coppola said at the time (1972, 223). The character of Harry Caul allowed Coppola to express his increasing isolation and lack of privacy. To help himself identify with Caul, he inserted autobiographical details in the character's background, like childhood polio and a fascination with recording equipment. Those details were "an almost desperate attempt," Coppola said, "to give [Caul] a real character that I could relate to" (1974, 31).

Coppola also thought the film expressed his religious culture.

> Well, I got into [Catholic sensibility and guilt] for three reasons: First, it's kind of like *Marty*: It's just something in my memory, so images of the Virgin Mary and the confession just seem comfortable. Second, there is the irony of it being a wiretapper, especially before 1968 when it was made illegal, was really a very hypocritical job. After all, he was doing one thing, which was really a terrible thing, yet it was all aboveboard—they even held conventions! But that also seemed very Catholic to me: to do one thing and yet believe another. And third was the image of confession, which may be, I think, the oldest form of eavesdropping. (1974, 31)

In the end, Coppola stripped Caul of all remnants of religious culture, such as his legalistic confession and a plastic statue of the Blessed Virgin Mary. Caul's attempt to find solace in confession fails because he mentions only petty sins like a stolen newspaper instead of baring his soul and facing his conscience. In the final scene, he tears apart the icon of the Virgin Mary along with the rest of his apartment, while trying to locate a hidden microphone. To Coppola, the "tearing down of the room [is] to kind of be synonymous with a kind of personal tearing down in order to try to come back more to what [Harry's] roots were as a man" (1974, 23). Because the holy statue is the last item that Caul tears apart, the scene suggests that Caul's basic religious identity needs to be reformed. (The statue is also the least likely and therefore the best place to hide a microphone.) The final strip-down achieves for Caul "a kind of loneliness and simplicity," Coppola said (1974, 33). Caul's recourse is to play a reflective saxophone solo, music that in *One from the Heart* (1982) will lead a male loner back to romantic (familial) love and community.

Coppola also linked Caul to his own childhood guilt. "I think [Caul's] roots are roots of guilt," he said. "Ever since he was a little kid, everything that has happened he has in some way been responsible for" (1974, 34). What has happened mostly to Caul is a life of isolation, a condition which, to take Coppola's idea a step further, he mistakenly believed he deserved as a child. Coppola's narrator already confronted childhood guilt in *Dementia 13* and here looks more critically at consequent isolation, as dramatized in Caul's commitment to his career. To understand better the source of isolation in Italian-American guilt—the sense of being separated from others, especially from one's family—Coppola returned to his ethnic background as a metaphor for ethnic/American hypocrisy in the pursuit of success.

The Godfather, Part II portrayed Michael Corleone's hypocrisy more directly than before, shifting the satirical subject from that of a small besieged ethnic family in New York to an immensely wealthy clan in the West. The Corleone family out West was Coppola's Italian-American metaphor for mainstream success and WASP greed in the 1970s; if *The Godfather* chiefly criticized religious symbols and ethnic violence, its sequel castigated the young don's pervasive, indeed multiethnic (Italian, Jewish, Protestant) success ethic. The West has, of course, always symbolized a new frontier for outlaws and opportunists. In Coppola's cynical tableau of Nevada, however, everyone from the governor to the local citizenry is corrupt. Only vestiges of Italian culture remain under the new don's autocratic patriarchy. Instead of a unified family, we see a kindly Mother Corleone and the repentant Connie, each alone in her house. Michael's personal tragedy is clearest in flashback, when he recalls from long ago his father's cheery birthday party. An isolated Michael has followed the American success ethic at the terrible price of losing his Italian family.

The Godfather, Part II seemed to Coppola very much based on his own life.

> You know, in making *The Godfather II*, it was something like writing an original script except, because there was no story, I came to realize little by little that the subject treated in the script referred exactly to what was happening in my life at the time; for example, in my marriage and, even more, in my relations with *my family and my brother* [italics mine]. And I used this material, I did not know what else to do, to make another Godfather. . . . Then I simply looked about me. . . . I am from an Italian family. . . . People told me, "Hey, you know, this scene, it uses. . . ." Or else my wife said to me that we had already had this discussion. (1979c, 9 [translation mine])

To take Coppola's lead, the impact of his life on both films was largely
in terms of his relationships with his father and brother. Viewed from
the conclusive moment of Michael's final flashback, the two films
together tell a story of struggle against the successful patriarch.

At first, this struggle seems merely to be an Italian-American
son's predictable rebellion from his ethnic background, a rebellion
that opposes a lawful WASP society against a lawless mobster family.
Michael's relation to his family is strained after he graduates from
college because, like the undertaker at the wedding, he wants to be
an ordinary American; he expects that his Italian image of himself
as a familial individual will neatly match with WASP individualism.
Dressed in a U.S. military uniform at his sister's wedding reception,
he tells his Anglo girlfriend Kay he is different from the rest of his
family, a status the family ironically encourages by labeling him "a
civilian" and marking him for a political career. When later circumstances force Michael to team up with his brothers and defeat his
father's assassin, he draws a crucial distinction that will trouble him
the rest of his life. Trying to convince the assembled family men that
he is capable of shooting his father's enemy, Michael argues, "It's
not personal, it's just business"; as a familial individual, his affections and loyalties are to the family, while he regards outside affairs
as business to be conducted with an Italian-American sense of un-
restricted freedom. Michael's brothers, of course, continue to think
exactly the opposite, while respecting the cold calculated way their
younger brother commits himself.

So Michael's presence at his father's bedside in the hospital is
a personal statement. Taking the old man's hand, he tenderly tells
him, "I am with you now:" Michael's change moments later to a
business-like cool not only saves his father's life but establishes his
future approach to business; he is apparently a loyal, familial individual. Unlike Sonny, who clearly relishes revenge when offended,
Michael advances himself by asserting the hypocritical distinction
of saying one thing and doing another. After the brutal murder of
his young Sicilian bride, Michael dedicates himself completely to this
code, though in the end he eliminates not just all family enemies but
his capacity for kinship as well.

What neither Michael's family nor even he himself realizes is the
original twist he has put on Italian-American identity. Because he
no longer places his Italian background first but instead equal to
Anglo-American culture, he sometimes thinks of himself as an Italian
familial individual and at other times as a competitive WASP indi-

vidualist, according to the situation; that is, he plays both sides of reciprocal assimilation to his own advantage. But he pays a terrible personal price for his duplicity, since his double game requires that he also lie to himself.

Michael's tragic self-deception is the subject of a series of dramatic confrontations between his ethnic and WASP identities. In each scene there lies a deeply ethnic man beneath his cool, business-like exterior. First, he arrives in Las Vegas for business but turns in seething rage on Moe Green, who has disciplined the lascivious Fredo. Second, Michael seems to make a routine business call to Frank Pentangeli only to talk angrily about the recent assassination attempt that threatened his children. Third, at the end of his Cuban business trip, Michael kisses his brother Fredo, the betrayer, hard on the mouth, telling him, "I know it was you, Fredo. You broke my heart." As a result of mixing ethnic values with business decisions, Michael eventually loses both his admirable familial identity and his good business sense: He further alienates Tom Hagen, his one remaining (adopted) brother, by demanding vengeance against an ailing Hyman Roth.

The American success ethic and a Sicilian passion for revenge together vitiate the young don's positive Italian personalism. By denying his intense desire for power, Michael has come most to resemble not an Italian familial individual but a ruthless WASP individualist devoted to business. He does not seem to mind that he has increasingly less time for his family: He orders Hagan to purchase presents for his son; and for weeks he is unaware of his wife's abortion. Michael evidently never heard his father's earlier advice to Frankie Fontaine, "A man is not a real man unless he spends time with his family."

Because Michael no longer respects the restrictions imposed by Italian familial values, he loses his sense of Italian compassion. He may tell Fredo never to put anyone else before the family, but he himself lets business constantly get in the way. He plays the hypocrite in forgiving Fredo and then ordering his execution; the singular attempt at Marian intercession in *The Godfather, Part II*, Connie's plea that Michael forgive Fredo, falls on deaf ears. The only Italian tag to survive is a pitiful, superstitious prayer: A few minutes before his execution, Fredo tells his young nephew that the best way to catch fish is to recite a Hail Mary.

Because Michael has lost his Italian familial identity and with it his sense of compassion, he is in the end a truly tragic figure. This tragic ending suggests that the basic conflict between a supportive fatherly narrator and an all-powerful patriarch was far from resolved. Coppola later noted that in order to confront the successful symbolic father, one must have a keenly critical conscience.

> I know a lot of bright young writers and directors in Hollywood who are very successful—some of them I gave jobs to four and five years ago—and they're making a lot of money; but they're no longer talking about the things they used to talk about. . . . They don't even see or hear the changes in themselves. They've become the very people they were criticizing three years ago. Like Michael, they've become their fathers. (Johnson 1976, 149)

Coppola was of course himself struggling with the spectacular success of his Mafia saga. His next project became for him an intensely personal journey about a father-son relationship, as imaged in America's experience in Vietnam.

If *The Godfather, Part II* was Coppola's double-edged Italian/ American satire, *Apocalypse Now* was his American metaphor for an Italian confession of struggle against the self-destructive father. Filmed in 1979 with uneven results, the film is a soldier's long confession about his difficulty in facing a successful but morally disoriented father figure, a subject that for Coppola was both universal and deeply personal. In the early scene in a Saigon hotel, young Captain Willard, played by a taciturn, introspective Martin Sheen (well-known in public life as a liberal and highly political Catholic), is close to a mental breakdown from his many missions. But he receives yet another assignment: to locate and terminate Commander Kurtz, a fast-rising older officer who has been operating on his own in Cambodia.

Coppola, in recounting his experience filming, describes a project that began as a standard Hollywood production and became something freighted with autobiographical, Italian meaning. First, he listed all the elements and characters to be expected in a film about Americans in Vietnam: U.S.O. shows, helicopter attacks, black soldiers at the front, etc. (Coppola 1972). He soon decided, however, to cut through the American war clichés.

> I tried to make *Apocalypse Now* more of an experience than a movie. It starts out as a movie. A guy has to go [up a river]. We've all seen that movie. Like you have to blow up a bridge. But along the river, the story becomes less and less important.

What becomes important are the things you experience and see: what it's like to be in a helicopter when 30 of them swoop down and annihilate a native village. What does that feel like? But as you get further up the river, there are no more of those movie scenes, and for me there couldn't be. In other words, it would have been a very great dissatisfaction for me if in the last ten minutes Martin Sheen pulls the gun on Kurtz and they fight and the Army attacks and the bridge is blown up. (1979d, 142)

As months passed for Coppola and his crew in the Philippine jungle, he gradually saw the film more as a myth than as a historical picture of American involvement in Vietnam.

I didn't know how to finish it like a movie, so I kept taking it more and more into some sort of MYTH. I struggled with the end, as you know. I kept writing other endings, wonderful end-ings like *Godfather I*. I finally realized that I had a murderer who has come to kill a king, and the people know the king must be killed because they need a new king so the rice can grow and everyone can live. I thought that must be the oldest myth in the world. And that's what I did. (1979d, 142)

Coppola's interest in myth-making in general reflects an Italian sen-sibility keyed to metaphor. What he calls "the oldest myth in the world" is the fall of an oppressive patriarchy so that a society may flourish. Significantly, he associates the film's emotions with those of *The Godfather*; he was again trying to face his own private concerns with the symbolic father, while helping American audiences come to terms with the bewildering experience of Vietnam.

As in *The Conversation*, Coppola associated violence and a reli-gious culture with hypocrisy, only this time his protagonist is keenly aware of the issue: as a brutal war based on America's supposed moral superiority. The truth of American morality as entertainment is all too evident when soldiers wildly applaud buxom U.S.O. enter-tainers, and when a young San Diego soldier surfs during combat. The moral hypocrisy turns grisly when a trigger-happy G.I. on the river guns down an entire peasant family. Willard, a man with an Ital-ian familial conscience, notes this pervasive hypocrisy and deduces the institutional and familial responsibility of higher-ups: The U.S. commanders "cut [soldiers] in half and give them a Band-Aid," he wryly observes.

Later in *Apocalypse Now*, Catholic ritual seems ineffectual, especially in a wartime setting. During an outdoor mass not far from battle, a helicopter passes overhead with an ox in a sling, a half-mad image of war booty that trivializes the priest and worshipers as little more than blurred figures in the smoke and noise. The ox image also foreshadows the natives' later sacrifice of an ox, a symbol of Kurtz's assassination; religious ritual will regress to a pre-Christian sacrifice for the removal of the royal father. Still, Coppola did not entirely reject Italian tradition. If the American army's hypocrisy is generally analogous to that of the Church, then perhaps Catholicism might also show a way out of the moral morass. Coppola turned in particular to an Italian sense of confession to help audiences face the overwhelming experience of the Vietnam war. The bizarre early scene in Willard's hotel room dramatizes the burden of a critical conscience in a mind-numbing war. Willard stands before a mirror (a symbol of critical self-examination) and, in a drugged frenzy, cuts his arms and legs (a parallel to Scorsese's *The Big Shave*). Willard, like Charlie in Scorsese's *Mean Streets*, talks about his story as a confession, which he understands chiefly in terms of penance. "For my sins they gave me this [mission]," Willard says in a voice-over. Because sins are countless in war-torn Vietnam, the penance will indeed be heavy. In subsequent scenes Willard's voice-over counts the sins of his American military fathers, focusing finally on Kurtz as his key metaphor for the destructive patriarchy.

Coppola candidly admitted that the film's chief subject was the creation of a critical conscience.

> As a filmmaker, I thought that this metaphor of the journey up the river is like a journey in life. There is only one place that the journey can take you and that is inside yourself. . . . As you go up the river, there are things on your right that you can choose and there are things on your left that you can choose— and usually possibilities are contradictions. I began to realize that I was not making a film about Vietnam or about war, I was making a film about the precarious position that we are all in where we must choose between right and wrong, good and evil —everyone is in that position. (1979d, 140).

In his own Italian way, Coppola associated the use of metaphors (journey, river, Vietnam) with an examination of conscience. Through this critical lens, he critiqued the war while grappling with the issue of the symbolic father.

Strangely, Willard's breakdown is not just a synecdoche for Vietnam but also a metaphor for starting over. And Vittorio Storaro's opening cinematography pictures a thickly textured, almost lyrical Nature, a jungle aflame with napalm. The combination of lush colors and slow motion creates a rich Italian-American sense of the physical world. More specifically, as the whir of Willard's hotel ceiling fan triggers his flashbacks of helicopter blades and napalm drops, the scene is about a self-destructive Italian-American success ethic.

Willard begins his new life and long confession by introducing us to his military family. In another of Coppola's family meal scenes, Willard seems just as alienated as was the young Michael Corleone. When Willard later meets a war-happy squadron leader, played by Robert Duvall, the older man brags about his troops and helps Willard learn the territory; he behaves in fact like a worldly-wise older brother.

Willard himself talks like a cynical, ambitious teenage son. "Everyone gets everything they want," he says, "and I wanted a mission." But he soon realizes he wants most of all to face the patriarchal Kurtz: The "thing I felt the most, much stronger than fear, was the desire to confront him." While Kurtz represents an extreme example of the military's success ethic, he is also the symbolic father whom Willard will supplant.

This overthrow of the WASP individualist, which is what Michael Corleone in *The Godfather, Part II* eventually became, begins with Willard's warm, fatherly compassion for the innocent. A key figure of innocence for Coppola, who has lived for many years in California, was the California soldier Lance. Lance triggered strong feelings of fatherly responsibility.

> [Lance] was the one who took the LSD. I chose to have him live because he had gone to a state of such total [ethnic] innocence. I wanted a scene after Willard kills Kurtz, where he comes down the steps and takes him by the hand and takes him back. I wanted this idea: that we drove our children mad and that we must take them back, that we must make them whole again. (1979d, 146)

This is Coppola's barely disguised hope to feel whole by replacing the old patriarchy of success with a new fatherhood. Although Willard begins as a son figure and an assassin, he shows in the end the possibility of a new (Italian) father. But first, he must become aware of his responsibility in a series of innocent figures—Lance, the butchered natives, and Kurtz's own son. Willard even talks about his confused soldiers as if they were children looking for a home. "The more they tried to feel like home, the more it didn't," he notes sadly. Before any such sense of place or family, however, Willard must face Kurtz, the successful father who here presents himself as an omnipotent god.

Coppola's Kurtz is both the epitome of individual military initiative and the chief of a tribal (radically Italian familial) ethos that is ultimately self-destructive. Kurtz achieves a fatal isolation because he has used the same double (Italian/American) tack as Michael Corleone; consequently, each leader sits alone in the end with a dark conscience. But here the duplicitous jungle patriarch actually desires his own death. Kurtz, as much as his natives, asks for his ritual murder; the growth of both the familial tribe and the repressed son requires it. Kurtz asks only that he not be judged. "You have the right to kill me," he tells Willard, but "you have no right to judge." In order for Willard to be a more compassionate father figure, he must forgo self-important judgment and regard the old destructive patriarchy for what it is; harsh judgment and hasty rejection would only lead him to recreate the same patriarchy.

Coppola was acutely aware that Willard might become another Kurtz. Describing the river massacre, the filmmaker explained Willard's moral choice. "I always saw [Willard and Kurtz] as different aspects of the same man, and at that point you're midway in the journey, and that gesture [of the massacre] was the mark of [Willard] turning into a Kurtz" (1972, 215). But Willard does not become another Kurtz, partly because he avoids self-righteous, public judgment. He meets Kurtz instead in private chambers, where the commander looks like an isolated, crazed man rather than a living god. In sharp contrast to this everyday image is the omnipotent father, as described by the fearful, overwrought photojournalist (Dennis Hopper) who talks about Kurtz as would a terrified young son. Whispering in awe, he claims Kurtz "knew more about what I was going to do than I did." If Willard adopted this attitude, he could never face Kurtz or walk away from the godlike aura of his success.

Kurtz himself implies a new father-son relationship when he asks the young man to eventually tell his small son all that has happened. The next generation must know his (Italian)American story and its self-destructive outcome.

Coppola later recalled how much he and his crew felt like the disoriented Willard.

The way we made it was very much like the way the Americans were in Vietnam. We were in the jungle, there were too many of us, we had access to too much money, too much equipment; and little by little, we went insane. I think you can see it in the film. As it goes up the river, you can see the photography going a little crazy, and the director and the actors going a little crazy. (1972, 137–38)

It was at this moment of near-total disorientation from Hollywood filmmaking that Coppola decided on his mythic, ambivalent ending.

Coppola worried that in choosing a clear-cut finale, he would himself be guilty of moral hypocrisy. "I was a nice Kurtz, but I could do anything that I wanted," he said (1972, 146). A definitive last scene would turn him once and for all into another Kurtz.

But when I cut the film I couldn't, in truth, have Willard go back. . . . So I wanted to end the film on a moral choice: Does he become the new prince and have anything he wants, or does he go back enlightened, and talk to Kurtz's son and go that way. Since the film right here is about moral choice, I wanted to leave it here, because what would you do? . . . I don't know for certain that's what he would do and I don't want to lie. (1979d, 146)

Willard does not yet choose a new fatherhood, for he is only at the beginning of a new order. Coppola's major focus instead was the first stage of a confessional conscience, as it works through a violent Anglo patriarchy based on written and verbal orders. By using graphic wartime violence to strip away an Italian/American success ethic, Coppola could begin to see himself as a father working for a family-like community of innocent soldiers.

The Flight from Italian/American Patriarchy

Coppola's most recent stage of filmmaking began in the 1980s, a time when his screen protagonists repeatedly flee from Italian/American patriarchy. *One from the Heart* pictures another Coppola breakdown, though this time with a happy musical ending. After this hopeful note, Coppola brought back the Irish-American in a multiethnic musical that ends with all good ethnics—blacks, Irish, Jews, and WASPs —fleeing a ferociously violent Mafia. Coppola then turned, in *Peggy Sue Got Married*, a small project with a similar theme, to flight into the past; a blonde WASP woman struggles with nearly forgotten anger against a man with Dracula-like power over her creative life force.

Coppola's most recent three films are all flights of fantasy that specifically address the tragic death of his son Giancarlo. *Gardens of*

Stone tenderly talks about a seasoned veteran who takes on a young assistant, only to have him die needlessly. *Tucker: The Man and the Dream* celebrates a strong father/son relationship, while American popular technology fails the (ethnic) family. And in "Life Without Zoe," virtually a Coppola family production, a regressive narrator imagines a heroic, larger-than-life Italian father to compensate for his frequent absence from home. Taken as a group, these symbolic flights show Coppola's great talent for psychological fantasies that, like the early *Dementia 13*, never fail to intrigue. Only now Coppola's work has a much fuller, Italian sense of natural beauty and family joy.

If in the late 1970s Coppola pursued his personal vision of an Italian/American confession in the jungles of Southeast Asia, he returned home wondering if there were not easier ways to make a movie. So, he decided to film *One from the Heart* entirely in his Zoetrope studios. There he returned to his early filmic passion—the romantic musical. Whereas his Vietnam film introduced the idea of a new father, his Las Vegas romance proposed a warm, fatherly narrator who encourages a young man to bare his love in public.

One from the Heart (1982) is the story of Hank (Frederic Forrest) and Frannie (Teri Garr), a Las Vegas couple who split up because she wants more excitement in their relationship; the working couple of the 1980s has sexual freedom and financial security but no vital (Italian) sense of family. There only family consists of two best friends —Maggie, Frannie's co-worker in a travel agency, and Moe, Hank's partner in the junk company Reality Wrecking.

Coppola's theatrical opening compares the filmic narrator to God looking down on creation. The shot looks head-on at a bright orange klieg light, Coppola's metaphor throughout the film for the narrator's eye and its divine-like presence as richly colored light. A blue stage-curtain parts to reveal an evening sky and the planet Earth suspended in it. Like the brief scene of starry heavens in Frank Capra's *It's A Wonderful Life*, the stage setting suggests God's idea of earth as his special creation. Similarly, the narrating camera approaches Frannie's workplace in a series of smooth dissolves (with elevator shots and elaborate tracking) that consciously celebrates the world's space. In the subsequent, happy communal context of a Las Vegas gambling strip, we see Frannie arrange a travel display in her office window, a metaphor of her desire to escape the routine, impersonal patterns and hollow materialism of her job, her town, and her home life; she vaguely senses that the superficial culture of success is getting her down. Confused, frustrated, and angry, she is a less desperate version of the housewife in *Rain People* who had to leave town to survive.

Critics complain that Coppola's colored filters and strong lighting are consistently and self-consciously artificial. But the startling break with conventional Hollywood lighting suits well the story of a couple's struggle with the routine of middle-class success. Coppola, like John Ford with his riveting pictures of Monument Valley, has an ethnic Catholic's sacramental regard for locale, which here helps substantiate the artifices of musical comedy.

Coppola's opening sequence establishes a brotherly narrator, a figure (part camera and part voice-over) that prods Hank's conscience. At first, the camera/narrator, personified by the klieg light's warm orange eye, adopts the cheerful attitude suited to a musical. But as the focus shifts to the couple, Coppola's narrator turns into a thoughtful, slightly amused older man: The deep throaty voice on the jazz soundtrack frequently comments on Hank's handling of situations. When Frannie leaves Hank a second time, the experienced voice tells him plainly, "She's got big plans that don't include you. Take it like a man." Curiously, this all-knowing, brotherly figure seems both to speak from outside Hank and also from within, as if he were the young man's emerging conscience.

Coppola's narrator is also visible as special background lighting. "Basically, *One from the Heart* is an experimental prototype for this ulterior film," Coppola said, "from the point of view of the light, the color, the sets, the songs" (1982b, 31). The narrator's sympathetic eye appears in the shifting colored light that marks so many scenes. When Frannie stomps out of her house, she is bathed in red light, while Hank stands in blue tones; their argument boils down to her frustrated, angry boredom and his coolly distant view of change in their relationship. When she tries to tell him about her frustrations, he, still in blue light, goes off by himself in a corner to play his trumpet, like Harry Caul in *The Conversation* with his saxophone; Hank feels blue, having chosen to play the music of his life for himself. Coppola further emphasizes Hank's closed-off feelings in a tour de force of theatrical scrims and two-way mirrors. When Frannie and Hank first appear at their respective jobs, they each look into a mirror, as each feels trapped by the tensions of their life together. Only after familial feedback from close friends do Hank and Frannie acquire outside points of reference for their relationship.

Moe, played by a well-weathered Harry Dean Stanton, is another of Coppola's older-brother figures. But for the first time the figure is fallible and also believably human: Moe confesses to the jealous Hank that he once kissed Frannie. Unlike the fantastical helicopter commander in *Apocalypse Now*, this brother figure seems neither dangerous nor boastful, and shows a family-like concern by sharing his friend's problems.

With this support, Hank and Frannie each try out their romantic fantasies in two new relationships. The circus-performer Leila and the singer-waiter Ray are kind, gentle people who add to Coppola's warmhearted vision of Las Vegas. (In fact, most of the film's secondary characters are well-meaning, good-tempered folk.) Most telling of all, the two new lovers, played by an easygoing Raul Julia and a precocious, pixie-like Nastassia Kinski, let go as soon as they perceive that Hank's and Frannie's hearts are elsewhere; unlike angry lovers in Coppola's past romances, neither figure seems capable of emotional violence or sudden demands.

The rest of America, however, is in trouble. "You know what's wrong with America, don't you? It's the light," says Hank. "Oh, there's no more secrets, you know, phony bullshit man—nothing is real." Hank is attacking the self-centered lifestyle of the 1980s. As he angrily observes, "Ain't nobody committed to nothing except having a good time." When Hank surrenders his pride and sings "You Are My Sunshine" at the airport, he has reached a critical moment of conscience, finally admitting his private love to a family-like community. Thus, Coppola's narrator has shone a personal light on the Italian ideal of a family where individuals mediate in one another's lives.

Coppola's next two films likewise featured sweet innocence and family love, as he continued to develop the idea of the good father in relation to troubled boys without parents. S. E. Hinton's *The Outsiders* (1983) is the story of three orphaned brothers and their friends, all "greasers" living in the poor part of town. Their rivals, the Soshes, are middle-class boys from the west side. Ponyboy, a fourteen-year-old greaser played by Ralph Macchio, enjoys writing fiction and hangs out with Johnny, his sixteen-year-old buddy. Ponyboy lives with his two older brothers—Sodapop, who is sensitive and likeable, and twenty-one-year-old Darrel, who behaves like a stern father.

Coppola takes an Italian-American approach to his characters, who are nothing like the boys in Hollywood teen films. Ponyboy, for example, openly shares his feelings with brothers and friends. In a dramatic moment that establishes the narrator's fatherly attitude, Coppola even added a scene of two young boys crying in the cold and falling asleep together. Through Ponyboy in particular, Coppola expresses a keen Italian-American sense of natural beauty in art. Ponyboy praises the film's bucolic sunsets which, Coppola said, imitate watercolors (1983, 43); or, as Ponyboy says, "I stepped out into the brightness." This brightness is not only an idealized Nature but also a cherished sense of community.

Poor children, Coppola thinks, should at least be able to find shelter in the (Catholic) church. As in *The Godfather*, the church is again guilty of hypocrisy, dramatized here as a large stone church next to which an advertisement reads—"urself save." By comparison, the boys learn to survive by relying on their strong sense of family and their closeness to Nature. In the film's last scene Ponyboy reads a letter from the deceased Johnny that celebrates youth. "You're gold when you're a kid," a sentiment clearly associated both with earlier golden sunsets and with Johnny's commitment to help his friend. In effect, this message from the grave brings to the surface Coppola's brotherly narrator.

Coppola next adapted Hinton's novel about a fatherly twenty-one-year-old who tries to guide his troubled younger brother. In *Rumble Fish* (1983) sixteen-year-old Rusty James (Matt Dillon) worships his older brother, known locally as the Motorcycle Boy (Mickey Rourke), a one-time gang leader who helped end citywide gang wars. Rusty James hangs out with Steve, a middle-class friend since childhood. Steve observes that although he can never be sure what the Motorcycle Boy is thinking, he always knows what is on the guileless Rusty James's mind; the younger brother lacks a critical conscience.

The success ethic of teen gangs encourages violence, competition, and male authority that only changes with a new ethos of compassion. Like a concerned father, the Motorcycle Boy realizes he must somehow erase the ideal of gang success that clouds his younger brother's vision. But Rusty James complains that if he only had had his brother's backing, the two could have run their side of town, whereas his problems actually lie in his family history: When he was a child, his alcoholic father (Dennis Hopper) got drunk and left him alone in a house for three days. The complaint to the older, successful brother echoes a scene from another famous ethnic film: The Catholic young man in *On the Waterfront*, played by Marlon Brando, tells his older brother, "I could have been a contender."

The Motorcycle Boy attempts to turn his brother around by setting himself up to die at the hands of the police, hoping to shock Rusty James into leaving town and starting life over in California with their mother. The noble attempt to spark Rusty James' conscience begins in a pet shop, where the older brother seems obsessed with a tank of rumble fish. Like tough urban youths, these creatures fight to the death when they see their own reflection on the tank's glass walls. That same night, the Motorcycle Boy breaks into the store and frees all the caged birds and animals. On his way to the nearby river with the tank of fish, he is fatally shot by a policeman and, with his last breath, tells his brother to follow the river all the way to the ocean.

The film's credits include Coppola's autobiographical tribute, set to the tune "Don't Fence Me In": "This film is dedicated to my older brother, August Coppola, my first and best teacher." Coppola also added to Hinton's story a final scene of Rusty James at the Pacific Ocean to further dramatize the dependent young man's final separation from his older brother.

Coppola's extensive use of metaphor once again points to an Italian aesthetic. In the final police scene, he tersely developed the central metaphor of rumble fish, Hinton's symbol of self-destructive teenagers trapped in urban poverty. When Rusty James is arrested, he stands with his hands raised against a police car, sees his own reflection in the car window, and begins angrily hitting it; like the rumble fish, he will kill himself unless he escapes from his social tank. Unlike the vengeful policeman in Hinton's novel, however, Coppola's officer orders Rusty James let go. Coppola set up this final choice of freedom, whereas Hinton's novel ends with Rusty James living in California years later and trying not to think about the past. For Coppola, Rusty James has learned to stop fantasizing about success in gang wars because of his older brother's fatherly compassion and suicidal self-sacrifice—Italian traits that will also be highly visible in Martin Scorsese's Little Italy.

The Cotton Club was likewise about flight from destructive violent competition. Set during the 1920s in Harlem's famous Cotton Club, Coppola's story is about the pursuit of success by blacks and whites, Irish and Italians, musicians and gangsters. This urban epic spins parallel ethnic plots about a pair of Catholic brothers, Dixie and Vinny Dwyer, and a pair of black brothers, Delbert and Clay Williams (Coppola 1983a, 75). Dixie, played by a hip Richard Gere, blows a hot coronet but has trouble getting steady work in a mostly black profession. By comparison, the Williams brothers work hard to get gigs in the Cotton Club. Dixie, in the course of his work, meets and falls in love with the ambitious Vera Cicero, the lover of mobster Dutch Schultz.

After the exposition of main characters, Coppola focuses on the issue of Vera's (WASP) lack of conscience. At a gangster's party, she and Dixie watch Schultz brutally murder a rival. While Dixie is physically revolted, Vera becomes Schultz's girlfriend to get a nightclub of her own. By the film's last scene, Dixie has brought new hope to this cynical Anglo blonde. Coppola's strategy is akin to one of Frank Capra's social comedies, in which a young (ethnic) man is willing to sacrifice himself to save the WASP soul of a savvy, big-city dame.

The (Italian) issue of a critical conscience flares up a second time, moments after Dixie and Vera make love in his mother's flat. Pointing out Vera's hypocrisy, he asks, "You can't see a murder, then come home, fuck your friend who loves you, leave him, go home, wake up in the morning, have tea and toast with a psychopath?" Vera implicitly replies later by talking about her sordid adolescence; because she has been hustling men since she was twelve, she has come to believe that only money counts in life. But once she realizes she has paid for her nightclub with her freedom, she leaves to start life anew in California with Dixie. The former altar boy helped the cynical 1920s WASP get a critical conscience and choose a life separate from a violent success ethic.

An underlying Italian-American aesthetic also emerges here. Coppola's Harlem epic focuses more on Dixie Dwyer, raised a Catholic, than on Delbert Williams, a choice that suggests a hierarchy of the competing ethnic groups—Irish, Jewish, Italian, Black—associated with the Cotton Club. Despite the extra attention devoted to Dixie's character, Coppola's musical community has a pervasive sense of similarity in difference, that is, of rough equality. Among the various gangsters, on the other hand, there are only extreme differences fleshed out in greed and murder.

The most sympathetic follower of the success ethic is Delbert Williams. Delbert slights his brother Clay by secretly arranging a solo for himself. Ironically, in romance, Delbert must face a mirror of his own self-centered desire for success: He falls for a woman who puts her career before his love. Once Delbert has argued that she should put their relationship first, he is able to take a less competitive attitude towards his own brother: Sitting in the audience for one of Clay's performances, Delbert graciously calls him the finest dancer in Harlem. When an amiable black gangster asks the two brothers to dance together again, Delbert and Clay end by falling into one another's arms, while hoofing to the lyrics of "You Go Your Way."

And Delbert says, "I'm sorry." This sentimental portrayal of black community life depends on an (ethnic) mediator, while dance itself is a joyful sacrament of family unity.

The film's climax again features (Italian) mediation and community in dance. During Delbert's solo in the Cotton club, Boss Schultz draws a gun on Dixie, but Delbert kicks it out of his hand. Delbert's dance fully expresses his rage over earlier scenes of racism: Throughout Schultz's assassination, Coppola's cross-cuts show Delbert dancing a fierce tap solo perfectly in sync with machine-gun bullets. Delbert has survived and triumphed by saving the innocent Dixie and pouring his energy into his art. Coppola likewise dealt with his anger against patriarchy by channeling his talent into film musicals.

Critics panned *The Cotton Club* for not offering more dance numbers. But Coppola was basically trying to show, in the club's multiethnic world, the communal functions of music and dance. Unlike an Astaire-Rogers classic in which dance routines support a flimsy plot, the nightclub numbers here are essential to plot and character; instead of a distant observant camera for dances, quick medium shots and close-ups encourage filmgoers to feel and hear the dance, to experience not so much dance per se as the joyful people who create it.

Cotton Club's singers and dancers and club managers are finally all members of Coppola's theatric family, an artistic group that outlasts self-destructive white gangsters. Among the film's white men, only Dixie and the Cotton Club's owner Onnie Madden (Bob Hoskins) realize that escape is the single answer to brutal competition. In the closing scene at Grand Central Station, the two men's departure by train turns into a grand homage to the American musical; Coppola asserts that flight from a violent patriarchy is a happy act of survival and community. Just as at the end of *Rumble Fish* Rusty James heads for the Pacific Ocean, Madden happily goes to Sing Sing where he can enjoy testing new club shows. Thus, in Coppola's spectacular cross-cuts, the departing whites at the train and the black performers at the club constitute one musical family.

In the same way that escape to the West Coast is Dixie's only answer, a comic escape to the past is the solution for Coppola's heroine in *Peggy Sue Got Married* (1986). Like Natalie Ravenna in *Rain People*, Peggy Sue is unsatisfied with her marriage and leaves her husband. More important, Peggy Sue's (time) travels similarly help her develop a critical conscience and reestablish a basic sense of family.

Here, however, the heroine rediscovers innocence not in a childlike football player but in her best childhood memories of family.

Coppola's film opens with an anxious Peggy Sue Bodell (Kathleen Turner) getting ready for a high school reunion. A middle-age mother and a businesswoman, she is about to divorce her husband Charlie for being sexually unfaithful. In high school, the two had been popular sweethearts. Later, the fire went out of their marriage after he gave up musical performance and college to take over his father's music store. Hurt and angry about Charlie's love affair, Peggy Sue would just as soon never see him again. Still, she has strong feelings about him as part of her happy adolescence. So, Coppola uses the comic device of Peggy Sue fainting at her high school reunion to take her back in time (without any physical change) and to show an adult critically examining her youth. Although Peggy Sue gets a second chance to decide whether to marry, she does not change the present (always an easy comic trick) but instead realizes the source of her marital problems and her husband's caring musical nature. Once again, a Coppola plot dramatizes the so-called feminine self's recovery of innocence and creativity.

The core of this psychodrama stresses Peggy Sue's underlying fear of the husband/father as predator. A betrayed wife, she feels deathly afraid of Charlie. She works through this fear by returning to the past, a trip that climaxes in a dream-like night scene outside her bedroom window during adolescence. She imagines Charlie flexing his hands like Dracula and entering to kill her; that is, she is simply terrified that if she again marries him, she will be one of the (married) undead.

Peggy Sue overcomes her fundamental fear of the bloodsucking patriarch after dream-like encounters with two outsiders, both men of noncompetitive values. These male figures help her to conquer her fear and enlarge her idea of men in general. Classmate Michael Fitzsimmons is a rebellious young writer, a type known well in Irish literature but seldom seen in recent American film. At school, Fitzsimmons lambasts Hemingway's Anglo-American idea of the virile male, and later helps give Peggy Sue a feeling for both love-making and life as sweet romance by awakening her desire to be a dancer; after making tender love to her, he asks her, paraphrasing Yeats, to find "the pilgrim soul" in herself.

The second man in Peggy Sue's life, brainy Richard Norvic, is a comic foil that helps her realize just how much her attitude towards men has changed. When a bully shoves Norvic, Peggy Sue quickly says, "You macho schmuck." Norvic's non-masculine character recalls Coppola's confidence, as he said for *Playboy*, in non-traditional men, an opinion that here strikes an autobiographical note: Coppola was known in high school as "Mr. Science." In sum, the Norvic character helps Peggy Sue completely reject an all-American model of men based primarily on physical strength.

A man of ideals committed to music is exactly what Peggy Sue finally recognizes in Charlie. Her husband's initially idealistic and innocent nature is the chief reason, she now realizes, she married him. Overhearing Charlie in a singing audition, she recognizes his basically artistic character. Despite herself, she is again charmed by his honest, goofy ways (played by Coppola's nephew—Nicolas Cage). In the final hospital scene, a mirror confirms Peggy Sue's full-blown critical conscience and renewed faith in family, two implicitly Italian issues. After Charlie repents for his extramarital affair, first the couple and then their daughter appear in a hospital mirror. The reflection reveals Peggy Sue's new view of herself: She can see herself again as part of a couple and a family. Because she has overcome her fear of an oppressive, Dracula-like husband, she is ready to listen to Charlie and finally forgive him.

Coppola's shot of the hospital mirror, as a critical conscience, brings full circle the film's opening montage. In the first major scene, the subject of Peggy Sue's conscience slowly becomes evident, beginning with a tight close-up of Charlie in a television advertisement. As the camera pulls back to the bedroom, and then back further to show the entire scene reflected in a dressing-table mirror, we realize that the camera's gaze is that of Peggy Sue glancing in her mirror. The remainder of the film is her internal dialogue with her earlier, scared self about her husband. Although the dialogue begins with an anxious televised image of Charlie, actually Peggy Sue's mental picture of her husband, she gradually pulls back from this image of the success-oriented salesman to the realities of her bedroom and her awkward conversation with her daughter. Her subsequent conversation reveals that anger towards her husband has blocked out her larger, familial sense of herself with her daughter. By comparison, Coppola's last mirror shot frames Peggy Sue in a cheerful family context.

Coppola might be criticized for passing quickly over the family roots of Peggy Sue's relation to her husband. When she travels back in time, she unearths mostly holy pieties about her family. More important than the event that triggered her underlying fear is Coppola's fascination with the trip itself, as a technological wonder.

A much franker film about the autobiographical source of Coppola's work is his second war film, *Gardens of Stone* (1987). Ostensibly the story of the Honor Guard at Arlington National Cemetery during the Vietnam War, *Garden* pictures "toy soldiers" in training under sergeant Clell Hazard (James Caan), a brusque career soldier who feels fatherly toward the son of an Army buddy, a new recruit named Jackie Willow (D. B. Sweeney). After Willow marries, volunteers for Vietnam, and later returns home in a coffin, Hazard feels torn apart.

Coppola's strong sense of family dominates this uneven, small film. "I care about the United States Army," Hazard says. "That's my family. The only one I got." (Coppola himself attended a military school as a boy.) On the rebound from a divorce, which includes separation from his son, the patriotic Hazard grows close to Willow and to his girlfriend, Samantha Davis (Angelica Huston), an anti-war reporter for *The Washington Post*. The three-some quickly develop quiet familial bonds. Last of all, sergeant Major Nelson (James Earl Jones) is Hazard's best friend, filling the Coppola role of the gregarious older brother.

These familial ties and political conflicts seem to reflect Donald Bass's screen adaptation of the Nicholas Proffitt novel. Coppola nevertheless shaped the project himself, stressing Hazard's ability to survive by treating an institution like the Army as family. Frustrated by the daily "drops" at Arlington Cemetery and stunned by Willow's death, Hazard decides, in the best tradition of (Italian Catholic) subsidiarity, to dedicate himself to the lowest level of decision-making: He transfers to a camp where he can train new recruits headed for Vietnam.

Coppola's story of paternal grief has distinct personal overtones. During filming, Giancarlo Coppola, the director's twenty-three-year-old son and assistant, was killed in a tragic boating accident in Chesapeake Bay. Coppola expressed his grief partly through his own father's elegiac film score, which is heightened by echoes from past films: a plaintive trumpet solo from *The Godfather* and a song by The Doors from *Apocalypse Now*. These musical associations blend with a pervasive sense of family, including the real parents (Peter Masterson and Carlin Glynn) of the actress who plays Willow's girlfriend (Mary Stuart Masterson). Even the stoic Hazard cries out at Willow's funeral, "I just wonder if we're getting better at knowing [our young men]." As a whole, the film suggests little compassion and a weak sense of the American people; in Hazard's Army, as in the Corleone family, women take secondary roles and men experience only brief moments of uncritical bonding. Far outweighing any sense of family here is the U.S. military as a civil religious symbol.

In another, more idealistic film about family unity, Coppola let his all-American fascination with technology dominate. Set in 1948, *Tucker: The Man and the Dream* (1988) is Coppola's study of post-war fatherhood, the story of an idealistic inventor, Preston Tucker, who tries to market and mass produce a "car of the future." The Tucker Torpedo features disc brakes, a popout windshield, and three head-lights. But when Tucker cannot meet production deadlines manipu-lated by powerful Detroit manufacturers, his dream eventually comes crashing to earth. More important, these business events lead him to temporarily forget about family values.

Coppola sets his all-American dream in a family atmosphere, in-cluding Tucker's Jewish partner who adopts the role of a gift-bearing uncle to Tucker's kids. This warm extended family includes as well Tucker's mechanics and his engineer, who work together in a shed next to the Tucker house. For major public occasions, such as the un-veiling of the first Tucker or a courtroom trial, all are present as one family.

Autobiographical echoes resound throughout the film. Coppola's own father was devoted to a career at the expense of his family. Re-lated to this, Tucker's relationship to his teenage son seems especially important, especially after Coppola's own loss of Giancarlo. Tucker's son, a high school senior, decides not to attend college in order to learn the car business from his father. And in all the important scenes, son and father work together. The only thing to put distance between them is Tucker's over-reliance on salesmanship and technology. This problem is most evident in an angry confrontation in the Tucker workshop, when Eddie, a longtime friend and mechanic (Frederic Forrest), balls out his boss for paying more attention to a production deadline than to a nearly fatal accident. Similarly, the son has more common sense than his father. Tucker behaves, in fact, more like a gregarious older brother than a father to his boy.

Tucker seems to belong squarely in the tradition of Frank Capra's social comedies. It has a bright-eyed optimism, occasionally touched by sadness. And the court scene, in which Tucker is crucified finan-cially, recalls both Jefferson Smith and John Doe. *Tucker* in sum seems an updated version of *Meet John Doe*, minus the happy ending. Yet, there are key differences in Coppola's style, beginning with his fascination with technology and salesmanship that together weaken his Capra-like feeling for the little people. Coppola's Tucker, instead of protecting the common folk from greedy capitalists, as does George Bailey in *It's A Wonderful Life*, sees himself as the go-between for car consumers and his own imaginary world of inventions and prosperity.

Coppola's next film, "Life Without Zoe," is a return to the candidly dreamlike center of his canon. The contemporary fairy-tale is ostensibly about Zoe, a twelve-year-old rich kid in New York City who seldom sees her parents, strikes up a friendship with a new Arabic boy at school, and, eventually, returns a jewel to a princess. In Coppola's fanciful ending, Zoe purchases plane tickets to Greece for herself and her mother so they can sit together and listen in adulation to her father, a world-famous musician (Giancarlo Giannini) and the mostly absent core figure in this fantasy.

The autobiographical ties to Coppola's own family background are unmistakable. Raised by a father fiercely dedicated to his musical career, Coppola creates for Zoe a musician dad who is easily forgiven for many absences from home. The daughter-figure recalls Coppola's early script for *Dementia 13*, in which a dead Irish girl expresses a young man's frustrated creativity in a family torn apart by American success. In "Life Without Zoe" the strong young protagonist has only a manservant for parental care yet remains lively and imaginative. Adding a personal family touch, Coppola cast his sister Talia Shire as Zoe's mother, his father Carmine Coppola as a street musician, and his daughter Gia Coppola as Baby Zoe. (He also worked on the script with his daughter Sofia, who designed the costumes.)

Bad dreams, musicals, and finally fairytales are the narrative strategies that Coppola frequently explores in his autobiographical works. With surprisingly candid material, he reworks old family issues in psychologically fascinating ways. Because as a boy he constantly changed schools and homes, as an adult artist he does not often portray permanent family situations, preferring instead the ad hoc community and shifting locale of the American musical. This belief in the musical, in turn, has fueled his interest in the Tucker-like showmanship of filmic technology. His few tragedies, *Apocalypse Now* and *Gardens of Stone*, are on the other hand, relatively formless narratives. With their uneasy sense of political and social satire, he remains deeply ambivalent about ethnic identity; without a clearer idea of his ethnic and religious roots, Coppola has been unable to pin down enduring values as fully developed dramatic actions. This is hardly a fault, however, in the aftermath of the moral and social upheaval of the 1960s. At his best, Coppola creates psychologically intriguing instances of flight from patriarchy, films that end with an idealized Italian sense of natural beauty and family unity.

The previously irritable (ethnic) artist in Dementia 13
*(1963) begins his marriage to a WASP American woman
with renewed creativity, symbolized here by the female
figure in the foreground. (Museum of Modern Art/Film
Stills Archive; courtesy of Film Group, Inc.)*

Shirley Knight, as the pregnant mother figure in The Rain People *(1969), may flee from Italian-American patriarchy but cannot shirk her sense of family (James Caan). (Museum of Modern Art/Film Stills Archive; courtesy of Warner Bros.–Seven Arts)*

Al Pacino, as the don in The Godfather *(1972), earns respect for himself and his business family. (Museum of Modern Art/Film Stills Archive; courtesy of Paramount Pictures)*

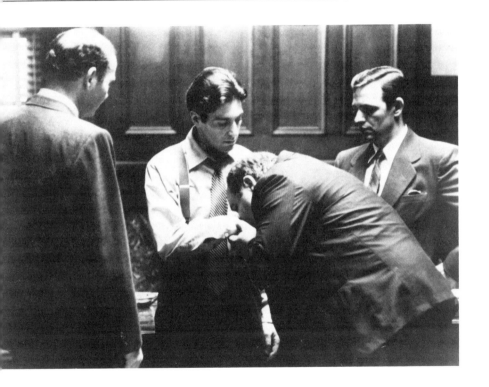

As Vito Corleone (Robert DeNiro) rises to power in The Godfather, Part II *(1974), he distorts his Italian heritage of Marian compassion, symbolized here by a badly hung religious print. (Museum of Modern Art/Film Stills Archive; courtesy of Paramount Pictures)*

Martin Sheen, as the confessional narrator and captain in Apocalypse Now *(1979), faces at last the radical representative of Anglo success and patriarchy (Marlon Brando). (Museum of Modern Art/Film Stills Archive; courtesy of United Artists)*

Harvey Keitel, as Charlie in Mean Streets *(1972), finally realizes he cannot choose his own penance in the streets. (Museum of Modern Art/Film Stills Archive; courtesy of Warner Bros.)*

CHAPTER 6

MARTIN SCORSESE

Martin Scorsese spent much of his childhood in bed with pleurisy, wishing he could play in the streets. When he did get outside, he immersed himself in Little Italy—in an insular, often self-destructive world. Years later, as a young filmmaker, Scorsese translated this world into film with religious-like devotion. Typically, he pictured an intelligent and morally sensitive young man who, in one violent moment, purges his Italian familial community. After thoroughly mining his ethnic boyhood, Scorsese turned to greater Manhattan where he envisioned non-Italian men either confronting or satirizing a WASP society based, not on the family, but on individual success.

Although all Scorsese's films are rooted in his early experiences of Little Italy, his themes generally resemble those of John Ford and Frank Capra—namely, home and family, decency, law, and democracy. In each case, however, Scorsese imbues his material with the perspective of a second-generation Italian American. For example, he sketches home and family as both an uncritical mother (who tells her son to "eat good") and a small crowd of buddies. In this ethnic milieu, decency means a familial compassion for young men and women rigidly ruled by a local patriarchy. In order for anyone to be free of (ethnic) patriarchy in Scorsese's films, they often must break the law and temporarily disrupt the neighborhood. In this way the entire community gets a glimpse of a better democracy, before the old patriarchal ways again take hold.

Scorsese developed his fatalistic vision in two stages that directly reflect the major challenge of his career: the shift in settings from Little Italy to the outside world. Scorsese, always the Italian ironist, began his career with mock portraits of a mob underling and an earnest young artist; that is, he poked fun at the clichéd ideas and stereotype of the Italian hood, while saving some ridicule for himself as the self-

in Little Italy and Greater Manhattan

absorbed artist. When he next focused on an idealistic and morally sensitive young man, his lens widened to include the fellow's pals, his mother, his girlfriend, and the Italian fathers who run local businesses and thus control employment. In this social context, Scorsese has put a new twist on the Christmas story of rebirth so dear to Frank Capra and John Ford. Scorsese's men, true sons of the 1960s, are reborn through great personal and social upheaval, typically a violent strip-down that reveals a primitive babe within.

Outside Little Italy, Scorsese continued to work with intelligent, morally responsive protagonists, each attempting to start life anew in the American mainstream. The emotional and financial struggle to survive there again leads to outbursts of violence, as it did in Little Italy, and sometimes to the creation of art, especially music and painting. As part of his own Italian art, Scorsese continued to look closely and ironically at each milieu. At the same time, he shifted his critical gaze from ethnic patriarchs to comparable WASP figures. Thus, Scorsese's Italian-American narrative schema for Little Italy proved to be perfectly adaptable to Manhattan, New Mexico, and even Palestine.

Scorsese's canon, when compared to Francis Coppola's, is far less ambivalent about the tensions between the Italian and American halves of his identity. The films set in Little Italy primarily treat conflicts within Italian-American culture, conflicts that Coppola never had to face. The films set outside Little Italy, all narratives of seeming Anglo conformity, do not so much erase Italian culture as place it in strong ethnic parentheses. (Even the nonethnic housewife in *Alice Doesn't Live Here Anymore* has kitchen curtains decorated with tiny eggplants, intimate signs of Italian culture.) In terms of plot structure, Scorsese rediscovers in Manhattan and elsewhere a violent purging of society remarkably similar to that of Little Italy, while his earlier ironic tone turns darkly satirical in every instance of WASP individualism and its success ethic. Only in his most recent work does Scorsese, now very much a New York success story himself, suggest a new stage marked by the ambivalence of ethnic double vision.

Boyhood in Little Italy

When Scorsese was growing up in Little Italy, Irish priests and nuns ran the local parish. St. Patrick's Old Church was an institution left over from when the neighborhood was mostly Irish immigrants and saloons. By the 1950s, the neighborhood had been transformed into a tight Italian-American community, where the Catholic Church was still a stabilizing social force, especially for Scorsese's family. At age eight, Scorsese moved with his parents and brother from Queens to Little Italy. Only then did he begin to pick up Catholic ideas from the instructors at St. Patrick's School (Scorsese 1986a). Today, he still vividly remembers the Church's presence.

> The Sisters of Mercy were Irish nuns with Irish brogues, which was very interesting in an Italian area. The area was originally Irish. So, for some reason the Church kept sending Irish nuns there even though it had changed to Italians. No Irish at all. . . . I became aware of the Catholic Church, nuns' trappings, and ritual. (1986a)

Over time, Scorsese realized that the Irish-founded parish, with its robust institutionalism, had brought order to his early family life.

> The thing about the nuns who taught us, they made us aware of a sense of order in the world, a sense of purpose of what we were supposed to do. And having moved from Corona, Queens to Elizabeth St. in Little Italy was quite a traumatic thing for certain personal reasons. I don't quite understand to this day why my family had to move. [But] we had to get out of Corona. For some reason, we had to live with my grandmother on Elizabeth St. until we got rooms of our own. So it was like a very big thing in the family that had happened, and there was no sense of order; there was a sense of chaos. And out of this chaos came the Church. (1986a)

The Church and its visual rituals gave Scorsese a new sense of order. Similarly, in his early films he often confronts social chaos by turning to religion and rituals of social rebirth to anchor his Italian-American values.

Scorsese's sense of lasting values is rooted in Irish as well as Italian culture. The Irish played a key role for the youth in Little Italy, Scorsese says.

> The Italian-Irish thing is very interesting in the sense that where I came from was an Irish neighborhood, and Italians took over. . . . there was an incredible amount of respect on the part of the third generation of Italians for, let's say, the films of John Ford. Anything to do with the Irish—Irish poetry, *anything*. We felt a great deal of fascination, even obsession, with Irish history because of the Catholicism and because of the family structure. (Occhiogrosso 1987, 96)

The Irish nuns at St. Patrick's were a mixed blessing. Strict ones like Sister Gertrude, whom Scorsese still recalls, taught that the road to salvation is paved by decisions of conscience (Scorsese 1986a). These decisions determine whether one goes to heaven or burns for eternity in hell. The nuns also stressed the painful self-sacrifice needed down the long road to Calvary and salvation. Poor Italian-American children had no trouble appreciating the worth of self-sacrifice; after all, their parents worked long hours at physically demanding jobs to support the family.

Besides the nuns, there was a young parish priest who shaped Scorsese's life. Blessed with a vibrant personality, he befriended the local boys and talked to them about music, acting, and especially the movies. The young priest, Scorsese says, provided him with his first role model of a man in the arts.

> Anyway, this one priest, who was a neighborhood priest, was very much involved in modern culture and played us classical music and talked about certain kinds of films and certain kinds of acting. He became very much of a role model for me. I liked him a lot. I wanted to be like him, and that sort of thing. . . .
>
> When I saw the priest, I liked him, a lot. I liked his ideas. He would make fun of—"Sure you like that kind of music, but listen to this." But with him, rock-and-roll happened, for him, "I hate it, I hate it. Listen to this." Then he plays a symphony. "Yeah, that's good too," we'd say. So he's a very important formula in my life *right now*. (1986a [italics mine])

The cultured priest was someone whom a boy with a quick mind and a keen interest in the movies could easily emulate. When Scorsese finished grammar school, he decided to enter a minor seminary, a school for boys seriously considering the priesthood. When Scorsese talks now about those days, he does not attribute his interest in the priesthood to the young parish priest, whom he associates only with the arts. He gives the credit for his vocational feeling instead to the nuns, while noting the few opportunities open to a boy from Elizabeth Street.

> There were no options [in Little Italy]. And here [in the Church], at least you had a sense of, "Maybe if I could be like these people and grow into this, then maybe what is really important —what they are telling me and I believe it—is not when you're living but when you're dead is what's important. That when you die, where you, where your soul goes, that's what's really important. Then I might be able to have an inside track, some sort of an edge in the sense that the average person has to for salvation of his soul." (1986a)

Scorsese's idea of an "inside track" betrays the pervasive influence of the Anglo-American success ethic, as filtered through Irish nuns.

Scorsese's idea of religion was to match the strong personalism of Italian-American culture with Anglo-American individualism. This deeply personal sense of religion was quite different from Irish or Roman institutionalism, which stresses the Sunday obligation to attend mass.

> And then the idea was also to be living the good life, which is living a life of practicing the tenets of Christianity. . . . Let's get down to basics here: Basic is love. Not hate, not retribution, not revenge. Love. And here, with the Church. I love to start from one again, and to have people understand how to lead one's life through love, rather than making mass on Sunday, making that important.
>
> I understand what they say about the action, I understand that point of view: [Because of] the action of going to that mass on Sunday, and being there, and being fed the party line of the Church coming through one man, the Pope, who is assigned by God, you will have an inside line. But not when you go home, not when you're in the street, not when you're on the film set. . . . That's the religious thing that came out [in my attraction to the priesthood], more so than the priest. (1986a)

Scorsese draws several crucial distinctions. First, he separates routine, uncritical church attendance from Christian ideals like love. In his adult years, he has cast off his earlier notion of having "an inside track," if that means unthinking obedience to Church laws; the Irish-American institutionalism that once attracted Scorsese eventually repulsed him. The Church, in his opinion, values attendance at mass more than it does a basic all-pervading love. Scorsese, like many Catholic theologians today, begins with divine love as an integral part of people's lives, including on a film set.* In his films, introspective characters likewise struggle to figure out love's meaning as a sacrament of the streets.

While condemning Irish-American institutionalism, Scorsese's words surprisingly echo Irish rhetoric: The metaphor "inside track," adopted originally from horse-racing, suggests an Irish influence and perhaps echoes early catechism classes. The American idea of success helped Irish nuns get across to tough Lower East Side kids the ideal of working for salvation. In his films, Scorsese repeatedly takes up success stories about a man with a strong conscience who tries to work out love in the streets.

Scorsese was asked to leave the minor seminary because he could not concentrate on his studies. He had fallen for a girl.

I went to the minor seminary when I was thirteen, and I really fully intended to be a priest, but then I fell in love with this girl who was fourteen, who was going to another school. There was no sex, but people said this is what it is. You have to see women. You have to understand that if you don't have a vocation, you don't have a vocation. But part of it is getting attracted to girls and that sort of thing. What I did, though, is I concentrated so much, became so obsessed with the young lady, I think, that I rolled all the class work, and I finally got thrown out because my grades were so low. (1986a)

A teenager's ordinary sex drive quickly became a major problem in a seminary, where Irish-American prohibitions against sex prevailed. But after Scorsese transferred to the local Catholic high school, his studies greatly improved (Scorsese 1986a). Years later, when he directed *Boxcar Bertha* (1972), he would look closely at women's identity.

In 1975, Scorsese's first marriage ended in divorce and he became

---

*See also Lawrence Cunningham's description of "Sacramentality and Life" for a Catholic sense of commitment to religion in everyday life (1987, 95).

estranged from the Church. Today, he calls himself a Catholic layman who strives for the Italian-American ideal of St. Francis of Assisi.

> In my films, my theme is how you live, how an average person, not a person as extreme as, say, St. Francis, how an average person can live a saintly existence. "Saintly" meaning, again, practicing the tenets of Christian love in my work. Now you can do it in the office, now you can do it on the set. And this I think, since I couldn't be a priest, since I changed my mind, since all of that, then what is the layman? Outcast, dispersed? No, you have to go through the Church.
>
> Well, wait a second. What if you don't necessarily agree with everything the Church is saying. There still has to be a church between you and God. Maybe utilize that. . . . In other words, you can't just say St. Francis was the greatest and we're nothing. No. We still exist; therefore, there must be a road for us to follow, for the layman to follow, the Catholic layman. (1986a)

As a filmmaker, Scorsese hopes that his intense focus on characters' inner lives will show a radically Christian aesthetic with a sacramental vision of everyday life. In defending this religious vision, Scorsese is quick to criticize autocratic institutions that cannot, in his opinion, look beyond their initial purpose of social order. He has likewise been critical of his ethnic heritage.

The Italian-American Family on Set

Working closely with family and friends was a hallmark of Scorsese's early urban films. (He has spent all but a few years of his life in New York City.) His rudimentary attempt at filmmaking in high school, *Vesuvius VII*, spoofed Anglo-American culture in an Italian-American context. The brief film is an Italian-American parody of the television show *Surfside 6*, featuring Scorsese's buddies in makeshift togas (Kelly 1980, 38). For *It's Not Just You, Murray!*, his 1964 parody of a small-time hood, Scorsese commandeered neighborhood streets and his parents' apartment. And his father helped finance the project, while his mother organized production materials. As his father later fondly recalled, "Those two, mother and son, working together" (Kelly 1980, 104–5). Scorsese eventually gave his mother walk-on parts in several films, including big-time projects like *Taxi Driver* and *New York, New York* (in a scene later cut). *Italianamerican* (1975) was a short documentary of the Scorseses in their apartment.

Mrs. Scorsese is the talkative, outgoing one in the family, and

she regularly attends the openings of her son's films, alone if necessary. Mr. Scorsese, a clothes presser, is more retiring in public. On
the opening night of *Italianamerican*, he preferred to greet friends in
the theater lobby rather than watch himself on screen. In 1985, at
his son's request, he screened a troublesome ending for *After Hours*,
along with professionals like Steven Spielberg and Michael Powell
(Scorsese 1986a).

Whenever Scorsese talks about his Italian-American family, it
seems inseparable from his style of moviemaking. As in Frank Capra's
films, the family atmosphere on set gets into the movie. "I think [a
family atmosphere is] probably it," he says. "I think it's probably the
only thing. Maybe some of that feeling comes out on the screen"
(1986a).

Scorsese also strongly agrees with Capra's idea of a family-
oriented approach to filmmaking, with the director as the final authority. While Scorsese gives full credit to others' for their input, he
places all final responsibility on his own shoulders. This approach is
close to Capra's idea of "one man, one film."

> You have a collaborative effort. I don't believe literally that every
> detail is one man. You hire people, you work it out. You get
> other people to get your mind going. You get other people to
> keep constantly questioning you to make you think further. You
> work collaboratively with these actors. You work collaboratively
> with writers. In the final analysis when you peel it all away, you
> have got to say—it's work that I did. Nobody else. (1986a)

On set, Scorsese carefully guards an atmosphere of familial intimacy.
"If there's too many people on the set, I don't like it," he says. "I just
like to have it private. It's very intimate, yes. And then when you're
doing a big scene, you have a lot of fun. But that's big scenes, and I
usually have the assistant directors work for me then." Otherwise, "I
like to be out of the limelight as much as possible when directing, so
that nobody knows, nobody can see what I'm doing" (Kelly 1980, 23,
26). (For his 1985 cameo appearance in *After Hours*, Scorsese briefly
appeared as a lighting technician on a catwalk above the actors.) Privacy and personal rapport are of chief importance on Scorsese's set.
Even though he works closely beforehand with writers, he frequently
re-works a script with his actors, hoping to capture the best moments
of improvisation. "I do a great, great deal of rewriting, a great deal
of it. Usually with the actors" (Kelly 1980, 22). This accounts for the
spontaneity and naturalness of performances in Scorsese's films.

Scorsese first learned how to get close to actors while working with Robert DeNiro. Together on set, the two men created a special electricity, said filmmaker Michael Powell. "To see this quicksilver genius work with Bob DeNiro is a breathless business. They have worked together so closely and so long that they can almost be said to have invented each other. Martin's thoughts becomes Bob's actions. The dialogue becomes dense and taut, the looks and gestures are subliminal. . . . Visual and verbal points are made with rapier-like touches" (Kelly 1980, 1). About his long history with DeNiro, a working relationship that has deepened over the years, Scorsese says:

> With me and DeNiro, it was a very special situation because we kind of grew together in each picture. And we kind of lost trust, and gained trust, and gained trust, and lost trust and gained trust, until in the final analysis we were almost like secondhand dialect. We would say, "Listen, do one this way." Then he'd come over to me, "Listen, I got an idea." And I'd say, "Great, don't even tell me. Shoot, shoot, let's shoot." It was exciting, like playing a game: Like kids, you want to see what he is going to do. Then we get other actors involved with that, the actors and actresses, and you get the cameraman excited about it. That's fun. (1986a)

After a childhood cooped up indoors, Scorsese was finally out in the street having fun. Of course *fun* here means concentrating on the dramatic moment and paying close attention to each interaction. It also means developing trust in the other guy's ideas. Ideally, the emotional spark between actors and Scorsese should catch everyone else's interest. For this reason, Scorsese, like John Ford and Frank Capra before him, tried for many years to maintain a stock company of familiar faces: Murray Moston, George Memoli, Barry Primus, Bill Minkin, and Steven Prince.

Scorsese very much values actors' input as an important part of Italian personalism on set. He remembers well, for example, the quick give-and-take during the filming of *Mean Streets*.

> It was totally planned, the film. We had it completely planned out. Every shot was drawn. But we still allowed for improvisation from within. And with that sort of thing—Harvey Keitel, DeNiro, David Provall, Richard Romanus, Amy Robinson—we all worked together. In a way, we had to at times do some of the directing right in front of the crew. (1986a)

When Scorsese found solid financial backing for later projects, he had to fit his highly personal, interactive style of directing to a much larger crew. For his film starring Ellen Burstyn, he again improvised.

> But when you got to a situation where I had a little more space, a little bigger budget, like on *Alice Doesn't Live Here Anymore*, which is another $500,000 I had, we were able to rehearse privately and shoot the film away from any producers watching, by shooting in Tucson, Arizona. I would always rehearse without the crew on the set and with the actors alone. And this way we could make our mistakes and do our things by ourselves and not feel embarrassed. (1986a)

An Italian-American director who worries about actors feeling embarrassed on set is an artist who believes in filmmaking as familial creativity.

When a project required huge crowd scenes and downtown sets, Scorsese took firm measures to protect family intimacy. "In *New York, New York* everybody was all over us. We had sound stages, people waiting, the whole thing. So eventually we went into the rooms and worked. And then we came out when we were prepared. It's a hard thing to do. I find it's a little embarrassing at times" (1986a).

Occasionally, an actor prefers to remain separate from the family on set. For *The King of Comedy* (1983), Jerry Lewis asked to be treated just as a reliable professional. Scorsese recalls vividly the emotional situation.

> [A family atmosphere] makes me feel good. . . . And then sometimes you get a person who comes in who's a total professional and doesn't want to. . . . Jerry Lewis was very much that way in *The King of Comedy*. He said, "Hey, I'm the total pro." And he was great that way. You didn't have to feel that if you . . . in that family atmosphere that he always had to be included or his feelings would be hurt or something. In a sense, he was very, very good that way because the family atmosphere he was coming into was between me and DeNiro, and that had already been five films. I guess with four films prior to that, no way he could compete with that *in terms of filming* [italics mine]. But what he did was as a pro he would come in, come out. (1986a)

Like Frank Capra, Scorsese believes in the tolerant perspective of an open family, with compassion for anyone whose feelings might be hurt. It is this careful attention to family feelings that protects the family atmosphere "in terms of filming."

Once Scorsese has finished a scene on set and begins to edit, he continues to think of the project in communal terms. On the one hand, he believes that his editing, perhaps more than any other aspect of filmmaking, reflects a personal style. "My rhythm and pacing [as an editor] reflect the way I think and talk and move" (Flatley, 1976, 42). But seated at his editing table, he also sees himself as mediating between his family of actors and the filmic story.

> I guess it is like a benevolent despot. By the end of it, [the actors and crew] gave you so many ideas that finally I'm the one who is going to be stuck with the final print and the final cut. They say, "well, whatever, Marty. You try it this way, drop that scene, maybe that will help you. Whatever you want to do. If you don't like it, call me, let me know. Just let me know, what you are going to do." That's all. There's never any, "You do this or I'll. . . ." Never. (1986a)

Scorsese knows his actors and they trust their Italian-American director.

Doing Penance in the Streets

Scorsese's films set in Little Italy are a changing portrait of the filmmaker as a young man. In his neighborhood, he grew from a clever and playful satirist to a young professional deeply concerned about the forces that tear apart a familial community. Scorsese's protagonists, for example, struggle with intense feelings tangled up with Irish notions of penance and Italian ideas of family responsibility. Given as well conflicting stereotypes of ethnic and WASP women, the road to salvation is indeed rocky for Scorsese's morally sensitive, self-sacrificing, and deeply confused young men.

Scorsese is quite frank about the pervasive influence of Catholicism in his life and work. "It always will [be there]," he says. "In every piece, in every work I do, even in the way I act" (Scorsese 1975c, 14). Sacramentality appears in his films not just in intimate close-ups of holy statues, but also in lively color shots of church festivals; public rituals of community are as sacramental for Scorsese as traditional church icons. Scorsese views his work as part of a popular religious tradition in which sacramental symbolism is an integral part of everyday life.

An early film like *Mean Streets* (1972) pictures young fellows at a neighborhood bar, as they jokingly use sacramental actions like a priest's ritual blessing. The comic scene recalled to Scorsese, after the fact, an early scene in James Joyce's *Ulysees*.

What I liked about the Joyce thing, maybe nothing original to put into a movie or whatever, but it was original to me . . . was these guys living in this tower. They had Catholicism just the way we had it in our daily life. And they can make fun of it, and still have a kind of attraction to it the way we had. Here's a guy with a bowl of shaving cream, saying "Ad altare Dei." And here we are, we do it all the time, blessing things and fooling around. I wanted to put that in movies. (1986a)

For Scorsese's Italian-American youths, sacraments are both intimately familiar signs and a fading part of childhood.

Quotidian life in Little Italy also includes individual acts of violence and much community anger. Scorsese has long had to struggle with these problems as part of the self-destructive character of third-generation Italian Americans. To begin with, this generation must come to terms with their elders, men who in Scorsese's films regularly advance their own interests instead of serving as selfless mediators in community disputes. Sometimes, Scorsese portrays this destructive patriarchy as young men who gradually destroy themselves while trying to fit their ethnic family values to the Anglo-American success ethic.

On a more positive note, Scorsese's ethnic background afforded him an ideal of social action, as embodied by St. Francis of Assisi. Commenting on a reference to St. Francis in *Mean Streets*, Scorsese describes the social path to sainthood.

[St. Francis] "has it all down" in the sense that he actually had a communication, an inside track. Now we don't know what Francis of Assisi went through in the Crusades. I can imagine he was just as ruthless and criminal as all the others were. But when he came back, whatever happened to him, he was able then to live his life on a basic level in which he had communication with God. He had communication with animals, communication with Nature. One of the best films ever made was about St. Francis of Assisi, *Flowers of St. Francis* by Rossellini. There is this wonderful scene where a leper is going by at night, and he just looks at the leper, and then he goes up to the leper and stops him, embraces him, cries. Leper looks at him. Leper goes on, goes away. That amount of love and actually applying it day by day, and actually shedding all possessions. And living without possessions, living without money, that's the way to go. (1986a)

Scorsese raises again his ideal of a fundamental love. St. Francis adopted a primitive life-style that allowed him to feel, in the passionate way of Italian Catholicism, close to nature and to human suffering. In the streets of Little Italy, Scorsese envisioned a similarly primitive setting for compassionate love and a direct relationship with God. Describing the fighter Jake LaMotta in *Raging Bull*, Scorsese said,

The thing that fascinates me about it is that [LaMotta is] on a higher spiritual level, in a way, as a fighter. He works on an almost primitive level, almost an animal level. And therefore he must think in a different way, he must be aware of certain things spiritually that we aren't, because our minds are too cluttered with intellectual ideas and too much emotionalism. And because he's on that animalistic level, he may be closer to pure spirit. Which means that maybe animals are closer to God than we are. It could be. At least, those are some of the things I've been thinking. That's the idea around the film, and that's what I like about it—that, and the idea of being born again. (Kelly 1980, 32)

By striving to recover his sense of the primitive, as opposed to both the intellect and the emotions, Scorsese charts a course of rebirth for his protagonists.

The early films in Little Italy on the whole reflect the startling growth of an Italian-American talent. In these uneven yet still riveting works, Scorsese the Italian ironist spoofs both the small-time ethnic hood, who boasts of his all-American success, and the self-absorbed young artist. After these social stereotypes, Scorsese undertook an ambitious Italian-American trilogy rooted in religion, starting with a film treatment of a bright, sensitive Catholic boy on retreat. Following this adolescent drama of conflicted religious ideals, Scorsese tried his hand at a traditional ethnic romance (Italian boy meets WASP girl), while continuing to explore the issue of a critical religious conscience. In *Mean Streets*, the concluding segment of his trilogy, Scorsese examined closely men's sexual stereotypes and discovered the root source of Italian youths' anger and violence: a rigid Italian patriarchy that controls jobs and thus the opportunity to marry. In summary, Scorsese recognized conflict with ethnic patriarchy both on the streets of Little Italy and within the sensitive conscience of his young male protagonist.

In 1963, Scorsese, still an undergraduate at New York University, began the first in a series of autobiographical films. *What's a Nice Girl Like You Doing in a Place Like This?* is the story of Harry, a young urban writer who, like St. Augustine, has decided to write his life's confessions. But Harry cannot seem to write, sleep, or eat because he is obsessed with one of his wife's paintings, a seascape of waves to which he feels deeply drawn. Neither advice from an analyst nor counsel from an Italian elder in dark sunglasses is any help. In the end, Harry solves the boredom of urban life by withdrawing to the painting's safe world; from the small frame we hear his voice call out that ordinary "life is fraught with peril." Scorsese's playful film reflects his own concern about finding a public medium for his talents and somehow also remaining in the safe childhood world of the visual imagination.

Scorsese intended *What's a Nice Girl* to be a horror film, but in production it turned into a comedy. Its waggish tone helped parody film styles Scorsese had learned at university, adding a reflective note that made tolerable an obsessively self-absorbed Harry. The title, for instance, is a dig at an artistic young man who remains stuck in a dreary urban environment. Even Harry's marriage is conventional since, as he says in an off-hand way, he has wedded a painter as a matter of course. Harry finally hopes that by confessing the humdrum facts of his life, he will gain new freedom. But his confession only leads to more self-pity and a clichéd escape—the peaceful isolation of floating alone at sea. In this condition, he cannot write his confessions. Scorsese's later protagonists would learn to use the visual arts to work through their troubled feelings about the city.

In 1964, Scorsese drew closer to his own neighborhood by spoofing a mob underling in *It's Not Just You, Murray!* Murray, a boastful Italian-American hood, recounts his rise to prominence. Seated at a business desk with an American flag, he humbly credits his best friend Joe for the "empire" they have built together, a business that seems to show the "love of one fellow man in friendship." Several flashbacks reveal other important people in Murray's life, such as his Italian mother (Catherine Scorsese in a black shawl) who advises him to "eat good." We see Joe and Murray in their first business—producing and selling illegal gin. After police raids force the partners into organized crime, Murray brags: "All peoples, places, things have been effected by us."

Murray's story is pathetically funny because he chooses to ignore reality. As an Italian American striving for all-American success, he sees himself as a big shot, while deluding himself about failures in marriage, friendship, and even worldly experience. Despite his visions of conquest, he has never travelled farther than Staten Island, and his friend Joe is not only "like a father to his children," he probably is their biological parent. In response to these unpleasant facts of life, Murray, like the obsessed artist in Scorsese's previous film, turns a deaf ear. He adopts an escapist, self-destructive attitude: "When people bother you, abuse you, curse you, don't do nothing."

Scorsese based *It's Not Just You, Murray!* on family stories about his uncles. Shot entirely in the basements and streets of Little Italy, the film is the most visually accurate depiction of Scorsese's old neighborhood. He even knew several Sicilians named Murray (Kelly 1980, 16). The film's Fellini-esque finale, half fantasy and half documented reality, impishly parodies Italian-American life.

Once Scorsese had toyed with the filmic stereotype of the Italian-American gangster, he turned to explicit autobiography about his youth in Little Italy. Not expecting his early films ever to be widely distributed, he did not hesitate to use personal material. In 1966, he wrote the treatment for *Jerusalem, Jerusalem*, "the first part of a trilogy," he said, "that never got made. The second part was *Who's That Knocking at My Door?* and the third *Mean Streets*" (1986a). The trilogy was to be his most deeply ethnic and most explicitly religious work (Kelly 1980, 19).

Jerusalem, Jerusalem is about high school boys who leave Little Italy for a religious retreat directed by Irish-American Jesuits. Scorsese himself attended such weekend retreats while a student at St. Patrick's School (Scorsese 1986a). Only after finishing the project did he read *A Portrait of the Artist as a Young Man*. "I was eighteen. And the stories were the same. Then I read *Portrait of the Artist* after and I said, 'My God, it's the same thing'" (1986a). To capture the feeling of Italian culture in a semi-documentary style, Scorsese initially wanted to use actual clergy. "At one point, I was going to hire real priests to do it, just to let them do their own sermons" (1986a). J. R., the main character, is Scorsese's alter ego, while Bud is his childhood friend Dominic Lo Faro (Kelly 1980, 42). The following discussion of the film's plot and themes is based on excerpts from Scorsese's original film treatment (Kelly 1980, 42–56).

Scorsese's story of Catholic boyhood opens in a Chinese restaurant where J. R. and Bud joke about the way a priest consecrates wine at mass. Revealing a roguish, earthy sense of the sacramental, J. R. holds up his cup of hot tea and intones, "Introibo ad altare Dei" [I will go to the altar of God]. Later, on retreat with their friends, the boys endure Irish institutionalism in the guise of Father McMahon, who tells them the retreat's "underlying ideals, its rules, and its schedule." (In the confessional, J. R. also shows an Irish-American attitude towards sex: He euphemistically calls masturbation "self-impurities.")

Unlike his friends, J. R. is a visually and morally sensitive boy unnerved by the gruesome scenes of hell depicted by the Irish clergy. As a result, he sleeps with his light on. A puerile young man, he expects his mother to pack his favorite pair of pants. He is also highly impressionable and has a surprisingly graphic imagination. For instance, he daydreams of a contemporary crucifixion in which the police lead a young man with a cross down a city street, while his own mother stands nearby in mourning. Meanwhile, at the actual retreat, the boys begin an outdoor Stations of the Cross, the traditional liturgy of fourteen moments before and during Christ's crucifixion. As the boys progress slowly up a hillside, they sing the Marian hymn "Stabat Mater." Quick cross-cuts reveal J. R.'s imaginary version of the liturgy back in the city. In his mind's eye he pictures a "young man's hands with thick spikes through the wrists. The blood shoots out." At the same time, a voice recites traditional prayers about Mary's feelings at the foot of the cross.

Scorsese shifts from somber religious images of suffering, self-sacrifice, and Marian devotion to J. R. and Bud on a hilltop, where they view the surrounding countryside. The two Catholic boys immediately think of Nature as a sacrament created by God, and they argue whether God should be considered an artist. The importance of a legalistic conscience for Irish Americans surfaces when the boys hear a sermon that ends with a dire warning not to "go all the way" before matrimony. With fearful references to sexuality, the preacher focuses intensely on the threat of hell in a parable about a modern couple who die suddenly in an accident, after yielding to sex a week before marriage. The cynical boys in the pews either ignore or lambast the parable, except for the sensitive J. R.

After J. R.'s return home, Scorsese concludes on a joyful, hopeful note about religion in the hands of a young artist-to-be: In his small bedroom, J. R. looks over a prayer manual and then goes to sleep as "music bursts in—glorious and beautiful." Scorsese's self-tailored treatment included Italian religious symbols like a Pietà, a Mater Dolorosa, and a Shrine of the Sacred Heart; and the film ends with a Jesuit dedication, "For the Greater Glory of God" (*Ad majorem dei gloriam*).

As the religious biography of an emerging artist, the film treatment carefully explores J. R.'s vision of the Stations of the Cross. In his empathic imagination, he quickly translates age-old liturgy and symbols into a contemporary idiom, stressing a son's self-sacrifice and a mother's devotion. Religious solace, moreover, is available in the form of Marian intercession: "O Jesus, by the compassion which Thou didst feel for Thy Mother, have compassion on me and give me a share in her intercession." Scorsese next investigated Marian psychology in great detail. The priest reads to the boys,

> "Later Joseph of Arimathea and Nicodemus take the Body of [Mary's] Divine Son from the cross and deposit it in her arms." The boys answer, "O Mary, Mother of Jesus, whose grief was boundless as an ocean that hath no limits, give me a share in thy sorrow over the sufferings of thy Son, and have compassion on my infirmities. Accept me, with the beloved disciple, as thy child. Show thyself a mother unto us; and may the Divine Son, through thee, receive our prayers." (Kelly 1980, 51)

Marian veneration here is in three stages. First, the boys concentrate on Mary's suffering. Second, they hope that by understanding her pain they will draw closer to her Son. And third, they ask pity from Mary as they would from their own mother. In Scorsese's later films, his proud male protagonists undergo suffering and often feel hope, but rarely ask for pity or understanding. Because of the American success ethic, each believes he can make it on his own.

Scorsese's ending counters earnest Irish instruction with an Italian-American sense of joyful, sacramental art. "Here something negative has happened," Scorsese later said, "and yet there's a sense of celebration about it" (1986a). The music celebrates a young man's struggle to find himself. Like the boys surveying the countryside from the last station of the cross, the ending focuses on the joyful side of religion for boys raised by mothers as warm and caring as Mother Mary.

By the mid-1970s, Scorsese had stopped attending mass regularly and was in a period of transition. And he was no longer, he said, "a political virgin" (Occhiogrosso 1987, 100). Before he continued his Italian-American trilogy, he directed *The Big Shave* (1967), a violent surreal short and the most intensely personal, angry film in his canon. The brief film, he said, reflects the terrible impact of the Vietnam War (Kelly 1980, 197). Yet, except for a reference to Vietnam tagged on to the credits, the film has no overtly political content. It simply, directly expresses an Italian young man's basic feelings about his masculine identity.

At first, *The Big Shave* seems a bizarre experiment, a surreal performance without words. After a mellow jazz trumpet simmers on the soundtrack, a young man enters a small white-tiled bathroom where he repeatedly removes his t-shirt, an Eisenstein-like montage that quickly builds filmic tension. Once he begins to shave, areas of his face appear in extreme close-ups in the bathroom mirror. Then, slowly and methodically, he gouges his cheeks and neck with his razor, ending with a firm sweep across his neck. The shockingly visceral scene closes with a medium shot of blood trickling onto the man's chest and into the sink.

Scorsese's drama of self-confrontation speaks brutally through actions, music, and camera positioning. If at first the young man enjoys the male ritual of shaving, the mirror image of his body triggers a self-destructive impulse that culminates in the violent destruction of that image. (Throughout the shave, the camera focuses only on the young man's mirror image.) By cutting himself, or rather, his conventional male image of himself, the young man exposes his rage towards conventional male identity.

Scorsese has hinted at the very personal roots of the film: "It grew out of feelings about Vietnam. Consciously, it was an angry outcry against the war. But in reality, something else was going on inside me, I think, which really had nothing to do with the war" (Kelly 1980, 197). More recently, Scorsese has said that the film's anger "has to do with my whole makeup and, I guess, the kind of person I am" (1986a).

Whatever the source of this psychodrama, its dramatic elements reappear often in the angry moments of later works, often during celebratory male rituals that typically isolate young men and lead to scenes of self-destruction. Yet, by purging both themselves and society through violence, Scorsese's protagonists serve a social function.

Violence has several sources in Italian-American male identity. In Scorsese's Little Italy, an established patriarchy oppresses the community, forcing young men to take desperate action. For example, in *Mean Streets* young men's rage is implicitly a response to male elders who tightly control the ownership of small businesses and thus the chance to marry. A second source of violent emotions is Irish-American prohibition towards sex. Scorsese's protagonists, in the latter segments of his trilogy, are repeatedly anxious about sex with a virtuous woman. The implicit conflict between Italian-American sensuality and Irish-American self-denial explains why J. R. is so troubled, and why he leaves his light on all night.

Who's That Knocking at Your Door?, the second part of Scorsese's trilogy, continues the story of J. R., now a young man in love with a non-Italian from outside the neighborhood. Originally titled Bring on the Dancing Girls in 1965 and then I Call First in 1967, Who's That Knocking was released in 1969 as a documentary-like portrayal of life in Little Italy, with a special focus on J. R.'s confused ideas of women and religion.

As the film opens, Little Italy is a distinctive blend of affectionate motherhood and street violence. An Italian immigrant mother, played by Catherine Scorsese, serves homemade bread to several obedient children, while a statue of the Blessed Virgin Mary, highlighted in several extreme close-ups, stands nearby. Out in the street, a young man, perhaps played by Scorsese himself, makes the sign of the cross, kisses a holy medal around his neck, and then lets five punks beat him with sticks. J. R., like Murray the hood, believes in taking life's licks, though this time with an explicit, if ambiguous religious angle. The beating dramatizes, in effect, what it must feel like for a sensitive youth to grow up with urban violence. Scorsese next generalizes this idea of Little Italy, cutting from the beating to a local butcher whacking a slab of meat. But throughout these scenes, J. R. also chooses to suffer out of a confused idea of a religious conscience.

By comparison, J. R.'s friends simply endure painful moments in several all-male rituals. In a club party, young men of weak conscience rapidly lose their admirable group spirit to pride, liquor, and greed; they may pursue pleasure together with the best of intentions, but they always end by hurting one another. At another party, one fellow even threatens a drunken friend with a revolver until the victim begins to cry.

Women are of little help to Scorsese's young men, because they are exploited for money and treated either as virgins or whores. Sally Gagga shows how women are often typically treated, when he kisses a girlfriend and, at the same time, picks her purse of forty dollars. Although J. R. at first seems different, he stops his tender lovemaking with his new blonde girlfriend, as soon as he sees himself as taking advantage of a good girl. (The bedroom set, including a statue of the Madonna and Child, was Scorsese's parents' bedroom.) J. R. explains, "Call it anything you want, old-fashioned, or what. I love you first as you. To me, you know, if you love me, you'll understand what I mean." But J. R. himself does not understand what he means, though his conventional idea of the virginal girlfriend is partly explained by shots of the nearby statue.

J. R. struggles to form a coherent picture of women by coming to terms with stereotypes such as the Blessed Virgin Mary and the raped girlfriend, the easy prostitute and the nurturing Italian mother. He does not, of course, realize that he feels torn inside because of his rigid stereotyping. He just restrains himself from "going all the way," as if he still could hear from *Jerusalem, Jerusalem* Irish-American warnings about sexual intercourse. Deeply frustrated, he finally lashes out at his girlfriend when he discovers that she is not a virgin, that his Irish self-denial has been for naught.

One escape from the narrow streets and fixed habits of Little Italy is again in Nature. J. R. and his buddy Joey leave Manhattan with a non-Italian friend who shows them his rural hometown. Atop a steep, tree-covered hill, J. R. stands transfixed by the grandeur of Nature, struck as in *Jerusalem, Jerusalem* by the sacrament and artistry of God's creation. In the end, however, the trip outside the Italian community is only temporary.

When J. R. is deeply upset at home, he seeks out a priest in a confessional to think through his problems of conscience. While acknowledging his sins, he vividly recalls the past and ends with extreme close-ups of saints' wounds and Jesus's pierced side on the cross; J. R.'s failings are for him forms of self-punishment. Imaginary pop lyrics help explain the mixture of violence and conscience in his mind, a mixture that leads him to identify completely with Jesus, speaking to God the Father from the cross: "Who's that knocking at my door, all last night and the night before? Bang, Bang, Bang, I can't stand this awful pain. Who's that calling my name?" Scorsese then points emphatically to the parallel between J. R. and Christ in a graphic Italian gesture: Twice the young man kisses the feet of the crucifix in the confessional, only to discover blood on his lips.

J. R. also seeks refuge from the compassionate Marian mother, a search made difficult by his confusing admixture of female stereotypes. A whirl of flashbacks shows J. R. enjoying lusty sex with a prostitute, or obeying a kindly mother, or listening to the story of his girlfriend's rape. Finally, in the midst of J. R.'s painful confusion, the camera focuses on a statue of St. Anne (an Italian cult figure and mother of the Blessed Virgin Mary) whose hand is outstretched in pity. Likewise, an abrupt cut focuses on the large crucifix hanging over the main altar.

J. R. also expects sympathetic understanding from his pals. He prizes most not religion found in church but in the streets. Suddenly, as the film ends, J. R. is standing again outside the Pleasure Club, while a song blares the plaintive lyric, "Baby, come back to me. I love you." In terms of J. R.'s attitudes towards women, his conscience is and will remain a confused jumble of male desires and religious ideals, as long as he is unable to recognize that his girlfriend cannot be defined simply by Italian-American stereotypes.

Throughout J. R.'s torturous struggle with images of women, his faith sustains him.* Relying on the traditional Italian Way of the Cross, he works out his confused conscience. The symbolism of blood on his lips in the confessional suggests an emotional Italian spirituality and a primitive self-surrender. Given this external image of his inner pain, J. R. is able to let his distress become part of Christ's on-going suffering on the cross. Scorsese later said he regretted the shot as simply "too much," that is, as too obvious (1986a). But at least the symbolism articulated for non-Catholics the complex religious emotions of J. R.'s confession. This Christ-like young man has offered up his pain. Because of this religious emptying of the self, he is able to return to the streets. Four years later *Mean Streets* portrayed him as a nobler, slightly wiser young man.

Scorsese got his first break in West Coast filmmaking with Roger Corman, a producer known for giving inexperienced, but potentially talented directors a start in the business in exploitation films. In 1972, Corman hired Scorsese to shoot the tumultuous life of Boxcar Bertha Thompson, a simple country woman who fell in love with a railroad union man, became a common robber with him, and finally witnessed her lover literally crucified on the side of a boxcar.

Scorsese has often downplayed the significance of *Boxcar Bertha*, saying it chiefly gave him the professional experience needed to shoot *Mean Streets*. The earlier film nonetheless shows him adapting an explicitly religious, sometimes violent script to his own idea of religion. Bertha, played with a sweet, earthy quality by Barbara Hershey, is a strong woman whom men quickly desire. When she innocently raises

---

*J. R. points to one source for his attitude towards women when he refers to John Ford's *The Searchers*.

her dress to scratch her thigh, Shelly, a railroad worker and union man, lustfully watches nearby. Although she later becomes a prostitute, she retains her idealistic, maternal character and repeatedly risks her life to save Shelly. She seems, in fact, constantly in search of a man to replace the father whom she saw killed in a plane crash. She finds in Shelly an emotional, religious co-mingling of father and son types.

As a character in a brutal crucifixion narrative, Bertha most resembles Mary Magdalene, the prostitute who became a devoted follower of another strong-minded, young speechmaker. The figure of Magdalene also appears painted on the back wall of a black fundamentalist church, where the Shelly gang hides out for several days. The mural shows a woman gazing devotedly at a redeemer dressed in white robes, with a small river flowing between the two larger-than-life figures. According to Biblical tradition, Jesus first appeared to Mary Magdalene after his burial; and in black American fundamentalism, Mary Magdalene has been celebrated in spirituals such as "Is There Anybody Here like Weeping Mary?" Scorsese accidentally discovered the church mural while on location in Arkansas and used it to match both his own Italian tradition and Bertha's character with religion practiced by the socially oppressed. The painting vividly symbolizes Bertha's flowing sexual energy as a pure, larger-than-life desire to follow her (political) saviour (Scorsese 1986a).

Because the optimistic, compassionate Bertha is a Magdalene with an uncritical conscience, she cannot comprehend the violent troubles that life brings her any more than did J. R. She explains her philosophy as simply "grabbing something good when it comes by." But this easy-going conscience provides little direction to her life. Stranded in a small town, she finds herself reading a movie poster about *The Man Who Could Work Miracles* (one of Scorsese's favorite movies [Scorsese 1986a]). Hoping for a miraculous event herself, Bertha is seemingly rescued by the proprietress of the local whorehouse, who quickly puts her to work. This critical obtuseness is again apparent when Bertha flaunts her outlaw status during a holdup, in a scene where, according to Scorsese, she and the gang are clearly "going down to hell" (1986a).

The script of *Boxcar Bertha* suited Scorsese for two reasons. First, the long-suffering yet consistently upbeat Bertha displays a primitive intuition that brings out the best qualities in Shelly and her sidekick Rake. Second, Shelly has a strong social conscience, while attacking the railroad company, a mainstream figure of Anglo power. Compared to Shelly's (ethnic) conscience, Bertha's uncritical (Italian) maternal attitude leaves her, despite numerous warnings, completely unprepared for her lover's death. What fascinated Scorsese most about *Boxcar Bertha*, however, was the Italian communal ideal of a church following the example of a saviour who mingles with ordinary sinners. Shelly's gang "are outlaws hiding out in the church. The church took them in. [Jesus] hung out with pharisees and prostitutes, didn't he? They all claimed that he was a glutton and a drunkard. . . . I just think it's wonderful to have the guts to hang around with the outcasts" (1986a).

Mean Streets, the third film in Scorsese's trilogy, returned to Little Italy to portray an older version of J. R. who, like Bertha Thompson, hangs around with outcasts and watches a loved one come to a violent end. Here, however, J. R. has the critical conscience and his friend is the one with a primitive approach to life.

Scorsese felt "compulsive," he said, about working through his religious background in *Mean Streets*; the film let "a lot out of my system" (1974, 30; 1975b, 33). He wrote the script just after *Who's That Knocking at My Door?* or six years before actual production. Because of the long gestation, the project finally seemed, Scorsese said, like "a fragment of myself" (1974, 29; 1981, 53). Given twenty-four days to shoot in Los Angeles on a low budget, Scorsese said he knew "nearly to the word what the characters should say" (1974, 29; 1981, 53). He had three-quarters of the film prepared ahead of time on storyboard, though he also allowed for improvisation on set with his friend Harvey Keitel and a new actor—Robert DeNiro (Scorsese 1975b, 33). This highly personal film was, Scorsese said, his "dream project" with the loose look of a documentary (1975c, 29; 1974, 30).

Mean Streets plunges into the lives of young men in Little Italy and includes plenty of authentic touches, such as a Sicilian uncle and Italian dialects (for instance, the word "Moog" is Neapolitan). But the heart of the project, Scorsese said, "has more to do with Catholicism than with being an Italian-American" (1975, 14). Because he was so heavily involved with Catholic ritual, he said, he later deleted many references to religion from the original script *Season of the Witch* (1986a; 1975, 33).

Charlie, an older version of J. R. played by Harvey Keitel, is, Scorsese has said, an image of himself (Occhiogrosso 1987, 100). As the film opens, the rock tune "Be My Baby," which ended *Who's That Knocking at My Door?*, is heard throughout Charlie's opening scene. As the lyrics imply, Charlie has a dark-haired girlfriend who grew up in his neighborhood, and he still has trouble with women. His ethnic situation is spelled out in three intertwined plots: The ambitious young man with religious ideals wants to continue his love affair with the epileptic Teresa; he wants to save his reckless cousin Johnny Boy from loan sharks; and he wants to open a restaurant of his own.

Scorsese's essential focus on religion begins with Charlie's idea of penance in the streets. As he says in the darkened screen of Scorsese's opening, "You don't make up for your sins in church. You do it in the streets. You do it at home. The rest is bullshit and you know it." Charlie has rejected the simple Irish legalism of reciting prayers for penance; as an Italian-American, he demands a more communal approach to confession. His penance, moreover, will be heavy, as Scorsese's summary opening implies. Awakening from a dream, Charlie immediately looks in a mirror, not far from a crucifix. Like the mirror in *The Big Shave*, this is a sign of the future, self-inflicted wounds of an Italian-American young man; male identity will again be a major source of conflict for the critical conscience.

Scorsese has said he believes that (Irish-American) institutional penance is at odds with an (Italian-American) commitment to community.

> You don't make up for your sins in the church. You make up for them in the street. And the rest is bullshit and you know it. The idea is that the practicing of Christian philosophy, Christian living, has to be done in the street, not hiding out in the church. Not practice it, go inside St. Patrick's Old Cathedral, when you come outside you can act any way you want. And when you go back inside you act OK. You can't do that. You have got to do it in your daily life. And the rest, everything they [the Irish-American priests] tell you, all that business of ritual, is not the main thing. The main thing is your actions.
>
> That making up for your sins is an allusion to penance, meaning that after confession you have to go to penance. They give you ten Our Fathers and ten Hail Marys. Oh great, then I can come out and act just as bad as I want. No. The idea is you take the penance, you do it outside, you do it out in the streets, you do it with your family, you do it with your friends. You offer up, as they say, the old intentions of taking on things as penance. It's almost like making Lent all year round. That concept, it's also implied in there. What [Charlie] does is he takes in the

Johnny Boy character as a penance. But he is really doing it for his own pride. (1986a)

From the opening of *Mean Streets*, Charlie's struggle to work out a penance for himself in everyday life deeply troubles his sleep because of all the conflicting variables—his hotheaded girlfriend Teresa, his reckless cousin Johnny Boy, and the financially powerful uncle who can help him open a restaurant. Both Teresa and the uncle repeatedly tell Charlie that Johnny Boy is a walking time bomb. The uncle also disapproves of the epileptic Teresa because, according to an old Italian superstition, the source of her disease is mental illness. Thus, Charlie has taken on a lot by remaining with Teresa and accepting Johnny Boy as a penance.

Charlie's idealistic, sometimes naive religious attitudes put him at risk in his tough neighborhood. We get a glimpse of his religious upbringing, the source of his attitudes, in home movies from childhood of his First Communion. Scorsese's subsequent jump cuts to the present seem to ask, does Italian piety suit a place where a self-reliant bar owner throws a junkie into the street? Will Charlie's religious education help him to handle the intelligent but underemployed, deeply frustrated and sometimes violent Johnny Boy? In a summary shot, Charlie kneels in church to talk to God about doing penance in the streets.

Charlie is also trying to work out certain Italian-American prejudices in his idealistic conscience in a series of violent episodes and wild club parties. To begin with, Charlie, like J. R. in *Who's That Knocking at My Door?*, is struggling with stereotypes of women. One moment, he makes tender love to Teresa, and the next he calls her "a cunt." But in the end he listens carefully to his conscience: He stops visiting prostitutes in order to put more effort into his relationship with Teresa.

In Charlie's friendship with Johnny Boy, however, his conscience, touched by pride, proves self-deceptive. Asked why he hangs around with his unpredictable cousin, Charlie says, "it's a family thing, it's complicated"; like a child raised to be responsible for younger children, Charlie believes he must watch out for his grown cousin. But in truth Charlie mistreats his cousin, as if he were a pawn sent to him by God. So, the morally self-righteous Charlie attempts to lay down rules for the hell-raiser, until the quick-witted Johnny Boy spits Charlie's pride back in his face: "I'm so stupid you got to look out for me?" Charlie may have a sensitive conscience and a genuine concern for his friends, but without a much more critical attitude, he is headed for tragedy.

Charlie is basically suffering from a naive Irish conscience, with a special Italian-American twist: He believes that religious judgments must work in the streets. His friends try repeatedly to point out his naiveté. Tony tells him, "You believe anything anybody says." When Charlie shrugs off the criticism, saying, "That's my charm," Tony quickly focuses on the source of Charlie's credulity, reminding him that he believed everything told him by the priests on their high school retreat (just as did J. R. in *Jerusalem, Jerusalem*). Tony also tries to dispel Charlie's idealized view of religion as an institution. It's "a business, it's work, it's an organization," he says.

The institutional Catholicism in Charlie's life was evident in the very first church scene, in which Charlie is preoccupied with his personal unworthiness and the exact penance necessary to pay for his sins. Unlike the young J. R. in *Who's That Knocking at My Door?*, however, Charlie questions the legalistic nature of Irish-American confession. Talking to God, he says,

> [We Catholics say just before communion, "I am] not worthy to drink your blood." OK, I just come out of confession . . . priest gives me the usual ten Hail Marys, ten Our Fathers and whatever. Now, you know that next week I'm going to come back and he will just give me another ten Hail Marys and another ten Our Fathers, and you know how I feel about that shit. [Close-up of the Christ figure in a Pietà with a live rose that someone has placed in Christ's hand.]

Irish-American clergy in the 1950s emphasized the number and degree of sins, while Italian-Americans stressed a more personal style of devotion, as suggested here by the live rose. As if educated by Irish nuns, Charlie is obsessed with punishment for his sins. As he says,

> It's all bullshit except the pain, right, the pain of hell—the burn from a lighted match increased a million times, infinite. You don't fuck around with the infinite. There's no way you can do that. The pain in hell has two sides—the kind you touch with your hand, and the kind you can feel with your heart, your soul, the spiritual side. And you know, the worse of the two is the spiritual.

Charlie might as well be quoting one of the retreat sermons referred to by Tony and parodied by Scorsese in *Jerusalem, Jerusalem*.

But as an Italian-American, Charlie realizes that if his religion is to have meaning, he must carry it into his everyday life. As he says in the opening scene, "You do [penance] in the streets." So, Charlie takes the logical but fatal step of viewing his life as one long penance. On first seeing Johnny Boy walk into Tony's bar, he makes a mental note, "OK, thanks a lot, Lord, thanks for opening my eyes. You talk about penance, and you send this in through the door. But we play by your rules. Well, don't we?" Preoccupied with penance, Charlie creates a God who assigns it to sinners. According to his twisted Irish-American logic, when the faithful do not follow the rules, God sends pain into their lives to help them atone for their sins.

The flip side of extreme unworthiness is self-importance, for Charlie regards himself as a kind of unordained priest. Even his friends jokingly call him Father. During the ritual of a private all-male party, Charlie stands at the bar and parodies a priest, washing his fingers in scotch and water as would a priest just before the consecration at mass (1986a). Unfortunately, Charlie confuses his priestly role of compassionate service with lifelong penance.

At one point, Tony tries to demystify Charlie's idealism about priesthood. "Why do you let those guys [the priests] get to you?" he asks. And Charlie replies, "Because they're supposed to be guys [and he makes a hand gesture to suggest real men]." Having admired Irish priests as masculine role models in his youth, he has uncritically accepted all their teachings; he has emotionally invested in the Church as a rule-dispensing institution led by a punishing God. The scene reflects Scorsese's own childhood sense of religion, his belief in one particular priest, and his later rejection of an institutional model of the Church.

Charlie's understanding of religion seems such a tragedy because of his noble spiritual ideals, in the Italian tradition of St. Francis of Assisi. As he tells the cynical Teresa, nobody today "tries to help people. . . . [but] Francis of Assisi had it all down." Charlie's belief in significant social action is all the more meaningful, given his Italian skepticism toward words. When he tries to negotiate his penance, for example, he tells God,

> Those things [like saying ten Hail Marys for penance] don't mean anything to me. They're just words. It may be okay for the others, but it just doesn't work for me. If I do something wrong,

I just want to pay for it *my way*. So I want to do my own penance for my own sins. What do you say? [italics mine]

Charlie does indeed pay in the streets for doing it "my way." He has overlooked his own selfish motives, while dedicating himself to the priestly service of others. Even as Johnny Boy spins out of control, there remains in Charlie a noble Italian sense of self-sacrifice for community. At great cost, he sticks close to Teresa and his cousin, two of the most unwanted, angry people on the mean streets of Little Italy. The film's violent ending, as also in *Taxi Driver*, calls for an ideal sense of law and order, which Scorsese himself learned from Irish-American nuns.

Charlie is the very best that a second generation of Italian Americans has produced. In contrast to the joyful outdoor festival of first-generation Americans, their sons get drunk in local bars. In summary, like the earlier J.R., Charlie is a morally sensitive young man who thinks a lot about confession and penance. Given his Franciscan ideal of social action, he repays for his sins by trying to help his hotheaded cousin. Unfortunately, Charlie's Irish conscience also confuses his cousin with penance sent by an angry God. In the end, Charlie's priestly attempts to mediate for both his cousin and his girlfriend prove tragically self-destructive. Without a more self-critical conscience, Charlie has missed the actual source of his friends' angry behavior—a superstitious, insensitive patriarchy that has no use for either an ill young woman or a clever hellion.

Outside Little Italy with an Italian-American Conscience

When Scorsese finally took his camera outside Little Italy, he continued his series of intelligent, morally sensitive main characters who run up against an unbending, success-oriented patriarchy. Before testing himself in Manhattan, Scorsese turned to *Alice Doesn't Live Here Anymore*, which blends the personae of the protective mother and the artist looking for work outside her neighborhood. The Arizona project was a warm-up for the explosive young taxi driver in Manhattan whose (ethnic) conscience slowly builds into rage against primps and a political WASP patriarch. By comparison, the angry Italian boxer in *Raging Bull* initially lacks a critical moral faculty; when the price of mainstream success is one's family, the Italian-American ending is sure to be tragic. If a non-ethnic lacks a conscience, the fellow gets the brunt of razor-sharp Italian irony: In *The King of Comedy* Scorsese ridicules the self-absorbed Jewish comic who feels excluded by a television patriarch; in *After Hours* he roasts the hapless non-ethnic who is repeatedly manipulated by others' patriarchal agendas; and in "Life Lessons," he toys with a famous male artist who half-way understands his lack of conscience, which has led him to compulsively destructive, patriarchal behavior. In all three cases, Scorsese's protagonist is a foil for quintessential Italian virtues such as familial sympathy and sensitivity to natural beauty.

Scorsese has remained surprisingly adamant about retaining religious themes. "No, there was no hesitation [to use religious symbols in *Mean Streets*]. There still isn't any. There won't be any in the future, any hesitation, whether it's embarrassing to me or not. Because it's like a purging—it's got to be done, and you just have to be honest with yourself" (Kelly 1980, 20). As in his early work, Scorsese's later protagonists struggle with an intensely moral conscience that boils over in violence because of confused female stereotypes and an oppressive patriarchy. Although violence here initially seems only self-destructive, it often serves a priestly function of social action; a violent act allows these anti-heroes to temporarily purge society. Scorsese thus added an entirely new twist to the Catholic-oriented, Christmas story of rebirth that was so dear to Frank Capra: These sons of the late 1960s are reborn through great personal and social upheaval, typically an extreme stripdown that reveals a primitive child within.

In 1974, Scorsese focused on two earlier issues: the need to recognize women outside of Italian-American culture, and, closely related, the need to face an impersonal patriarchy. Actress Ellen Burstyn sent Scorsese the script for *Alice Doesn't Live Here Anymore* after Francis Coppola had highly recommended *Mean Streets* to her (Scorsese 1975d, 22). The script was about a woman's struggle to support herself and her young son on their way to California. Shot mostly on location in Arizona, the final film does not at first glance seem to fit Scorsese's canon. He regarded the project, however, as an opportunity for personal growth, hoping to learn more about women raised outside his own ethnic background.

[The film helped] my struggle with learning about living with women, let's say. Living with women and understanding, because they were so different from the women I grew up with . . . [who had] a whole different way of thinking. And these women, the women who made that film—Ellen Burstyn, Sandy

Weintraub who was my friend at the time, Toby Rafelson who was the production designer, Marcia Lucas who was the cutter for the film—all these women together and me. It was very interesting in the sense of, Diane Ladd working on the picture and Leila Goldoni, it was really interesting to get. I just used it as a learning experience to see how they think, to see what they think. And maybe saying it was autobiographical, that's my way of saying it's my film too. It isn't just the women. [It is] just my way of putting my own stamp—what's the word?—of possession on it. (1986a)

Scorsese has also described the time spent working with these talented women as "a form of therapy" for himself (1975a, 13). The most personal aspect of the project was improvisation with the actors, especially the long rehearsals with Ellen Burstyn before the actual shooting. "It was an interesting thing to improvise all that," Scorsese said, "and through that improvisation to really get to know a little bit about the way [women] think . . ." (1986b).

A second autobiographical side of *Alice* was the central story of a mother and son. Scorsese was hesitant to discuss this issue with me, despite the obviously strong relation between mother and son in the Italian-American family. After production, Scorsese's own mother evidently advised him about the idea of learning from women while on the job. Scorsese said,

These [actors and crew] were the women of the real world in a sense. Not the people you grow up with, one aspect of the world. That thing about the real women, it's interesting. It's not that the people that I came from are not real women. They're very real. In fact, there's not any more real than my mother. And that was the woman, those were women, that I know, that I knew. But here I was in the outside world. And I had to get to know, I thought, a little more. I just don't learn about women in three months of shooting. And she said to me, what's the matter, you don't do that. Anyway, that was the impulse there. (1986a)

Scorsese mentions his mother only in a slip of the tongue, since his relationship with her was too private for general discussion.

But when I asked Scorsese about hints of Italian-American culture in this southwestern story, he immediately thought of his childhood home and his mother.

I'll tell you about my concepts for *Alice* by example. I grew up in a very structured family life, and my mother was always having people over to the house—for coffee or this or that. So in *Alice* you have a scene where Alice's girlfriend comes over for coffee. I used that to get across a feeling of being home. That's why Alice's house is filled with so many small details—some so small as to have merely a subliminal effect. The cups have names on them: Alice, Tommy, Donald. In one scene Alice is wearing an apron with little eggplants on it—eggplants because I'm Italian. Even the kitchen curtains have eggplants on them, though you may not notice them. The point is that all that detail was good for the actors and for me and consequently for the film as well. (1975a, 13)

Scorsese took great pains to place reminders of his own ethnic past on set so that even in Arizona he would feel at home. The small images of eggplants are not so much inside jokes as evocative clues. In Italian terms, they quietly helped to create a sense of community for Scorsese and his actors. Likewise, the film helped him work out feelings about women that began with his own mother. That is not to say, of course, that there is any direct correspondence between Scorsese's mother and the woman that Ellen Burstyn wanted so much to play on screen.

Alice Doesn't Live Here Anymore is the story of a housewife whose first love is singing and who hates her life in Socorro, New Mexico. Married to an autocratic husband, a truck driver who expects her to quietly clean the house, Alice spends her days raising their son and cooking the meals. Her sense of anger runs from the present deep into her past. In the vivid red-filter of the film's opening flashback, Alice is again a little girl in Monterey, California, where she first hoped to become a singer. Her mother angrily tells her to come in from play or she will be beaten. Thus, the grown-up Alice associates her anger as a housewife with this childhood, the first time she was not allowed to sing and be herself—a musically talented woman.

In Scorsese's filmic fairy tale wishes instantly comes true. One day Alice half jokingly mentions that she wishes her husband were dead, and her desire is instantly granted. After her husband's funeral, she and her son Tommy head out on the road back to Monterey, California; and along the way she searches for work as a singer, flees a wife-beater, and finally lands a job in Tucson waiting on tables. Supported by the female camaraderie of Mel's diner, Alice tries to work out a relationship with David (Kris Kristofferson), a divorced rancher.

In the last scene, mother and son decide that Tucson may perhaps offer all that Monterey ever could.

Scorsese intended *Alice* to reflect directly on his earlier ethnic trilogy. "I wanted to make a film that was radically different from *Mean Streets* on a superficial level, but that was the same if you looked deeper into its emotions and feelings. That's where the two films are similar" (1975a, 13).

Like Teresa and Johnny Boy, Alice is an angry character in a suffocating situation. The purgative moment of violence occurs not at the story's end, as in *Mean Streets*, but at the beginning—with the abrupt dispatch of Alice's husband. Later, she sympathizes easily with other women, just as Charlie has strong ties with his buddies. Mel's diner, moreover, is a Southwest version of Tony's club, a communal watering-hole where Alice works out her relationship with her new boyfriend David.

Alice begins her journey to a new world by explaining her identity as an artist. Just as *Mean Streets* was, Scorsese said, his first musical, the songs in *Alice* are essential to the protagonist's character. Practicing for her departure some day from Socorro, Alice sings,

> When you're awake, the things you think come from the dreams you dream. Thought has wings, and lots of things are seldom what they seem. Sometimes you think you lived before all that you lived today. Things you do come back to you as though they knew the way.

These sentiments help Alice celebrate the better self she remembers when she was nineteen in Monterey, as the music, like earlier pop tunes in Little Italy, takes on a deeply personal, almost ritualistic function.

Although ethnic religious culture may be less evident than music, it helps Alice grow just as much. Especially important are subliminal associations that perhaps only Catholic audiences would register. When Flo advises Alice in Mel's back bathroom, she wears a homemade Christian cross of safety pins, which she says "holds me together," as the two women stand against a background of royal blue walls. The three associations—women, cross, and a deep royal blue—strongly suggest a subliminal Marian presence. At the time, Scorsese was not consciously aware of this association, even though he chose the bathroom's color himself (Scorsese 1986a). But when asked years later if he could think of a particular link between the scene's images of blue, women, and a cross, he immediately responded, "Mary, I never realized" (1986a). It is appropriate, then, that the final image in *Alice* is the all-providing mother, as Alice and Tommy decide to stay in Tucson.

After directing a short documentary about his parents in 1974–1975, Scorsese totally absorbed himself in another project set outside Little Italy, this time in greater Manhattan. Here he further deepened his sense of a Marian spirit in *Alice* by again studying a non-Italian woman and by picturing a protagonist who rejects patriarchy. For *Taxi Driver* Scorsese adopted Paul Schrader's Calvinist-tinted script with few changes, improvising only the scene with actor Peter Boyle (Scorsese 1976b, 7). Scorsese has nevertheless said, "it was from the beginning an intimate work that I had to make at any price" (1981, 53). The dark side of Scorsese's Irish conscience matched well with Schrader's skeptical vision of human nature. Moreover, Schrader's morally righteous protagonist suited Scorsese's longtime fascination with an intelligent, morally sensitive young man.

Travis Bickel, played by a high-strung Robert DeNiro, has both an alert critical conscience and an attraction to blonde WASP women. After service in Vietnam, Bickel drives a night taxi in New York City because he cannot sleep. Gazing through the taxi's windshield, he records on his mind's eye endless scenes of violence: He is the city's conscience. Like Capra's Jefferson Smith, he is highly critical of downtown Manhattan; and he falls for a savvy blonde woman, Betsy (Cybill Shepherd). (For an inside joke about parochial school uniforms, Scorsese dressed Shepherd in a blazer and pleated, Scotch-plaid skirt [Occhiogrosso 1987, 98]). Bickel also introduces himself to a twelve-year-old blonde prostitute named Iris (Jodie Foster), to whom he takes a protective, fatherly attitude. After he fails to assassinate Betsy's political candidate, he guns down Iris's pimp and two cohorts; for the moment, he has purged the city's conscience with primitive violence. But when his wounds heal, he returns to driving taxis and meets Betsy one last time in a brief encounter.

Bickel is indeed a restless urban conscience. Just as Charlie stared in a mirror after a bad dream in the opening of *Mean Streets*, Bickel cannot sleep after watching an urban nightmare from his taxi. He also shares Charlie's credulity, taken to a nearly psychotic extreme. Speaking of the city as if it were his own body, he says on the telephone, "Too much abuse has gone on for too long." So, he himself chooses the penance (and male ritual) of intense physical training. Finally, in a twisted version of the Capra hero, he sees himself as the people's conscience. At the same time, he regards Palantine, a New

York political patriarch, as a rival for Betsy's attention. As in *Mean Streets*, the protagonist's urge to action stems both from an Italian social conscience and from a confused idea of women.

Bickel's cathartic violence suggests not just Schrader's righteous punishment of sinners at the hands of an angry God. It matches as well Scorsese's fierce Irish anger at the sexual abuse of a young girl, which dominates here. Whereas the letter from Iris's parents stresses (Italian) familial values, Scorsese focuses mostly on Bickel's (Irish) conscience. In Bickel's final ride with Betsy, for example, he seems to drive with a relaxed demeanor, although his furtive intense eye watches her in the rear-view mirror. Scorsese later explained this fast montage. "Basically, it is like a time bomb ticking; it's going to happen again. We don't know when, we don't know where. But he will blow again. It's like he saw something in the mirror, and he said, 'what the fuck was that?' " (1986a). The explosive anger of an (Irish) conscience, with all its suppressed sexual desire and righteous defense of women, is still very much with Bickel. It is ready to lash out again and purge society. More important, Bickel's terribly isolating judgment, especially in relation to blonde women, ruins his chances for both assimilative romance and (Italian) familial community; the Irish side of Scorsese's background essentially has undermined his Italian-American values. But then, Scorsese's narrator naturally feels defensive and self-critical outside Little Italy.

After the mean streets of Manhattan, Scorsese turned to a musical about romantic assimilation and mainstream success. In *New York, New York* (1977), Irish-American Jimmy Doyle (Robert DeNiro) is another one of Scorsese's self-destructive young men, a fellow who puts his pride on the line every time he directs his band, instead of thinking first about his talented, caring wife Francine Evans (Liza Minnelli).

Scorsese's film opens with one of the great community celebrations of American history—V-J day in New York City. But by the film's last scene, Doyle and his wife have separated over his incurable envy of his wife's career; the sacrament of music has nurtured her over the years, whereas his ethnic idea of competitive success has destroyed his sense of family. Doyle, unlike Scorsese's earlier protagonists, seems unable either to follow his conscience or to confess his past mistakes. Instead, he purges his anger by hitting his pregnant wife.

It is instead Evans who has a critical conscience. Years later, after both artists have successful careers, Evans meets her ex-husband briefly in her crowded dressing room. She first sees his face in her dressing mirror, an image from her past she still finds troubling. Minutes later, she decides not to accept his invitation for a drink. Scorsese said at the time that the plot reminded him of the struggle in his own first marriage, when he too was reaching for mainstream success (1978, 2, 3). More important, the choice of an Italian-American actor for an Irish-American role allowed Scorsese to express the sort of anger that an Irish American would not typically reveal within the family. On the other hand, this stubborn Irish individualist seems incapable of Italian-style familial mediation, despite the encouragement of Minnelli's palpably warm and partly Italian visage.

The root of Italian-American anger was the impetus for Scorsese's next major feature film. *Raging Bull* (1980) had one of the longest gestations of all his films and capped ten years of work (Scorsese 1981, 53; Kelly 1980, 33). After Mardik Martin labored on the script and Paul Schrader rewrote it, Scorsese and DeNiro were still not satisfied and reworked much of the material (Scorsese 1980b, 31). To adapt the life of Jake LaMotta, the famous Italian-American boxer, Scorsese hired nonprofessional ethnic actors, such as Joe Pesci and Cathy Moriarty, and returned to his earlier documentary-like style.

Raging Bull is a linear story about a "guy attaining something and losing everything, and then redeeming himself" (Scorsese 1980b, 31). The film shows exactly what can happen to a second-generation American obsessed with success. Although LaMotta wins the middleweight championship of the world, he drives himself and his family to ruin, losing first his brother and then his wife and children.

In Scorsese's aesthetic, LaMotta favors a primitive, self-destructive style of boxing: He wears out an opponent by first letting him land solid punches, and then hitting fast and hard. LaMotta's dogged style, Scorsese said, is like a priest's vocation (1981, 57). In his private life, LaMotta is just as self-destructive: Maddened with jealousy, he believes his second wife is encouraging men to make passes; and he even accuses her of sleeping with his married brother.

LaMotta's basic reason for betraying all sense of Italian family is his pursuit of success. Even more stubborn and proud an individualist than Charlie in *Mean Streets*, LaMotta wants the boxing title without having to feel he owes anyone. In the end, he lands in a Florida jail where he beats his head against a wall, an Italian American furious about his willful pride and futile, isolating pursuit of mainstream success.

After prison, LaMotta acquires an offbeat critical conscience. As a stand-up comic in a sleazy Manhattan bar, he presents an odd, half-ethnic medley of William Shakespeare and Tennessee Williams, Rod Serling and Budd Schulberg. Although he even tries to make amends with Joey, his brother will not forgive him for having insulted him in front of his family. So, LaMotta sits alone in his dressing room, rehearsing Marlon Brando's famous speech as a washed-up boxer, "I could have been a contender. . . ."

LaMotta's primitive, self-centered character is an ironic twist on Scorsese's earlier protagonists—morally sensitive young men like J. R. and Charlie. LaMotta most resembles Johnny Boy in *Mean Streets* (also played by DeNiro), the young man who continually puts himself in destructive situations. As Joey points out to his brother, "Why don't you come down off the cross?" LaMotta sacrifices not only himself but also everyone else to his career. Lacking Scorsese's Irish conscience, he finally turns to non-Italian writers like Shakespeare and Schulberg for a critical perspective on life.

Scorsese dedicated *Raging Bull* to the late Haig Manoogian, the film professor at New York University who offered a second home to the bright student from Elizabeth Street (Scorsese 1981, 61). In a strikingly personal dedication just before the film's credits, Scorsese wrote:

> So, for the second time, (the Pharisees) summoned the man who had been blind and said: "Speak the truth before God. We know this man is a sinner." "Whether or not he is a sinner, I do not know," the man replied. "All I know is this: once I was blind and now I can see."
>
> John 9, 24–26
> *New English Bible*

> Remembering Haig P. Manoogian
> May 23, 1916–May 26, 1980
> With love and resolution, Marty.

After Scorsese's earlier idea of penance in the streets, he strove for a specifically Italian image of Christ in everyday life, someone who is a healer. This was not just a movie concept. It was a deeply personal reality for Scorsese, who associated the human side of Christ first with a parish priest and then with a university professor outside Little Italy. These mentors helped the young filmmaker by encouraging his art, one that strongly identifies with Italian characters in pursuit of success. "Jake LaMotta, at least as he appears in the film, is someone who permits me to see more clearly," Scorsese said (1981, 61 [translation mine]). *The Last Temptation* would further flesh out Scorsese's extreme idea of a human saviour.

The biblical quotation touched as well on several personal parallels between Scorsese and his protagonist. First, like LaMotta, Scorsese has struggled to succeed in an intensely competitive field. Second, as a college student, he likewise favored the works of Shakespeare and Serling. And third, like the older LaMotta, Scorsese the big-time filmmaker has felt himself grow distant from his old neighborhood.

Since *Raging Bull*, Scorsese has not turned back to Little Italy. *The King of Comedy* (1983) and *After Hours* (1985) are parodies of the Manhattan success ethic in a Jewish comic and a WASP word-processor, respectively. *The King of Comedy* skewers the entertainment industry for its adulation of success at the expense of basic (Italian) values. This fantasy satire is the story of Rupert Pupkin, a young upstart comedian who overthrows a television patriarch. Played by Robert De-Niro with a disturbing mixture of determined ambition and sheltered naiveté, the Jewish Pupkin still lives with his parents as he plans a great career in television. Obsessed with success, Pupkin invents his own make-believe audience in his parents' basement; and his dream is to host Jerry Langford's top-ranked talk show. Langford, played as a street-savvy professional by Jerry Lewis, also lives in isolation—with unlisted telephone numbers and a private country estate. After Pupkin achieves his dream in one blow by kidnaping Langford, he is sentenced to jail where he writes a book that makes him a celebrity. Pupkin's wacky talent, then, is to realize that the 1980s Anglo success ethic will reward even an urban terrorist for trying to get to the top. From Scorsese's ethnic perspective, however, Pupkin has no more familial concern for others or sense of conscience than Jake LaMotta. Once again, a bright, willful, ethnic protagonist has followed his gut instinct to success.

Critics accused Scorsese of taking black humor here too far, so he pulled back in his next project to a tone of disturbing irony. *After Hours* satirizes Paul Hackett, a mundane word-processor in New York. Like Pupkin, Hackett seems thoroughly self-absorbed and lacks basic compassion: In the film's opening scene, Hackett barely pays attention to a trainee sharing his own dream of success. At first, Hackett seems to deserve our pity as he accidentally slides into a nightmare world of manipulative women and angry homosexual

men. Hackett's fall from (WASP) grace begins when he makes a care-
less step outside his safe, self-contained world: After picking up a
new girlfriend, he ignores hints of her bizarre life-style. His lack of a
critical conscience also leads him to miss the basic similarity between
himself and the lonely people he meets, each as self-absorbed as he.
At every new encounter, he tries to use a stranger to get back to his
home in the Upper West Side, only to discover that each person has
his or her own (patriarchal) agenda. Without the compassion for little
people of a Capra protagonist, this word-processor just hacks away
at life.

The film's first scene quietly introduces the values lacking in
Hackett's life, when the young man's attention drifts to photographs
of children on a worker's desk. But Hackett, we soon learn, has no
family and chooses to live alone in a silent apartment. Even his wall
hanging pictures an empty room.

Hackett's inadequate confessions force the issue of his uncritical
conscience. He first strikes up a romance with Marcy, a sexy but flaky
and possibly kinky young woman (Rosanna Arquette). Later, through
a bizarre series of coincidences, Hackett is forced to apologize to
Marcy for having deserted her that same night. But his confession,
the climax of this story line, proves futile: He acts only under duress (a
muscular fellow threatens to pulverize him), and he soon realizes
that Marcy is dead. Hackett's next attempt at confession is both religious and ironic. After a series of disasters, he finds himself pursued
by angry vigilantes who mistake him for the neighborhood burglar.
Falling to his knees in the street, he looks up to the night sky and
complains to God, "What do you want from me? What have I done?
I'm just a word-processor, for Christ's sake." Hackett has still learned
nothing about himself and takes no responsibility for his actions. The
camera next segues to another potential saviour—a timid young man
whom Hackett begs for help, only to realize later that the fellow assumes he is a homosexual pickup. Once again, Hackett tries to take
an easy out: He phones the police who dismiss him as a nut. Finally,
he starts to confess to the patient young man. "I just wanted to leave
my apartment, maybe meet a nice girl. And now I've got to die for it?"
Hackett has still not understood his basic mistake, which is his self-
centered way of using women and men. (Scorsese has said cryptically
that the film "has a lot to do with the sexual aspects" of Catholicism
[Occhiogrosso 1987, 100]). No wiser, Hackett recognizes a familiar
female face on the street and rushes out again into the dangerous
city.

Hackett's final attempt at confession is in Club Berlin, a punk nightclub where he hides from a fierce vigilante mob. There he desperately tries to pick up a lone woman, a regular whom patrons usually ignore. Unrepentant, he lies once more. "I can't seem to find anyone to just sit with me, without yelling at me or something." Then he fatally adds, "I obviously wouldn't have approached you in this state if I wasn't intrigued." Because of his duplicity, he soon finds himself in the grip of yet another stranger's agenda: In the woman's basement apartment he encourages a motherly embrace, only to be encased in plaster of Paris. This ironically maternal care is tied, by association, to an earlier sculpted figure associated with Edvard Munch's painting "The Scream." Hackett clearly wants to scream about life's troubles, but that is not enough; without a critical conscience, he is literally stuck in a self-centered, womb-like world. By sheer luck, he is able to return to the more mundane version of that world, namely, a pleasant office where piped-in music and a computer greeting await him. But he still has not learned his lesson.

After Hours is a devastating satire of the worst fears of 1980s yuppie culture. Just as films from the first decade of this century perceived ethnics to be a dangerous mob, Hackett fears that women and gay men will turn into a threatening, uncontrollable crowd. In this way, Scorsese, by substituting SoHo for the fearful Lower East Side, expanded his Italian social vision.

Yet, Scorsese seems at times almost too clever and too distant from his characters, in effect denying Italian personalism. *The Color of Money* returned to passionately human, troubled characters who grow up close to poverty. Scorsese also showed a new interest in the Anglo man who, having succeeded in the mainstream, is looking for ways to recover his former sense of success; Scorsese, drawing closer to Coppola's ethnic double vision and to 1920s ethnic romantic comedies, sees himself both as part of established success in New York and as part of a young, up-and-coming ethnic culture. For this cultural mix, *The Color of Money* pairs together Italian-American and Anglo-American buddies, with Paul Newman reprising the role of Fast Eddie Felsen from *The Hustler*. After Felsen has retired from professional pool, he spots a potential moneymaker in Vincent Lauria, a young pool ace played by an innocent-eyed yet flaky Tom Cruise. Felsen takes the naive Lauria and his streetwise girlfriend on the road to train for a national tournament in Atlantic City. Halfway through the tour, Felsen drops out to retrain himself. In the end, Lauria has learned how to dump games for big money, while Felsen has regained his own self-confidence from the cocky young man. In effect, the buddy plot is a clever twist on the 1920s ethnic formula of the successful WASP man who teams up with an ethnic (woman) to restore his sense of Anglo success.

But Scorsese's film is not just about American success. Once the threesome are on the road, the film quickly becomes a family story: The fatherly Felsen teaches Lauria to survive in a brutally competitive world. When Lauria gives Felsen a hug to thank him for all his advice, Newman's expression of pained pleasure strikes a personal, familial note. Scorsese thus avoided the possible story-line of an older man simply reliving old victories through a young turk. Scorsese instead used the skeleton plot of a training film to show an inexperienced, incredibly naive young man acquiring a critical attitude towards his talents and himself. At first Lauria, a spokesman for 1980s youth, is convinced that only winning matters. But there are hints he is also morally sensitive: As an employee in a children's store, he pointedly tells a young couple about a cheaper but superior baby carriage. As morally alert as J. R. and as success-oriented as Paul Hackett, Lauria has both an Italian-American's drive for success and basic Catholic innocence.

Ironically, it is the non-ethnic Felsen who forcefully steers the impressionable Lauria away from his Anglo-American idea of success as winning toward a more aesthetic and deeply personal view of the game. "Pool excellence is not about being excellent," he tells the young man. "It's about becoming something." Felsen sets Lauria up for a brief beating to teach him that indiscriminate Italian compassion, what he calls "Our Lady of the Cue Ball," is not smart. But after Lauria graduates from "child care" by learning to hustle big money, he turns, in the words of Felsen's girlfriend, into "a little prick": Ignoring his friend's feelings, he brags about the championship game he dumped with Felsen. The pleasure of shrewd success has blinded Lauria, leaving his conscience barely developed. Unlike Scorsese's earlier protagonists, he has not really suffered.

Scorsese chose not to film a final pool match, mano-a-mano, between Lauria and Felsen. The focus instead is Michael Ballhaus's kinetic shots of pool as a dynamic and visually thrilling art. The film's end is not about winning but about "becoming something," as both men start life from a new position. As Felsen notes at the start of the final game, even if Lauria wins there will be many matches to come, each a challenge of character; pool builds a self-critical conscience. The film's chief short-coming is that "becoming something" may simply mean self-improvement through hard work, another form of the success ethic.

On set, Scorsese worked hard to maintain a family atmosphere. Although he could not rely on the emotional shorthand he had developed with Robert DeNiro, he cultivated a close work relationship with Newman. Scorsese later recalled,

> [I could have said] "All right, Paul, I'll shoot one cover your way." You can't do that with a new relationship. You have to battle it out all the way, until in the final analysis you say, "Listen, this scene I could shoot two or three ways. So let me do it. We have the time, let's do it." And you look in the rushes and you say, "No, no, okay, all right, we'll do it this way." It could be his way, it could be my way. But whatever way, I want to see it up on the screen. So it kind of balances out. (1986a)

Collaboration with Newman included work on the script, where the generation gap between the two men was more evident.

> The script suggestions were always with me and [screenwriter] Richard Price, or, me, Richard, and Paul Newman. And it started to shape, and do a lot of the work I did with the actor, with Paul Newman, right there in the script sessions, saying, "Yeah this," but he said, "But what about this. And I don't know, I feel something missing here." And sometimes Paul is a different generation, so I don't even know what he is talking about. So I'd say, "Well, Paul." We'd question that. We kind of look at each other. We all found a common . . . we all got to like each other that way. And it was exasperating but it worked out. It worked out very interestingly, I think. (1986a)

Trust and intimacy, Scorsese went on to say, are the basis of family atmosphere on set.

The intimacy of Scorsese's film family appealed to Newman who quickly assimilated the personal, Italian-American style. Scorsese recalled, "We had a very good time making [*The Color of Money*] in terms of that feeling comfortable with each other, because then, when you feel comfortable, you can do anything. You can make a fool of yourself. As Paul Newman keeps saying, you can drop your pants and it's okay" (1986a).

In 1973, Scorsese began raising money to film Paul Schrader's script of *The Last Temptation of Christ* (1988), another complex portrait of a protagonist who is naive, intelligent, and apparently proud.

Based on Nikos Kazantzakis's novel, the film, Scorsese said, "repre-sents my attempt to use the screen as a pulpit in a way, to get the message out about practicing the basic concepts of Christianity: to love God and to love your neighbor as yourself" (Occhiogrosso 1987, 101). He has long struggled to shoot the film, which adopts a goal as radical as its offbeat saviour. "People no longer had open lines of com-munication with churches," Scorsese said. "Maybe the film would reinstall a better open line of communication with God" (1986a).

Once again, Scorsese pictured religion in the streets, this time in Biblical Palestine. The film, a cause célèbre after church protests, has striking parallels to Scorsese's early Italian-American work, imag-ing even miracles in down-to-earth cinematography—blood and fire and a Brooklyn-accented voice-over. Kazantzakis' story virtually in-verts Scorsese's idea of the modern primitive saint: An age-old figure suffers from twentieth-century angst.

Scorsese relied heavily on Kazantzakis's novel as adapted to the screen by Paul Schrader. The novel is a highly eclectic mixture of "Henri Bergson's *élan vital* and Friedrich Nietzsche's Superman, with a strong dash of Sigmund Freud thrown in for good measure" (Greeley 1988, 1, 22). The Calvinist-raised Schrader, who first began working on the novel in 1982, included even Kazantzakis's anachro-nistic scenes of penitents flagellating themselves.

Still, the flesh-affirming sensibility of *Temptation* has numerous precedents in Scorsese's Italian Catholic canon. In *Jerusalem, Jerusa-lem*, J. R. imagines a contemporary crucifixion in which blood spurts when Roman soldiers nail Jesus's feet to the cross, a graphic detail recaptured in *Temptation* at the political prisoner's death. And Scor-sese used similar, if more subdued, images in other films: in *Who's That Knocking on My Door?*, the blood that appears on J. R.'s lip in the confessional; in *Boxcar Bertha* the crucifixion of a thief; and in *Taxi Driver*, the redemption of a magdalene.

Scorsese has long favored ethnic narratives that violently strip men to a primitive state for rebirth. In *Temptation* this psychological process takes an odd twist. Jesus suffers from terrible inner conflicts, the worst of which entails a predatory God; like J. R.'s vengeful deity in *Mean Streets*, Yahweh here repeatedly sends an invisible bird to feed on Jesus's desire for earthly existence, attacking him unawares. This gruesome dynamic between the holy and the primitive develops toward a surprisingly clever, if distracting reversal of fortunes: Jesus on the cross suddenly fantasizes he has a wife and children. This satire of a small comfortable life argues implicitly for Christian existentialism, as Scorsese translates his religious interest in the primitive into an existential struggle against routine everydayness.

Scorsese's and Kazantzakis's angst-ridden saviour could not be further from the innocent confidence of the American Catholic experience of the 1940s. John Ford, picturing a very different Christ figure in *The Fugitive*, asserted his faith in a triumphant, institutional Catholicism. Scorsese, a product of the 1960s, undercuts the institutional values of his Irish-American schooling. His post-Freudian redeemer is riddled by self-doubt and seems incapable of mediation. Preparing for the Sermon on the Mount, he agonizes aloud, "What if I say the wrong thing? What if I say the right thing?"

Once again, Scorsese has bypassed community structures in search of a primal, direct relationship with God. "One does not need an intermediary. I love the Chruch's ceremony. . . . [and yet] this is not a film taken from Christianity. It is solely a matter of restoring a face-to-face relationship with God" (Scorsese, 1988 [translation mine]). Unwittingly, Scorsese draws closer here to a Protestant tradition of direct grace and prayer than to a Catholic world of mediated grace. On the other hand, the film reverts to an earlier, sensual spirituality far from Protestant culture when an apple tree or demonic animal suddenly appears. The jarringly graphic magic suggests a Catholic, specifically Tridentine, perspective, in which the Eucharist is an event of transubstantiation. Missing in this pre-1960s view is the Eucharist as the holy bread of a Christ-centered community. Thus, Scorsese's Last Supper features an isolated shot of the Eucharistic bread, as if it existed in a nonmaterial world and separate from Palestine's political troubles.

More to the point, Scorsese's handling of Kazantzakis' ideas denies his best sense of Italian community. Although he pictures crowds that multiply like loaves and fishes in time-lapse photography, his Jesus is essentially a loner who trusts only his future betrayer. Judas and Jesus together, moreover, constitute a psychodrama as bloody and self-destructive as the lone young man in *The Big Shave*. Just as important, Scorsese's decision to pack so many events from Jesus's life into a feature-length film leaves no time for him to develop the lively male camaraderie of his early work in Little Italy.

"Life Lessons," the first third of *New York Stories* (1989), is an urbane, witty portrait of the artist (and filmmaker) as an older successful man. Big-time painter Lionel Dobie (played by Anglo-looking Nick Nolte) is faced with a three-week deadline before his annual abstract show. At the same time, he is trying to rekindle a romance with Paulette (Rosanna Arquette), his live-in ethnic assistant and a struggling, if mediocre, artist. Hounding his ex-lover to return his affections, Dobie stirs up enough anger to motivate himself artistically and produce excellent work on time.

Behind Richard Price's witty script, loosely based on Dostoyevsky's *The Gambler*, is an ethnic story of success. All the elements of a 1920s ghetto comedy are present in new guises: A well-to-do man renews his sense of success by falling in love with an ambitious ethnic woman (Paulette wears a Catholic holy medal throughout the film).

Scorsese's chief interest is, once again, the self-destructive but artistically and spiritually productive artist. Just as *The Last Temptation* ended in a Calvary with a highly imaginative fantasy, "Life Lessons" builds to an intense, painful outburst of creative energy. This is the reason why Dobie gazes up woefully at Paulette's dark bedroom window during the climactic aria from Puccini's *Turandot* (the story of a coldhearted princess who orders all her admirers to be slain). After the ethnic Paulette finally flees this and similarly patriarchal fantasies of rejection, the WASP artist triumphs once again in mainstream competition.

Dobie's tormented art also has autobiographical overtones for Scorsese. As Dobie's hand (actually that of painter Peter Gabriel) strokes color onto a large blurry canvas titled "Bridge to Nowhere," Scorsese cuts twice to a small head peaking through the grimy grays —a personal statement of Dobie's sexual anger reworked into art. Similarly, the film is about Scorsese's early internal anger with male identity, reworked here in basic cinematic media: tactile, fluid camera movement; Nestor Almendros's cinematography; Nolte's and Arquette's performances; and a savvy co-mingling of Puccini, Bob Dylan, and contemporary rock music.

All of Scorsese's recent work is still pervaded by an intensely Italian sense of natural beauty. Yet, increasingly, Scorsese seems less interested in traditional themes of family and home, decency and law and democracy. He has supplanted these earlier ethnic concerns with issues of individual achievement and self-expression in the big city. As a result, his narrators now identify not so much with young ethnics, like a flaky pool hustler or an insecure woman painter, as with older WASP professionals who are trying to maintain their creative powers.

Scorsese's identity theme as a filmmaker has arrived full circle in "Life Lessons," where Dobie's painterly figure beneath an urban bridge is another portrait of the artist. Only now he is an older man who, having crossed over to Manhattan and achieved success, has little sense of family or home. Yet, compared to Scorsese's first confessional artist who cried out from a painting, this latest voice in the New York wilderness is a more weathered and wiser man.

As otherwise ordinary Travis Bickel in Taxi Driver *(1976), Robert DeNiro not only listens to his conscience but also transforms himself into a modern primitive saint. (Museum of Modern Art/Film Stills Archive; courtesy of Columbia Pictures)*

*Griffin Dunne, the Anglo young man without a critical
conscience in* After Hours *(1985), stumbles across a
sign of his own sorry fate. (Museum of Modern Art/Film
Stills Archive; courtesy of Geffen Film Company)*

Willem Defoe, as Jesus in The Last Temptation of Christ *(1988), is an angst-ridden man of this world. (Museum of Modern Art/Film Stills Archive; courtesy of Universal City Studios)*

*Nick Nolte, as the Anglo painter Lionel Dobie in "Life
Lessons" (1989), hopes to repeat his artistic successes by
holding onto his ethnic girlfriend (Rosanna Arquette).
(Museum of Modern Art/Film Stills Archive; courtesy of
Touchstone Pictures)*

List of Films

To Save Her Soul (1909)
Riley and Schultze (1912)
The Madonna of the Storm (1913)
A Healthy Neighborhood (1913)
Tess of the Storm (1914)
Hearts Adrift (1914)
The Italian (1915)
The Eternal Grind (1916)
Poor Little Peppina (1916)
The Immigrant (1917)
A Hoosier Romance (1918)
The Hoodlum (1919)
Little Orphan Annie (1919)
Molly O' (1921)
Puppets of Fate (1921)
All Soul's Eve (1921)
Made in Heaven (1921)
Hold Your Horses (1921)
The Supreme Passion (1921)
Little Miss Hawkshaw (1921)
Diane of Star Hollow (1921)
When the Clock Struck Nine (1921)
Society Snobs (1921)
Little Italy (1921)
The Love Light (1921)
Fortune's Mask (1922)
Come on Over (1922)
The Man with Two Mothers (1922)
Head over Heels (1922)
The Scrapper (1922)
Peg O' My Heart (1922)
The White Sister (1923)
The Wages of Virtue (1924)
Conductor 1492 (1924)
The Perfect Flapper (1924)
Painted People (1924)
Flirting with Love (1924)
One of the Bravest (1925)
The Beautiful City (1925)
Irish Luck (1925)
The Man in Blue (June 1925)
Cobra (1925)
The Greatest Love of All (1925)
The Beautiful City (1925)

The Manicure Girl (1925)
Irene (1926)
Puppets (1926)
Don Juan (1926)
Rose of the Tenements (1926)
The Silver Treasure (1926)
Sea Horses (1926)
Blarney (1926)
Irene (1926)
Sweet Daddies (1926)
The Shamrock Handicap (1926)
Fighting Love (1927)
Mountains of Manhattan (1927)
Hangman's House (1928)
Smiling Irish Eyes (1929)
Clancy at the Bat (1929)
Kathleen Mavoureen (1930)
The 3 Sisters (1930)
Oh, For a Man (1930)
Mean Streets (1972)

C H A P T E R 3 : John Ford and the Landscapes of Irish America

For the most up-to-date and complete filmography of Ford's films, see Tag Gallagher's *John Ford* (1979), pp. 501–46. This is also the best book for a general overview of Ford's themes.

The Iron Horse (1924)
The Shamrock Handicap (1926)
Three Bad Men (1926)
The Blue Eagle (1926)
Mother Machree (1928)
Hangman's House (1928)
Four Sons (1928)
Riley the Cop (1928)
The Lost Patrol (1934)
The Informer (1935)
Mary of Scotland (1936)
The Plough and the Stars (1936)
The Hurricane (1937)
Wee Willie Winkie (1937)
Stagecoach (1939)
Young Mr. Lincoln (1939)
Drums Along the Mohawk (1939)

The Grapes of Wrath (1940)
The Fugitive (1947)
3 Godfathers (1949)
The Quiet Man (1952)
The Bamboo Cross (1955)
The Searchers (1956)
The Last Hurrah (1958)
7 Women (1965)

C H A P T E R   4 :   Frank Capra and His Italian Vision of America

Fultah Fisher's Boarding House (1922)
The Strong Man (1926)
For the Love of Mike (1927)
That Certain Thing (1928)
Say It with Sables (1928)
Ladies of Leisure (1930)
Platinum Blonde (1931)
The Miracle Woman (1931)
American Madness (1932)
The Bitter Tea of General Yen (1933)
Lady for a Day (1933)
It Happened One Night (1934)
Mr. Deeds Goes to Town (1936)
Lost Horizon (1937)
You Can't Take It with You (1938)
Mr. Smith Goes to Washington (1939)
Meet John Doe (1941)
Arsenic and Old Lace (1944)
It's A Wonderful Life (1946)
State of the Union (1948)
A Hole in the Head (1959)
Pocketful of Miracles (1961)

C H A P T E R   5 :   Francis Coppola and Ethnic Double Vision

Dementia 13 (1963)
You're a Big Boy Now (1967)
Finian's Rainbow (1968)
The Rain People (1969)
The Godfather (1972)
The Conversation (1974)
The Godfather, Part II (1974)
Apocalypse Now (1979)

One from the Heart (1982)
The Outsiders (1983)
Rumble Fish (1983)
The Cotton Club (1984)
Peggy Sue Got Married (1986)
Gardens of Stone (1987)
Tucker: The Man and His Dream (1988)
"Life Without Zoe," in *New York Stories* (1989)

C H A P T E R   6 : Martin Scorsese in Little Italy and Greater Manhattan

For a filmography of Scorsese's canon up to 1983, see Michael Bliss's *Martin Scorsese and Michael Cimino* (1985), pp. 269–81.

What's a Nice Girl Like You Doing in a Place Like This? (1963)
It's Not Just You, Murray! (1964)
Jerusalem, Jerusalem [treatment] (1966)
The Big Shave (1967)
Who's That Knocking at My Door? (1969)
Street Scenes (1970)
Boxcar Bertha (1972)
Mean Streets (1972)
Alice Doesn't Live Here Anymore (1974)
Italianamerican (1974–75)
Taxi Driver (1976)
New York, New York (1977)
American Boy: A Profile of Steven Prince (1978)
Raging Bull (1980)
The King of Comedy (1983)
After Hours (1985)
The Color of Money (1986)
The Last Temptation of Christ (1988)
"Life Lessons," in *New York Stories* (1989)

Selected Bibliography

Adams, Henry. [1904] 1933. *Mont-Saint-Michel and Chartres*. Boston: Houghton Mifflin.

Ahlstrom, Sidney Y. 1975. *A Religious History of the American People*. 2 vols. New York: Doubleday.

Albanese, Catherine L. 1981. *America, Religions and Religion*. Belmont, Calif.: Wadsworth.

Anderson, Lindsay. 1981. *About John Ford*. New York: McGraw-Hill.

Andrew, Dudley. 1984a. *Concepts in Film Theory*. New York: Oxford University Press.

————. 1984b. *Film in the Aura of Art*. Princeton, N.J.: Princeton University Press.

Atkinson, Clarissa W., Constance H. Buchanan, and Margaret R. Miles, eds. 1985. *Immaculate & Powerful: The Female in Sacred Image and Social Reality*. Boston: Beacon Press.

Ayfre, Amédée. 1954. *Conversions aux Images? Les Images et Dieu; Les Images et Homme*. Paris: Les Editions du Cerf.

Banner, Lois. 1983. *American Beauty*. New York: Knopf.

Barton, Josef J. 1975. *Peasants and Strangers: Italians, Rumanians, and Slovaks in an American City, 1890–1950*. Cambridge: Harvard University Press.

Bellah, Robert N., and Frederick E. Greenspahn, eds. 1987. *Uncivil Religion: Interreligious Hostility in America*. New York: Crossroad.

Bellah, Robert N., Richard Madsen, William M. Sullivan, Ann Swidler, and Steven M. Tipton, eds. 1985. *Habits of the Heart: Individualism and Commitment in American Life*. Berkeley, Calif.: University of California Press.

Bliss, Michael. 1985. *Martin Scorsese and Michael Cimino*. Metuchen, N.J.: Scarecrow Press.

Bock, Audie. 1979. "Zoetrope and *Apocalypse Now*." *American Film* 4 (Sept.): 55–60.

Bogdanovich, Peter. 1978. *John Ford*. Berkeley, Calif.: University of California Press.

Booth, Wayne C. 1983. *The Rhetoric of Fiction*. 2d ed. Chicago: University of Chicago Press.

Braudy, Leo. 1986. "The Sacraments of Genre: Coppola, DePalma, Scorsese." *Film Quarterly* 39: 17–31.

Braxton, Edward K. 1987. "Is There an American Catholic Church?" *America* 157 (5 December): 422–26.

Breslin, John B., ed. 1987. *The Substance of Things Hoped for: Short Fiction by Modern Catholic Authors*. New York: Doubleday.

Briggs, John W. 1978. *An Italian Passage: Immigrants to Three Cities, 1890–1930*. New Haven, Conn.: Yale University Press.

Browne, Nick, ed. 1980. "The Politics of Narrative Form: Capra's *Mr. Smith Goes to Washington*." *Wide Angle* 3 (Fall: 4–11).

———. 1981. [Issue on Frank Capra.] *Film Criticism* 5.

Bygrave, Mike and Jean Goodman. 1981. "Meet Me in Las Vegas" [on *One from the Heart* and *American Film*] 7: 38–43, 84.

Canby, Vincent. 1986. " 'Peggy Sue' Visits A Changeless Past." *New York Times*, 19 October: H21, H24.

Capra, Frank. 1971. *The Name Above the Title: An Autobiography*. New York: Macmillan.

———. 1974. Interview with George Bailey. *Take One* 4: 10–12.

———. 1977. Interview with John F. Mariani. *Focus on Film* 27: 41–47.

———. 1978a. Interview. *American Film* 4 (Oct.): 39–50.

———. 1978b. Interview. *Dialogue in Film* 4 (Oct.): 40–49.

———. 1980. Interview with Morris Dickstein. *American Film* 5 (May): 43–47.

———. 1981. Interview. *Literature/Film Quarterly* 9 (March): 189–204.

———. 1982. "America's Love Affair with Frank Capra." *American Film* 7: 46–51, 81.

Carney, Raymond. 1986. *American Vision: The Films of Frank Capra*. Cambridge: Cambridge University Press.

Caughie, John, ed. 1981. *Theories of Authorship: A Reader*. London: Routledge & Kegan Paul.

Cawelti, John G. 1965. *Apostles of the Self-Made Man: Changing Concepts of Success in America*. Chicago: University of Chicago Press.

———. 1976. *Adventure, Mystery, and Romance: Formula Stories as Art and Popular Culture*. Chicago: University of Chicago Press.

Cogley, John. 1973. *Catholic America*. New York: Doubleday.

Conrad, Joseph. 1902. *The Heart of Darkness*. Baltimore, Md.: Penguin.

Coppola, Francis Ford. 1968. "The Youth of Francis Ford Coppola, an Interview." *Film in Review* 19: 529–36.

———. 1969. "The Dangerous Age." *Films and Filming* 15: 4–8, 10.

———. 1972. "Coppola and the Godfather." *Sight and Sound* 41: 217–23.

———. 1974. Interview [on *The Conversation*]. *Filmmakers Newsletter* 7: 30–34.

———. 1975. Interview. *Playboy*, 22 July: 53–54, 56, 58, 60, 62, 64, 68, 184–85.

———. 1979a. [Biofilmography.] *Positif* 222 (Sept.): 54–56.

———. 1979b. Dialogue with Mario Puzo. *American Film* 4 (May): 33–34.

———. 1979c. Interview [on *Apocalypse Now*]. *Cahiers du Cinéma* 302: 4–23.

———. 1979d. Interview [on *Apocalypse Now*]. *Millimeter* 7 (Oct.): 136–38, 140, 142, 144, 146.

———. 1982a. Interview. *Cahiers du Cinéma*. 334/335: 42–51.

———. 1982b. Interview [on *Apocalypse Now* and *One From the Heart*]. *Positif* 262: 27–34.

———. 1983a. "Idols of the King." *Film Comment* 19: 61–75.

———. 1983b. Interview. *Cinéma* [Paris] 292 (April): 25–27.

Cordasco, Francesco and Eugene Bucchioni, eds. 1974. *The Italians: Social Backgrounds of an American Group*. Clifton, N.J.: Augustus Kelley.

Cox, Harvey. 1984. *Religion in the Secular City: Toward a Postmodern Theology*. New York: Simon and Schuster.

Cripps, Thomas. 1978. *Black Film as Genre*. Bloomington: Indiana University Press.

Cunningham, Lawrence C. 1985. *The Catholic Experience: Space, Time, Silence, Prayer, Sacraments, Story, Persons, Catholicity, Community and Expectations*. New York: Crossroad.

———. 1987. *The Catholic Faith: An Introduction*. New York: Paulist Press.

Curran, Charles E. 1982. *American Catholic Social Ethics*. Notre Dame, Ind.: University of Notre Dame Press.

Curry, Leonard. 1972. *Protestant–Catholic Relations in America: World War I through Vatican II*. Lexington, Ky.: University of Kentucky Press.

De Lauretis, Teresa. 1984. *Alice Doesn't: Feminism, Semiotics, Cinema*. Bloomington: Indiana University Press.

Dolan, Jay P. 1985. *The American Catholic Experience*. New York: Doubleday.

Dulles, Avery. 1974. *Models of the Church*. Garden City, N.Y.: Doubleday.

Eco, Umberto. 1989. "A Literary High-Wire Act." Interview with Marshall Blonsky. *New York Times Magazine*. 10 December: 42, 60, 62, 78, 79.

Eliade, Mircea. 1959. *The Sacred & the Profane: The Nature of Religion*. New York: Harcourt Brace Jovanovich.

Ellis, John Tracy. 1969. *American Catholicism*. 2d ed. Chicago: University of Chicago Press.

Erens, Patricia. 1984. *The Jew in American Cinema*. Bloomington, Ind.: Indiana University Press.

Everson, William. 1971. "Forgotten Ford." *Films on Focus* 6 (Spring): 14–17.

———. 1978. *American Silent Film*. New York: Oxford University Press.

Fitzgibbons, John. 1987. "Developmental Approaches to the Psychology of Religion." *Psychoanalytic Review* 74: 128–34.

Flatley, Guy. 1976. *New York Times*, 8 February: 34–43.

Ford, Dan. 1979. *Pappy: The Life of John Ford*. Englewood Cliffs, N.J.: Prentice-Hall.

Forsberg, Myra. 1986. " 'The Color of Money': Three Men and a Sequel." *New York Times*, 19 October: H21, H28.

Friedman, Lester D. 1982. *Hollywood's Image of the Jew*. New York: Frederick Ungar.

Gabler, Neal. 1988. *An Empire of Their Own: How the Jews Invented Hollywood*. New York: Crown Publishers.

Gallagher, Tag. 1986. *John Ford*. Berkeley, Calif.: University of California Press.

Gardner, Gerald. 1987. *The Censorship Papers: Movie Censorship Letters from the Hays Office, 1934 to 1968*. New York: Dodd, Mead.

Geertz, Clifford. 1973. *Interpretation of Cultures*. New York: Basic Books.

Getlein, Frank, and Harold C. Gardiner. 1961. *Movies, Morals and Art*. New York: Sheed and Ward.

Gilkey, Langdon. 1975. *Catholicism Confronts Modernity: A Protestant View*. New York: Seabury Press.

————. 1981. *Society and the Sacred: Toward a Theology of Culture in Decline*. New York: Crossroad Press.

Glatzer, Richard, and John Raeburn, eds. 1975. *Frank Capra: The Man and His Films*. Ann Arbor, Mich.: University of Michigan Press.

Glazer, Nathan. 1983. *Ethnic Dilemmas 1964–82*. Cambridge: Harvard University Press.

Gleason, Philip. 1979. "Confusion Compounded: The Melting Pot in the 1960s and 1970s." *Ethnicity* 6: 10–20.

————. 1982. "American Identity and Americanization," pp. 57–144 in *Concepts of Ethnicity* by William Petersen, Michael Novak, and Philip Gleason. Cambridge: Harvard University Press.

————. 1983. "Identifying Identity: A Semantic History." *Journal of American History* 69: 910–31.

Gombrich, E. H. 1969. *Art and Illusion: A Study in the Psychology of Pictorial Representation*. Princeton, N.J.: Princeton University Press.

Gordon, Mary. 1988. "'I Can't Stand Your Books: A Writer Goes Home." *New York Times*, "Book Review," 11 December: 1, 36–38.

Gordon, Milton. 1981. *America as a Multicultural Society*. Annals of the American Academy of Political and Social Sciences, no. 454.

————, and Richard Lambert. 1964. *Assimilation in American Life: The Role of Race, Religions & National Origins*. Oxford: Oxford University Press.

Greeley, Andrew. 1972a. *The Denominational Society: A Sociological Approach to Religion in America*. Glenview, Ill.: Scott, Foresman.

————, and Mary Greeley Durkin. 1984. *How to Save the Catholic Church*. New York: Viking Press.

————. 1972b. *That Most Distressful Nation: The Taming of the American Irish*. Chicago: Quadrangle Books.

————. 1977. *The Mary Myth: On the Femininity of God*. New York: Seabury Press.

————. 1985. "What Is Subsidiarity?" *America* 153 (9 November): 292–95.

————. 1988. "Blasphemy or Artistry?" [on *The Last Temptation of Christ*]. *New York Times*, 14 August: 1, 22.

Greene, Graham. 1968. *The Power and the Glory*. New York: Penguin Books.

Griffith, Mrs. D. W. 1969. *When the Movies Were Young*. New York: Dover.

Griffith, Richard. 1951. *Frank Capra*. London: British Film Institute.

Gunn, Giles. 1985. "The Literary and Cultural Study of Religion: Problems and Prospects." *Journal of the American Academy of Religion* 53: 617–32.

————. 1987. *The Culture of Criticism and the Criticism of Culture*. New York: Oxford University Press.

Halsey, William. 1980. *The Survival of American Innocence: Catholicism in an Era of Disillusionment, 1920–1940*. Notre Dame, Ind.: University of Notre Dame Press.

Handy, Robert T. 1971. *A Christian America: Protestant Hopes and Historical Realities*. New York: Oxford University Press.

Happel, Stephen, and David Tracy. 1984. *A Catholic Vision*. Philadelphia: Fortress Press.

Hellwig, Monika K. 1981. *Understanding Catholicism*. New York: Paulist Press.

Henderson, Robert M. 1970. *D. W. Griffith: The Years at Biograph*. New York: Farrar.

Hennesey, James. 1981. *American Catholics*. New York: Oxford University Press.

Henstell, Bruce, ed. 1971. "Frank Capra 'One Man—One Film.'" *Discussion #3*. American Film Institute.

Herberg, Will. 1960. *Protestant–Catholic–Jew*. Garden City, N.Y.: Doubleday.

Higham, Charles. 1973. "Directors Guild Winner: Francis Ford Coppola." *Action* 8 (May/June): 8–11.

Hollinger, David A. 1985. *In the American Province: Studies in the History and Historiography of Ideas*. Bloomington, Ind.: Indiana University Press.

Holloway, Donald. 1977. *Beyond the Image: Approaches to the Religious Dimension in the Cinema*. Geneva: World Council of Churches.

Hurley, Neil P. 1970. *Theology through Film*. New York: Harper & Row.

Hutchison, William R. 1976. *The Modernist Impulse in American Protestantism*. New York: Oxford University Press.

Johnson, Robert K. 1976. *Francis Ford Coppola*. Boston: Twayne.

Karp, Abraham J. 1962. *The Jewish Way of Life*. Englewood Cliffs, N.J.: Prentice-Hall.

Katz, Ephraim. 1979. *The Film Encyclopedia*. New York: Perigee Books.

Kazantzakis, Nikos. 1960. *The Last Temptation of Christ*. Trans. P. A. Bien. New York: Simon and Schuster.

Kelly, Mary Pat. 1980. *Martin Scorsese: The First Decade*. South Salem, N.Y.: Redgrave.

Keyser, Les, and Barbara Keyser. 1984. *Hollywood and the Catholic Church: The Image of Roman Catholicism in American Movies*. Chicago: Loyola University Press.

Kinder, Marsha. (1979/1980). "The Power of Adaptation in *Apocalypse Now*." *Film Quarterly* 33 (Winter): 12–20.

Kolker, Robert Phillip. 1980. *A Cinema of Loneliness: Penn, Kubrick, Coppola, Scorsese, Altman*. New York: Oxford University Press.

Kroh, Bill. 1984. "Coppola des studios Zoetrope aux studios Astoria" [on *Cotton Club*]. *Cahiers du Cinéma* 366 (Dec.): 4–9.

Lambert, Richard D., ed. 1960. *Religion in American Society. Annals of The American Academy of Political and Social Sciences*, no. 332.

Luhr, William, and Peter Lehman. 1977. *Authorship and Narrative in the Cinema: Issues in Contemporary Aesthetics and Criticism*. New York: Capricorn Books.

Maland, Chuck. 1980. *Frank Capra*. Boston: Twayne.

Maritain, Jacques. [1943] 1986. *Christianity and Democracy and The Rights of Man and Natural Law*. Trans. Doris C. Anson. San Francisco: Ignatius Press.

Marty, Martin. 1972. *Protestantism*. New York: Holt, Rinehart, and Winston.

Mast, Gerald. 1979. *The Comic Mind: Comedy and the Movies*. 2d ed. Chicago: University of Chicago Press.

———. *A Short History of the Movies*. 1981. 3d ed. Indianapolis, Ind.: Bobbs-Merrill.

———. *Howard Hawks, Storyteller*. 1982a. New York: Oxford University Press.

———, ed. 1982b. *The Movies in Our Midst: Documents in the Cultural History of Film in America*. Chicago: University of Chicago Press.

———, ed. and Marshall Cohen. 1985. *Film Theory and Criticism*, 3d ed. Oxford University Press: New York.

May, Henry. 1959. *The End of Innocence: a Study of the First Years of Our Own Time, 1912–1917*. New York: Knopf.

May, John and Michael Bird, eds. 1982. *Religion in Film*. Knoxville: University of Tennessee Press.

May, Lary. 1980. *Screening out the Past: The Birth of Mass Culture and the Motion Picture Industry*. Chicago: University of Chicago Press.

McBride, Joseph, and Michael Wilmington. 1974. *John Ford*. New York: Da Capo.

McBrien, Richard P. 1981. *Catholicism*. Minneapolis, Minn.: Winston Press.

Miller, Randall M., ed. 1986. *The Kaleidoscopic Lens: How Hollywood Views Ethnic Groups*. Englewood, N.J.: Prentice-Hall.

Mitchell, Thomas. 1964. "Ford on Ford." *Films in Review* 15 (June): 321–31.

Mitry, Jean. 1955. "John Ford." *Films in Review* 6: 305–9.

Monaco, James. 1979. *American Film Now: The People, The Power, The Money, The Movies*. New York: Oxford University Press.

Moore, Colleen. 1968. *Silent Star*. Garden City, N.Y.: Doubleday.

Munden, Kenneth W., ed. 1971. *The American Film Institute Catalog of Motion Picture Production in the United States, Featuring Films 1921–1930*. New York: R. K. Bowker.

Occhiogrosso, Peter. 1987. *Once a Catholic: Prominent Catholics and Ex-Catholics Reveal the Influence of the Church on Their Lives and Work*. Boston: Houghton Mifflin.

O'Flaherty, Liam. 1967. *The Informer*. New York: New American Library of World Literature.

Ong, Walter J. 1967. *The Presence of the Word: Some Prolegomena for Cultural and Religious History*. Minneapolis, Minn.: University of Minnesota Press.

Orsi, Robert Anthony. 1985. *The Madonna of 115th Street: Faith and Community in Italian Harlem, 1880–1950*. New Haven, Conn.: Yale University Press.

Palmer, James W. 1976. "*The Conversation*: Coppola's Biography of an Unborn Man." *Film Heritage* 12 (Fall): 26–32.

Parenti, Michael John. 1975. *Ethnic and Political Attitudes: A Depth Study of Italian Americans*. New York: Arno Press.

Phelps, Guy. 1975. *Film Censorship*. London: Victor Gollancz.

Pickford, Mary. 1955. *Sunshine and Shadow*. New York: Doubleday.

Poague, Leland A. 1975. *The Cinema of Frank Capra: An Approach to Film Comedy*. New York: Barnes.

Richards, Jeffrey, ed. 1971. [Issue on Frank Capra.] *Positif* 133: 1–88.

Ricoeur, Paul. 1976. *Interpretation Theory: Discourse and the Surplus of Meaning*. Fort Worth, Tex.: Texas Christian University Press.

———. 1977. *The Rule of Metaphor: Multi-disciplinary Studies of the Creation of Meaning in Language*. Trans. Robert Czerny. Toronto: University of Toronto Press.

———. 1978. "The Metaphorical Process as Cognition, Imagination, and Feeling," pp. 141–57 in *On Metaphor*, edited by Sheldon Sacks. Chicago: University of Chicago Press.

Rockett, Kevin, Luke Gibbons, and John Hill. 1988. *Cinema and Ireland*. Syracuse, N.Y.: Syracuse University Press.

Rose, Brian Geoffrey. 1980. *An Examination of Narrative Structure in Four Films of Frank Capra*. New York: Arno Press.

Roud, Richard, ed. 1980. *Cinema: A Critical Dictionary*. 2 vols. Norwich, England: Martin Seeker & Warbug.

Ruether, Rosemary Radford. 1986. "Crises and Challenges of Catholicism Today." *America* 154 (1 March): 152–58.

Scherle, Victor, and William Levy. 1977. *The Films of Frank Capra*. Secaucus, N.J.: Citadel Press.

Schrader, Paul. 1972. *Transcendental Style in Film: Ozu, Bresson, Dreyer*. Berkeley, Calif.: University of California Press.

Schumach, Murray. 1964. *The Face on the Cutting Room Floor: The Story of Movie and Television Censorship*. New York: Da Capo Press.

Scorsese, Martin. 1974. "The Filming of *Mean Streets*." *Filmmakers Newsletter* 7 (Jan.): 28–31.

———. 1975a. Interview. *Millimeter* 3 (May): 12–16.

———. 1975b. Interview and article by Paul Gardner. *Action* 10 (May–June): 30–34.

———. 1975c. "It's a Personal Thing for Me." *Film Heritage* 10 (Spring): 13–28, 36.

———. 1975d. "The Making of *Alice Doesn't Live Here Anymore*." *Filmmakers Newsletter* 8 (Mar.): 21–26.

————. 1975e. Transcript of American Film Institute Seminar. *Dialogue on Film* 4 (April).

————. 1976a. Interview with Guy Flatley. *New York Times*, 8 February: H34, 43.

————. 1976b. "Scorsese on *Taxi Driver* and Bernard Herrmann." *Focus on Film* 25 (Sum.–Aut.): 5–8.

————. 1977. Interview [on *New York, New York*]. *Image et Son* 323 (Dec.): 7080.

————. 1978. Interview [on *New York, New York*, and *The Last Waltz*]. *Positif* 213 (Dec.): 2–13.

————. 1980a. Interview [on *American Boy*]. *Positif* 229 (April): 5–10.

————. 1980b. "Martin Scorsese Fights Back." *American Film* 6 (Nov.): 30–34, 75.

————. 1981. Interview [on *Raging Bull*]. *Positif* 241 (April): 46–66.

————. 1982a. Interview with Paul Shrader. *Cahiers du Cinéma* 334/335: 6–13, 126.

————. 1982b. "Marty." *American Film* 8 (Nov.): 66–73.

————. 1983. Interview [on *King of Comedy*]. *Positif* 267 (May): 14–19.

————. 1986a. Interview with author. 14 May. Tape recording. New York, N.Y.

————. 1986b. Interview with Myra Forsberg. *New York Times*, 29 June: H19.

————. 1988. Interview with Michael Henry. *Positif* 332 (Oct.): 6–12.

Shannon, William V. 1963. *The American Irish*. New York: Macmillan.

Sharpe, Howard. 1936. "The Star Creators of Hollywood." *Photoplay* 50 (Oct.): 98–100.

Silk, Mark. 1984. "Notes on the Judeo-Christian Tradition in America." *American Quarterly* 36: 65–85.

Silverman, Kaja. 1983. *The Subject of Semiotics*. New York: Oxford University Press.

Sinclair, Andrew. 1979. *John Ford*. New York: Lorrimer.

Sklar, Robert. 1975. *Movie-Made America: A Cultural History of American Movies*. New York: Random House.

Sollors, Werner. 1986. *Beyond Ethnicity: Consent and Descent in American Society*. New York: Oxford University Press.

Stororo, Vittorio. 1979. Interview with Dean Tavoularis. *Positif* 222 (Sept.): 18–56.

Tavernier, Bertrand. 1967. "John Ford à Paris." *Positif* 82: 7–30.

Tavernier, Claudine. 1969. "La Quatrième Dimension de la Vieillesse." *Cinéma* 137 (June): 35–45.

Taves, Ann. 1986. *The Household of Faith: Roman Catholic Devotions in Mid-Nineteenth-Century America*. Notre Dame, Ind.: University of Notre Dame Press.

Teresa of Avila. 1961. *Interior Castle*. New York: Doubleday.

Tracy, David. 1981. *The Analogical Imagination: Christian Theology and the Culture of Pluralism*. New York: Crossroad.

————, and John B. Cobb, Jr. 1983. *Talking about God: Doing Theology in the Context of Modern Pluralism*. New York: Seabury Press.

Turner, Dennis. 1985. "The Subject of *The Conversation*." *Cinema Journal* 24: 4–22.

Wilkerson, James L. 1960. "An Introduction to the Career and Films of John Ford." Master's thesis, University of California—Los Angeles.

Williams, Martin. 1980. *Griffith: First Artist of the Movies*. New York: Oxford University Press.

Willis, Donald C. 1974. *The Films of Frank Capra*. Metuchen, N.J.: Scarecrow Press.

Wilson, John F. 1979. *Public Religion in American Culture*. Philadelphia: Temple University Press.

Wollen, Peter. 1972. *Signs and Meaning in the Cinema*. 3d ed. Bloomington: Indiana University Press.

Zuker, Joel S. 1984. *Francis Ford Coppola: A Guide to References and Resources*. Boston: G. K. Hall.

Index